Next Stop: *Gallup!*

Anne Overland

PublishAmerica
Baltimore

Hardcover 978-1-4560-9690-8
Softcover 978-1-4560-9691-5
PUBLISHED BY PUBLISHAMERICA, LLLP
www.publishamerica.com
Baltimore

Printed in the United States of America

The Indian summer of the heart!
John Greenleaf Whittier

The author wishes to give special thanks to *Ruth Herbert* for her direction and assistance in writing this manuscript,

Peter Lathwood, for his continued confidence in my work and Tom Kennedy of the Zuñi Tourism Department for filling the blanks in my memory.

And to Brandie Pittman, computer artist.

To Indians, the soul of New Mexico.

CHAPTER
1

A chill went through me when the door of the log hogan snapped shut behind me like steel jaws of a trap. I expected to see the furry head of a bear with yellowed teeth and glass eyes mounted on a wall as a ferocious reminder of what could crawl in if the sky hole wasn't covered.

I took the same defensive stance every white person takes who is unaccustomed to this innovation in the roof flooding the entranceway with light: neck stretched back as far as it would go, eyes averted, mouth slack-jawed looking at the deep blue of the New Mexico sky and looked forward to nighttime when it turned into a luminous bubble of plastic stars. But at the moment I marveled at the blueness of the sky and at how lucky I was to have my own personal observatory every time I walked into the hogan.

I have never slept in an Indian hogan before, not even a modernized white man's version, and while the thought of staying here alone was exciting, the thought of living here by myself for two years was unnerving nonetheless.

A framed chart on the wall caught my eyes and a few telltale words jumped out at me: Sun, Moon, and Stars like on a horoscope chart. With New Mexico's stars seemingly at close range, the chart made sense, but I'd wait till I was alone before examining it more closely to see if the director, Sr. Hyacinth, a heavyset woman about fifty, was a holdout from the sixties. Maybe she was a hungry stoner, the popular belief regarding munchies could explain her weight problem; I've been duped by addictive personalities before.

Nuns aren't supposed to use horoscopes either, horoscopes are like omens, astrology or palm readings; they're divination trying to see into the future. A glimpse into things to come might not be such a bad idea for me at the moment.

The walls inside the eight-sided hogan were smooth and painted white while the outside was made out of logs. The small hogan was chilly and had the stale odor of deodorant, aftershave and perfume of recent retreatants hanging in the air. Sr. Hyacinth opened each of the three doors leading to the bedrooms pulling open curtains and asked me to pick the one I wanted. The stocky nun reminded me that even though I would be living here by myself, if there was an overflow of retreatants, which didn't happen often, I would have to welcome them into the other two bedrooms and share the one bathroom. I told her I wouldn't mind; everything's all right when you're trying to land a position.

The moment we walked into the hogan, I had the impression we entered a hobbit hole and when she opened the doors to the bedrooms, I was sure of it. The rooms were so small I could touch the roof if I wanted. And, because the bedrooms were built to fit the octagonal shape of the hogan, the narrow passageways gave me the feeling we were burrowing underground as well and I expected to see Frodo scurrying around every corner.

The octagonal shape took some getting used to like it was a labyrinth consisting of intricate mazelike passages making me feel I should take notice of key turnings if I wanted to readily find my way out. After learning I would be staying here by myself, fear had become a constant companion and the benign figure of Frodo was replaced with an imprisoned Minotaur of Greek mythology, an angry monster with the body of a man and the head of a bull, growing larger with my panic.

Since the hogan consisted of only three bedrooms and not three thousand chambers like Egyptian labyrinths, I dutifully followed

Hyacinth who was showing the bedrooms with pride, her round face smiling as she pointed out little things like outlets, beaming when she came to the speckled white linoleum, making the most of very little allowing me to pick the room I wanted.

I walked from room to room quickly scanning each for some distinction on which I could base my choice but even the bedspreads were the same, tan with ribbing on top. The room on the left had a sliding glass door that looked directly into the next hogan, and unless I wanted someone watching me undress I would have to keep the curtains drawn for privacy; the room on the right faced east and would catch the direct rays of the sun and would be too hot; but the room in the middle when I pulled open the drapes, had a personal view overlooking the city of Gallup and made it just right.

"I'll take this one," I said, satisfied I had chosen the best overall fit to my personality which was turning out to be that of a professional vagabond; *all destinations considered, no place too remote.* At the back edge of the center, this room was private and had a few pine trees growing on the decline of the property to obstruct the view. As long as I wasn't facing directly into a man-made structure, drooping pine branches would be just fine; I'd see what the bed felt like tonight.

"Okay then," Sr. Hyacinth said, plunking my suitcase on the end of the twin bed. She laughed as she tried to wedge her way past me, I ended up sitting on the bed and pulling my legs up so she could pass; we had already exceeded the occupancy level of the small room.

She stepped toward the closet, opened the door, and pointed to the two drawers at the bottom. This was the same amount of drawer space I had in my last bedroom, socks and underwear didn't take up much room anyway. Leaning over, the Sister pulled out a drop-leaf piece of plywood attached to the side of the closet and turned it into a desk and moved the one hard back wooden chair in the room to face it saying, "It's not the biggest desk, but it will do."

A bed, a closet, a desk, and a view, these were the extent of the bedroom amenities. But instead of feeling the room was lacking in accessories, dressers, coat racks and shelving and the like, it was loaded one important feature people pay dearly for, privacy. Happy the little room met with my approval, the Sister looked at me like I must have come from a poverty-stricken background. Actually, it made me happy; it was the perfect heritage.

Hyacinth pushed her way through to the hallway. "Here's the kitchen; a sink and refrigerator. Retreatants eat in the large dining room at the Center at scheduled times. You won't have to use this kitchen either. We'll all eat in the small dining room off the kitchen but if you want to bring over a chicken leg or something as a snack, or keep a carton of milk for coffee, feel free."

I knew I wouldn't be spending much time in this small kitchen because I wasn't cooking; the *ultimate* perk involved in volunteering at a retreat center.

She led me back into the hall and explained how real hogans were usually made with mud mixed with brush. Here, they were made with cement. It doesn't look bad either, log, cement, log, cement, all the way up."

"Another way we differ from authentic hogans is the installation of thermostats. A bathroom, heat and running water, this really is a white man's hogan. Your thermostat's right here," she said, showing me how it worked while assuring me that the walls really do keep the heat in.

"Fine," I said, relieved I didn't have to carry wood in to a woodstove to use as fire for heat. Now *that* would be primitive.

"Okay then, if there's nothing else, I'll let you unpack and get settled in and when you're done, come over to the kitchen for something to eat.

"There *is* one more little thing," I said as I edged my way toward a chair by the kitchen table. "I debated the entire train ride whether to tell you this or not but it's not fair to you if I don't. I was diagnosed with multiple sclerosis last year. It affected my walking the most, but as I you can see, I'm almost all the way back to normal. My doctor said sometimes patients go for long times in-between episodes, sometimes even years, so I shouldn't have any problems while I'm here. I thought you should know."

Her forehead crinkled as she thought. "I'm glad you told me," she said with a serious look, no longer sprinkling her comments with laughter. "While you're here, work as long as you want, take plenty of rests, don't overdo, and you'll be fine. It happens that Sr. Celeste, besides being our cook, is also a nurse. You'll be fine," she said again in such a convincing tone. I believed her. It would take a stronger person than I to defy her by becoming sick, I hoped she was right. It felt like a ton of worry had been lifted from my shoulders and I knew I had done the right thing by disclosing my condition.

"I think there's some left-over pizza in the retreat kitchen," she said, her eyes widening at the thought.

"Great, I'm famished!" I exclaimed, relieved my tension had been disarmed and the hardest part of our getting acquainted was over.

"Work a week, meet Sr. Celeste and the girls from our group home and see if it's a place you'd like to work and let me know what you decide." Taking a quick look toward the retreat kitchen, I could tell her mind wasn't on my M.S. anymore but on dough covered with tomatoes and cheese. She smiled thinking of the mouth-watering meal languishing in the kitchen, and, like she was about to reveal a deep secret, said confidentially, "Wait until you taste Sr. Celeste's cooking," nodding her head knowingly, then left me to finish unpacking.

Alone in the hogan I went to the bedroom and sat on the bed and felt how quiet it was. My anxiousness having calmed, I began thinking about my good fortune: from the distance of my bedroom Gallup had turned into a beautiful city right before my eyes; the retreat location was more beautiful than I could have imagined, and I had been accepted as a retreat worker even with my condition. I picked up my cowboy lying on my suitcase and tossed it on the hook on the back of the door, and like it agreed with my thinking, it caught on the very first try.

I opened my suitcase and laid my clothes on the bed. God only knows what I would have done if Hyacinth hadn't been willing to give me a try. With a sigh of relief, I hung my blouses in the closet and flattened my jeans out in the bottom drawer. Closing the door bedroom behind me, I walked into the hall. I stopped short when I came to the chart on the wall by the door. Stepping closer, I saw that it didn't contain signs of the zodiac and positions of stars, it turned out to be something quite different as I stood there reading the framed poem written by the founder of the Franciscan order which was almost as unconventional:

*Praise be to thee, my lord, with all Thy creatures. Especially to my worshipful Brother **Sun**, which lights up the day and through him dost Thou brightness give, and beautiful is he and radiant with splendor great.*

*Praised be to my Lord for Sister **Moon** and for the **Stars** in heaven. Thou hast formed them clear and precious and fair. Praised be my Lord for Brother **Wind**, and for the **Air** and clouds*

and fair and every kind of weather by which Thou givest to Thy creatures nourishment.

*Praised be my Lord for Sister **Water**, which is greatly helpful and humble and precious and pure.*

*Praised be to my Lord for Brother **Fire**, by which Thou lighted up the dark; and fair is he and gay and mighty and strong.*

*Praised be to my Lord for our Sister Mother **Earth**, which sustains and keeps us and brings forth fruits, grass, and flowers bright.*

*Praise be to my Lord for our Sister **Death**, from which no living man can flee. Woe to them, who die in mortal sin; blessed those who find themselves in Thy most holy will.*

St. Francis of Assisi

I was relieved to know the head of this retreat center wasn't into psychedelics and mind altering drugs. Somehow this heavy set nun didn't strike me as being a carefree flower child advocating universal peace and love while scattering flower petals. My hunch was she was of the old school where love was something earned after proving yourself through years of hard service. This was the first time I ever worked with Franciscans so it was just a hunch and time would tell.

Closing the door, I stepped into the fresh air of the yard and took a deep breath of clean, trouble free air, absolved from my worries, breathing freely for the first time today. I grabbed the tallest weed the last in the intensified quiet. St. Francis retreat was made of older buildings and I was startled by each loud crack the kitchen made when it settled while drafts of air moving from place to place sounded like low moans of a ghost.

Then my eyes landed on the sign, God Bless the Cook, and remembered Celeste should be coming to check on me, and I relaxed somewhat. Nevertheless, being in a strange kitchen that was unfamiliar to me, I thought how being frightened was no fun, picked up the plate of pizza, locked the kitchen door and walked to my empty hogan, looking over my shoulder with every step.

It was growing darker by the minute, not a moment to lose. I went through my hogan making sure all the sliding glass doors were locked in the bedrooms and pulled a kitchen chair to the entryway and propped it against the front door as one more barrier against intruders. Satisfied I had done all I could to protect myself I went into the kitchen and sat at the table behind the plate of pizza. Realizing I hadn't eaten since 6:00AM I began to pick at the cold pizza but it was hard to eat when my stomach was constricted in a tight ball and put the food back in the refrigerator.

I changed into pajamas and slid into bed pulling the covers up to my eyes, glad this day was over. Hearing the fading whistle of a train in the distance, I fell asleep wondering how I ended up in the heart of Indian land by myself.

CHAPTER
2

It wouldn't have surprised me to see spirits rising from the desert, awakened by the rumbling of our train like it was a herd of stampeding buffalo. My eyes followed the swelling and sloping of a mountain range hundreds of miles away instead.

We had crossed into New Mexico long ago, a land heavy with superstition and folklore. There were no trains hundreds of years ago. Nothing had been sketched on walls or trickled in colored sand to warn inhabitants of the coming metal behemoth, one to awaken tribal members all the way back to prehistoric Anasazi times. Forcing rails down into ground soaked in blood from our nations' violent past wasn't adding to my peace of mind. I was sure disgruntled ancients from another world would be waiting for me in defiance at the station in Gallup.

Growing up in a middle-class white family, I was as far away as I could be from tribal legends and tales of Native Americans. With this limited exposure, it was with a growing sense of panic that I scrambled to find some kind of invocation in my memory to help restore sanctity to the land and remove the desecration brought on by our train's ungodly crossing. But my knowledge of counter-incantations and opposing charms was as devoid as the desert we were impiously racing across so I inconspicuously flicked a couple drops of holy water out the passenger window as we motored along at 60+ miles per hour hoping *some* of it would reach the ground.

I was riding on the *Southwest Chief* feeling about as disheveled on the outside as my insecure mind was making me feel on the inside. Each new town on the east-west thoroughfare filled me with dread because Gallup was fast approaching and with it, my new life. The guidebook stated every local street in Gallup ended at Route 66 and with growing certainty I was convinced myself this applied to life spans too.

In the reflection on a window I saw the incredulous face of a doctor reminding me I had no business being on a train. His displeased face was asking, "Are you insane? You shouldn't be on **any** conveyance that wobbles back and forth!" He would never react this way in real life but his opinion of my actions was coming through loud and clear in the refection.

He was right of course; I had no business riding on a train so soon after going through a severe case of vertigo. I had never ridden on a train and didn't know it would sway from side to side and in no time the remembrance of my non-stop nausea came back and I was right back in the 107' degree heat being driven to the hospital. I had never heard of *positional vertigo* before but it was a term I learned in a hurry, multiple sclerosis was another.

The very real fear of becoming physically sick in front of a group of passengers didn't outweigh my desire to get as a far way from the traumatic experience as possible. But seeing the long fibrous tendrils on a group of soaptree yuccas brought back how lucky I was a skilled emergency room doctor had hit the mark with the long needle on the very first try and the spinal tap felt about as painful as a mosquito bite sending a wave of gratitude through me like the heat.

I glanced in another direction over the vast expanse of desert but this did little to keep the images of my hospital stay from dominating my mind; it wasn't easy forgetting the discovery I made by accident, one that still amazes me—simply by turning my head a different way, the nausea had stopped. I remembered how it was just plain luck when I was driven to the hospital that I put the left side of my head on the car seat and my dizziness stopped. It was such a simple cause and effect, so subtle, the moment my nausea suddenly stopped it *still* didn't dawn on me I had caused it by tilting my head in a different direction. In fact, I would have to wait years before understanding how *positional vertigo* works.

I could feel impending doom holding me as I sat stuck to the hot vinyl seat on the train. Traveling into the heart of Indian land by myself after being diagnosed with multiple sclerosis two months before wasn't the smartest thing to do but my need to leave the clinical examinations, barbaric diagnostic practice and improbable diagnosis far behind was even greater. If I had known the gentle motion of a passenger car moving from side to side was like the listing of a boat, I would have thought twice about climbing aboard. Yawning from the effects of a motion sickness pill, I was glad my first spell of nausea had trailed away as gently as the ridge.

With the monotonous sound of the *driving wheels* of the train making it difficult for me to *run the line* without giving into drowsiness, I kept myself awake by considering all the new lingo I'd learned. Coupled with hospital jargon like *dysarthria*, the name for weakened speech muscles or motion sickness pills, my new vocabulary with its promise of healing bolstered my optimism with confidence.

More than ever I appreciated sitting next to someone who didn't want to engage me in conversation now that MS had literally slowed my ability to form words. I hoped my fellow passengers didn't take offense, but it felt so good resting the muscles used in articulation.

Clumps of teddy bear cholla aglow in the sunlight dotted the landscape like low voltage bulbs and I had the thought, to reduce my growing anxiety the closer we came to Gallup, I would bring up everything I knew about Indians. The most obvious came first, that Indians venerated their burial grounds and were overly protective of these hallowed places, burial grounds were sacred and not to be disturbed; it was the worst abomination anyone could inflict. Unfortunately, this was exactly what I was doing at the moment, profanely barreling across long stretches of land that may have been used to bury some Indian's mortal remains. It left me with an uneasy feeling.

I knew Medicine men and women were about as high on the Indian hierarchy as one could go and grew calmer recalling the simple way one tribe found to have the calling. Toddlers were placed in a tee-pee with a tomahawk on one side and a doll on the other. If a boy went to the doll, he was considered special, and if a girl went for the tool, her uniqueness was proven too; both were thought to have special powers and for the rest of their lives they were considered healers and taught about medicinal herbs and potions. I looked at the number of grass-eating sheep we were passing and had the feeling the combination of aspirin and sheep manure poultice still wouldn't be enough to stop my growing headache.

Seeing a spinning spiral of air moving erratically off in the desert I recalled how some Indians think these swirling winds were *devil winds* full of evil spirits and they were waiting for them to blow so they could drift more easily from place to place. Remembering this, the engineer couldn't go by fast enough for me and relaxed when he gave it full throttle and we went speeding down a grade away from the funnel full of imagined dusty spirits.

I remembered how indigenous south of the United States' border Indians like Yaqui, differed from American Indians and the farther we traveled into the Southwest, the more I wanted to see something that reflected Native Indian culture. I was disappointed when we zoomed passed a giant mustard yellow tepee positioned back from the tracks, I was expecting something more symbolic of the southwest Indian culture for my first tourist attraction. I wondered if there was an Indian inside selling local color, paintings of horse corrals, adobe dwellings, or mugs he had spent hours painting his likeness on reminding tourists they bought a souvenir inside a giant yellow tepee. If the tee-pee had been covered in buffalo hides or bear skins it would have been more authentic. But in the Southwest, where the soil is packed and dry and the prevalent animal is the jack rabbit, I gave up trying to calculate how many pelts it would take to cover a tepee that size.

The adventurous writings of Carlos Casteneda came to me and how he perfected *traveling* in the desert. He traveled, but without the help of a train, he relocated using his thoughts aided by peyote. His series of books became a religion for some readers, to the point die-hard followers moved south of the border in search of brujos and brujas like they were twentieth century protégés. Weren't followers of Castaneda's teachings still wandering aimlessly in the desert to this day? I was all for cultivating and expanding my consciousness as long as it left my thinking intact. Reassuring myself, I thought if I kept my wits about myself, I'd be okay.

A big part of me was actually looking forward to spending time on the last frontier while the other part was scared to death. I had never been exposed to Indians in real life, cowboys either for that matter, and what I did know I'd picked up from television. The little Indian knowledge I did retain, I wondered how much of it, if any, was true.

I sat back on the black plastic seat out of the glare of the sun realizing I had reached the end of my practical knowledge of Indians. My reflections did help me remember two important points though; that as big as the giant tepee was, it stood for something much bigger, it stood for the Old West, and I would be stepping back in time, and secondly, what I knew about Indians was as useful as a poisoned water hole.

It didn't seem possible when I heard the conductor announce in a long drawl from the car in front of us, **Next Stop, Gallup** even though I remembered crossing the city limits of San Bernardino and Barstow, then Kingman, Arizona, thinking with each loud holler newfangled instruments like microphones hadn't made it this far out in the country yet.

I directed my attention to the passengers on both sides of the aisle. Since our destination was Gallup, I understood why the handful of people riding on the *Southwest Chief* were ranchers wearing blue jeans and bold silver belt buckles. I wouldn't call the showy silver rings on their fingers gaudy but good fashion sense because they matched their large belt buckles perfectly. The men wore clean and buffed cowboy boots that had me shamefully tucking my dusty tennis shoes under my seat whenever anybody walked by.

Across the aisle I saw the back of a Native American woman wearing an elegant silver comb holding her black hair in place. She wore turquoise jewelry on her fingers, and when she leaned over to pick up a bead that had fallen from her necklace, I noticed a silver brooch decorating her lapel. Suddenly I wished I had taken more time fixing my hair.

Then there was me in my jeans, wearing no jewelry at all, clutching my old cowboy hat like it was a security blanket; I fit right in. Whatever the reason, shyness perhaps, but no one had said a word to me the entire trip. Maybe the passengers *couldn't* speak English, either that or they thought I was hiding a revolver in my hat.

Silence and I were old companions and I was used to not speaking after spending the last two years in a strict Catholic monastery where speaking was practically non-existent. I am proud of my two years in a place reputed to be the strictest of Orders, Trappist. I would keep this personal information to myself because even though monasticism is a voluntary lock up, some people see it as cult-like involving brainwashing. Still others, even other religious, who see monasticism as lunacy and priories as Bellevue-like clinics. In any case, monks are notorious non-talkers and I was used to keeping quiet.

My time with the Trappistines made me aware Indians aren't the only ones inundated with folklore, I was chock full, but mine were of the Catholic kind that included traditional beliefs, poems, oral literature, rituals and incense burnings; we stopped short of blood letting.

I patted the pocket of my blouse again to make sure I had my traveling essentials, the vial of Holy water I could use in many situations from warding off angry sleep-deprived forefathers to frustrated earth-bound human mashers who might be staking out the station waiting the arrival of the 2:15.

I felt my back pocket too, to be sure I didn't forget to pack God in the form of a small Bible for moral support; and to complete my spiritual trifecta, I ran my thumb and index finger along the chain around my neck, fingering the corpus at the end. I was ready for all contingencies. But nothing could prepare me for actually seeing Gallup for the first time.

Listening to the unmistakable slowing of the clickity clack of the rails keeping time with the rapid beat of my heart, we pulled in lined up with the platform. Rubbing my eyes, I felt we had pulled back in time to the previous century and I peered over the seat in front of me finding it hard to believe what I was seeing but it was true; I had stepped back in time into what looked like a cavalry outpost and expected to see hitching posts, watering troughs and gun-slingers; a U.S. marshal couldn't be far away.

I was startled when the sound of a loud whistle brought the crew out in the yard in a reluctant trot but it wasn't until the conductor pitched the train to a complete halt that a flurry of frenzied butterflies began fluttering in my stomach.

Outside, I could see people getting off benches in murmured gatherings, one lady was already crying, and another one looked like she just about to, in preparation to embrace and kiss in welcome. As a stranger in this strange new land, I was greeted by a familiar knot of fear in my throat.

"Gaaallup," a black porter announced loudly in a disinterested voice as he entered by a connecting door.

I straightened up quickly, rigid with anxiety.

I watched him walk up and down the isle in a routine manner, his black bolo tie swinging from his stiff white collar as he leaned in close making sure the passengers knew to get off if this was their destination. I thought, sure, he could be calm, he wasn't getting off here.

"Gaaaallup," he yelled again, his voice trailing away as he went into the next car taking the strong scent of cologne with him. I tried to look happy to be here but I was too nervous. I sat staring down the aisle like I was waiting for a quick draw from Mr. David L. Gallup himself who had been the paymaster for the Atlantic and Pacific railroads. I'd read after David Gallup established his office in Gallup in 1881, the town was literally named by the workers who where *going to Gallup* to get paid. I glanced around trying to figure out who looked like they were here to collect paychecks; nobody, if their bulging midriffs were thick money belts strapped around their waists.

Sitting so long on the train, I pointed my cramped toes out as far as they could go and stretched my legs before standing up stiffly and was caught up with the rest of the bucolic looking passengers inching their way toward the opened section of the car with everyone else.

Mentally, I took stock of my walking as I moved my hold from head-rest to head-rest. So far I was doing okay. My right leg felt heavy but manageable. Knowing this was the end of the line in more ways than one, I convinced myself no could notice my weakened muscle coordination except me and pushed forward.

When I stepped from the train I staggered slightly as I took my first unhindered steps in hours on an uncovered walkway beside the train but I think everyone was woozy after the 13 hour ride. It's hard to stop a day's worth of swaying just by *telling* yourself the train wasn't moving anymore; I knew I would be swaying way past dinner.

I gave the engine a scrutinizing once over as I passed, marveling at the harnessed power balanced on large steel wheels the size of small cars and levers like crow bars. As if it knew I was admiring it, the pent up power in the engine let out a sharp sputter and quit, its tonnage resting on the tracks incapable of being budged.

I could feel light puffs of a November breeze as I made my way through the crowd of disembarking passengers. The station reminded me of the depressed looking set of the *Honeymooners*, no frills, just the bare necessities, existing just above the poverty line and I couldn't resist searching the benches for Ralph Kramden holding his lunch box.

There was one good reason however, that kept me from not jumping off the platform and running for the hills away from the train, away from all the passengers and away from my new life. It was one line in the reply letter I received from a Franciscan Superior in answer to my query about volunteer work: "Just remember the Sisters stationed in Gallup have pioneering spirits." It had been all the pitch I needed.

I had recited the line to myself over and over like a mantra. On roads so low I could skim the sand with my hand, when we went through dark tunnels and into bright open country again; and, when, after hours of sitting on the hot sticky pad of flattened black vinyl, we reached Gallup's city limits, for the hundredth time I heard the line running through my mind like a challenge.

Then I saw a Sister, plump as a dumpling standing in the middle of groups welcoming loved ones. She was dressed in a knee length black habit and black veil and was searching the handful of disembarking passengers for one fitting my description. She wouldn't have to look hard, I was the only blonde on the train, maybe in the entire town; similarly, she was the only nun on the platform, maybe the entire town. Sr. Hyacinth a Franciscan nun and my contact, was diligently scanning the crowd with resolve.

She wasn't lithe and slender like a member of the lily family her name implied, although she did have a reddish-cinnamon complexion like the plant that sprang from the blood of the slain Hyacinthus. She was a large woman with a strong frame you could tell radiated an authority by the way she was pointing and guiding others with all the confidence of a conductor. Helpfulness emanated from her frame as she directed traffic balanced on a powerful base of low black pumps. Something told me that once she made up her mind, she was incapable of being swayed. Gulping, she looked more intimidating than the train.

I could tell she was a good schmoozer though, from the good natured comments she was making to others around her, happily going on about one thing or another talking to no one in particular. Seeing this made me feel less threatened as I can't think of one meet-and-greet encounter I ever looked forward to. I have never been overly-eager to go to on *any* interview and was greatly relieved someone actually showed up to collect me.

I stopped briefly to let a single woman using cardboard boxes for luggage pass, but long enough for my mind to question, how much did I *really* know about Franciscans, surprisingly little; they were probably kind to animals because of the reputation of their founder,

Saint Francis of Assisi, a friar known and for helping animals and for living a simple lifestyle. Maybe I play up the fact I was newly diagnosed with multiple sclerosis (something she could never discern from my bearing) so she'd see me as a wounded stray and take me in? Or should I not mention it at all, hoping I'd remain symptom-free during my two year stint of volunteer work. But if something unpredictable happened to my body like optical neuritis, how would I explain this weird vision problem? I didn't think starting my two volunteer years off by withholding important information about my health would be right and a guilty laugh escaped me when I wondered what it would be like lie to a nun.

What would she do I dropped both my bombshells at once; "Excuse me Sister, but I have something to tell you, 'I was forced to end a novitiate in a monastery recently due to my failing health.' How would she take it? Not very well and imagined her throwing her veil to the ground and walking away in disgust.

There didn't seem to be much point telling her I was in the same Order as Thomas Merton either, the Order that followed the strict *Rule of St. Benedict.* Admitting this would have its advantages though, that I was Catholic, for one thing, knowing we had the same values would surely be a plus. Then again, I was only volunteering here, not joining. It might give her the impression I was some sort of religious nut, but if reading everything Merton ever wrote qualified me, then I might just be. He was such a prolific writer, to this day I'm not absolutely sure I *have* read everything he authored.

Finally, the woman blocking the aisle cleared the walkway, smiling apologetically for taking so long. I forced myself to smile back but I was so tense, it felt like I smiled the wide-eyed grin of a psycho, reminiscent of how I used to snarl every time I would see the Novice Mistress in the monastery due to the fact I wasn't feeling particularly happy at the moment.

I repeated my mantra for the last time, *pioneering spirits?* I straightened my hair and made my way through the crowd to the Sister standing in front of the platform. I reminded myself even if lying wasn't considered a grave fault by St. Benedict, the ringleader of the Trappist Order, it still wasn't right to lie to a nun. The trouble was I didn't want to give my prospective director any reason to reject me by telling the truth.

I put on a wide smile that I hoped didn't make me look too desperate, moved in closer ready to introduce myself, but before I had the chance to say anything, she held out her hand in greeting and began pumping mine like it was a lever on a handcar. With a giggle that quickly developed into a hearty laugh spreading into a friendly smile across her face, she said, "*Yah-te-hey*, Anne, welcome to Indian country."

"Long trip?" she questioned while leading me toward bags being piled on the sidewalk.

I think I said hello back, but I can't be sure. "Yes, it was some trip," I heard my voice say as I leaned forward.

"I'm Sr. Hyacinth, the director of St. Francis Retreat."

"I'm so glad you wore your habit," I replied. "I had no trouble at all finding you," stopping before adding the *sore thumb* remark but she really did. There was no way I could miss her conspicuous black religious habit amid the sea of blue denim.

Sr. Hyacinth had the cheery disposition of a Mrs. Claus with rosy cheeks and a jolly nature to match and I liked her happy personality immediately. She was one of these people who liked to laugh; in fact, she was chuckling as she reached across and easily picked out the only suitcase marked from L.A. out of the line of bags. I noticed things like muscle strength after spending a week in the hospital re-learning how walk and talk just two months earlier. My progress had been encouraging, remarkable really, so much so, I wanted to give this new vocation in retreat work a chance.

We walked across the colorless depot to the parking lot. I looked around at the rotting fruit in crumpled trash cans, rusty benches with discolored arm rests, at the paint peeling off ticket counters. Nothing here was broken or falling apart; the depot wasn't wracked and ruined, just dissolving and wasting away in the after affects of a four season climate that went from blistering heat to icy cold. I made a mental note where the ticket office was located just in case I wanted to leave in a hurry.

Right then I made the conscious decision; no matter how unattractive and unappealing I personally found this frontier town, I would *force* myself to *try* to like it. After all, I had grabbed at this opportunity like someone had thrown me a life preserver now that I was officially *disabled.*

Hyacinth set my suitcase on the ground next to a dusty, white sedan, opened the door to the backseat and tossed my suitcase on the floor in front of the bench seat. "I have the car washed once a week," she said apologetically, "but it's pointless because most of the roads around here are dirt. You can't tell but I washed it this morning being it's a special occasion. Most people drive straight through Gallup, not many people choose to *stay* here."

The small station's parking lot was filled with old GMC trucks that were covered with dirt. As an introduction to Gallup, Sr. Hyacinth told me that in this town the letters GMC stood for Grand Mother's Car.

"That's nice," I said politely, not understanding her meaning.

"See there," she said, following a truck as it pulled into traffic.

Rolling the window down, I turned and looked, "I'll be darned," I said trying not to stare. "That's the grandmother sitting in the *back* of the truck?"

"That's how it is here. It's customary," Sr. Hyacinth stated matter-of-factly. I looked closely at the back of the truck as we pulled up close at a traffic light. Snuggled into a bed of blankets was indeed an older Navajo woman with a bandana covering her head comfortably nestled in, happy for the ride; there happened to be space in the back so why not climb in? It would save her a long walk into town. Speechless, I resisted the urge to gawk.

After the long train ride it was wonderful to be able to stretch my legs luxuriously across the carpeted floorboard, lean back against the soft cushions in the front seat and relax listening to Hyacinth drop occasional facts about the flora and fauna on the hills surrounding us like she was a botanist.

"It's a shame I didn't bring my camera," I complained.

"I'm glad you didn't. Out here you never take pictures without asking first. You're taking something from them, their spirit, and many Indians fear having their spirits stolen by the camera's eye. We have to respect that."

"You mean I could never take a photograph?"

"Not without getting permission first. I don't know if you'd actually be arrested for snapping a shot but I wouldn't try it," Hyacinth warned.

"Spontaneous Kodak moments aren't worth losing my camera over, don't worry," I reassured her, but already regretting my decision.

When the light changed and my unconventional welcoming party sped away into traffic, Sr. Hyacinth turned to me and with a knowing look, said, "That, Anne, was genuine Gallup, transportation is transportation, after all." I told her St. Francis would be pleased.

It was only a short time before we reached the downtown storefront part of Gallup. This frontier town looked like it had been pieced together by a brick mason who used red bricks exclusively. I saw pawn shop after pawn shop. In fact, the façade looked like the town had had a hard time keeping itself above water, literally and financially; and the longer I looked, the more I had the impression a red tide had washed the street soaking the buildings leaving them a rusty, copper color that were moist to the touch.

We passed cafes, loan offices and pawn shops, many displaying what were once colorful awnings, now dull and faded due to years of bad weather, historical museums, trading companies, and an Indian 'jewelry, rug and loan' store. Exchanging goods without money by borrowing and lending; investments seemed to be the backbone of this town. But for all the bartering being carried on here, the town didn't look very prosperous. It put me in mind of a pretend bank I opened when I was young; I did a brisk business but nothing over a dollar ever changed hands and bet the interest rate on this street was probably just as high.

It wasn't the prettiest town I'd ever seen. Faded ads and weathered store fronts disintegrated all my hopes and plans; suddenly, my future turned bleak. There was nothing I could do but watch my dreams crumble to the ground with the brick buildings. Here I was, yet again, making another new beginning with total strangers. This flat plate of a town in dark negative images was developing a picture of my sinking heart. My first train ride had been pleasant enough but actually seeing Gallup for the first time was a shock, and my prevailing thought was, *I don't think I can live here.*

As we passed washed out commercial buildings with torn and peeling advertisements selling healing oils for barbed wire cuts, toothache gums, rupture cures, and one with the likeness of a pallid green frog looking directly at me selling nerve pills that read, '**Don't Be Nervous**' like I was turning pages of a *Country Gazette*, giving the impression the residents here were falling apart like the town; and for a moment, I wondered how many other people entered the city of Gallup like me with goiter-like protruding eyes, fixed and staring, refusing to believe what they were seeing.

Not letting socio-economic culture shock take over my mind completely, I knew I *had* to give this retreat business a try and like it or not, this copper colored, underprivileged town came with the deal.

"Gallup is such a beautiful city, with so many interesting things to see and do, don't you agree?"

"To be honest with you Sister, I really haven't seen much of the town," explaining, "with the odor of oil and grease hanging in the air in the depot, to tell the truth, I felt a little homesick for L.A. smog."

"Ha, right you are," she said, laughing again, scrunching up her nose in disgust, like she could smell the dirty polluted air right then. Sr. Hyacinth's optimistic behavior put me in mind of an employer expounding the qualifications needed to fill the position as a driven, ambitious and focused individual, while the interviewee is looking out the window enjoying the view. It gave me a clue into her personality. Who was I to judge a town anyway, coming from Los Angeles, a city the rest of the country viewed full of residents having fallen out of a cracked pot, some falling farther away than others?

Hyacinth commented on how Gallup was situated at an elevation of 6,500 feet and the retreat center was a thousand feet higher. "Gallup winters are cold, but we have plenty of sunshine too." She told me how snowfall seldom stayed on the ground for more than two or three days, if there is snow.

As we drove north on the long uphill grade, I noticed the brown and colorless landscape surrounding us. The beauty of the scruffy brown rabbit brush lining the highway with its golden-yellow heads was lost on how good it was going to feel to finally stop moving. During the train ride I'd made it a point to concentrate on things in the distance to combat motion sickness and to relax, but after 13 hours of tensing it was hard to stop.

Pointing to the Navajo reservation we were passing on the right, I was surprised it wasn't marked at all, no signs, fences or barricades, only a few sheep wandering on the sloping hillsides. I was expecting to see at least a cow skull on a pole or dangling eagle feathers to warn visitors they were about to enter a tract of land set apart by the federal government for Native Americans. It surprised me how reservations looked the same as other land so a visitor would have to know beforehand they were passing over the boundary line.

"The Zuñi reservation is just up the road 26 miles. *Just up the road*, you'll find, Anne, is a phrase used a lot; try not to learn the hard way like when first arrived and picked up someone using a crutch and we were halfway to the Grand Canyon before I realized he must have dropped it out the window. I didn't mind though. We had taken the scenic route but then every place around Gallup is a scenic route."

I spied a shaggy brown dog roaming aimlessly over on the next hill and I was seized by a heavy pull on my heart. The sight of this poor pitiful dog, probably abandoned on the side of the road that was lost, homeless, and unwanted, I realized the likelihood I had drawn this four-footed wandering mongrel into my vision by the overall way I was feeling; we were both wandering from place to place, basically lost, and in search of a home. I could feel myself shrink visibly.

"We're here," Hyacinth said, and we turned off the smooth paved highway to climb a steep dirt driveway.

I tightened my grip on the bench seat to steady myself on a road that was so ribbed it looked like an old wash-board causing her voice to sound like someone was knocking on her Adam's apple. I was able to catch snippets of words here and there… "Ga ga ga llup, has pa pa pa pin yon yon yon trees, turk turk turk oise, and pa pa pa pers…," putting together her bits of words. I strained forward anxious to see what lay ahead but I was also keeping a close watch on the right side of the road if I needed to grab the steering wheel to keep the car from plummeting over the edge. I'd heard rumors about the erratic way nuns drove and I didn't want to find out it was true while lying in the bottom of a ditch.

I was feeling as jittery on the inside as the road was making me feel on the outside wondering what the retreat would look like and if I could really make myself stay in a place that was broken down and dilapidated. In my alarm, I questioned whether volunteering was like a lobster trap, easy to get into but hard to get out of. I would know soon enough.

At the top of the driveway, Sr. Hyacinth turned the wheel hard to the left and we joined a better dirt road for a few yards, and parked. We sat attentively at the top of the entrance in a cloud of filtering dust. Then she announced abruptly, "*This* **is St. Francis Retreat,**" like we had entered Vatican City.

We sat there a few moments scanning the yard for what I can only assume, for a sighting of the Pontiff, so pleased and proud she was of the center.

Taking in the full scope of the scene that lay before me, I calmly surveyed the property like an appraiser looking over a prospective property, over the main building, the out-buildings and the out of control state of the yard and summed up my assessment with the question, 'Where's the For-Sale' sign?, a natural reaction to a place that looked abandoned.

Even if it wasn't Cinderella's garden, it wasn't without potential either. Squirrels were scampering about and greedy dive-bombing blue-jays were zeroing in on distended branches at semi-shriveled grape sized red berries hanging from the shapeless shrubs. There wasn't a Disney score playing in the background but I could tell this place was powerful because something wonderful happened when Hyacinth finally had turned off the engine and I stepped into the most blissful feeling of quiet imaginable, so quiet it made my head pound and I understood why this site had been chosen for a spiritual center.

And in an instant, I was aware of the presence of Fr. Walchars, the visiting retreat director from my former monastery, standing beside me pleased I had recognized the subject of his many lectures, *stillness*, on top of this remote hill at St. Francis retreat. I could feel my opposition to living in Gallup giving way when I realized he had been right; a retreat center might be the ideal place to practice what I learned in the desert monastery. So even if it wasn't Cinderella's garden with bluebirds tying bows in the air and squirrels festooning my hair with ribbons, this place felt special.

Weeds had taken over for the most part growing in flower beds, covering walkways, climbing up porch posts. Bumpy crab grass was crowding good turf grasses on a small section of lawn but at least the paths gave the illusion of order as their worn trails cut through the yard. Lopsided junipers hung over the paths in places blocking the sun to at least one *hen-and-chicken* plant, but to a cactus lover like myself, the cactus patch was a delight as I tried to distinguish the entangled cactus from the weeds.

Having spent two years in southern Arizona, I was excited to see oval shaped clumps of *barrel* cactus in dense coats of brownish-gold spines on one side of the patch. These useful cacti had spines to keep their bodies from caving in, and pictured Native Americans using them as storage containers by hollowing out the barrels for bowls that never developed into a line of cookware and handy kitchen implements and marveled at the foresight of using natural cookware.

A column of blue-green *hedge* cactus was poking its way through the mat of weeds, and stooping I scraped my thumbnail on a waxy *strawberry* cactus and gingerly pushed away the dead weeds enveloping it with a stick looking for small edible fruit. Pink instead purple, the dehydrated crop looked like shriveled strawberries and I couldn't bring myself to taste one; I left them lying there.

As dry as the planter was, shaggy columns of *robust hedgehog* cactus had managed to survive, and if I looked hard, I was able to pick out the curved variety of spines of a *pincushion* cactus, the curved spines protecting *chillitos* I resisted tasting, too, in among small inconspicuous clusters of areoles. The garden had a good mix of pointy plants to make up the succulent portion of the yard and as a cactus devotee I knew I was going to derive pleasure from watering this odd array of differing species.

Towering over this horticultural fray were tall pine trees surrounding the property with branches that had been stripped thin from years of holding back wind, sleet and snow while enhancing the air with their clean pine scent. A large rusty bell in the center of the yard was squashing a circle of grass next to a wooden frame, its clapper forced into silence by a group of weeds like they were a committee of disapproving librarians.

Encircling the yard were five irregularly shaped log cabins hewn from real logs followed the road as it wound around the yard leading cars back to the entrance again. The five cabins were for retreatants and they weren't called cabins, they were called *hogans* after Navajo dwellings in an effort to give guests a sense of authenticity. "We call them white-man hogans because they have running water and electricity unlike on reservation land."

"Indian hogans don't have running water?" I asked, only moderately surprised; after seeing the matriarch of the family riding in the bed of a truck, not having running water somehow didn't seem so unlikely.

"There's a well at the top on the hill on parish property," pointing over a slope past the entrance away from the retreat. "Wells are drilled on neutral ground, like church property, so it won't cause friction between the tribes, or else they can't afford to hire people to do the drilling, I'm not sure which. Up and down they carry water in their own barrels to their homes on the reservation from the well. You'll hear the trucks. They ramble up the driveway at all hours with large empty barrels clanging in the back of their trucks. That's one of the reasons the driveway is in the shape it's in. It gets plenty of use."

Shaking my head, I asked, "And they don't complain about doing it this way?"

"No, I honestly think they are just grateful there *are* water wells like this."

"I guess having to make water runs would keep a person humble," I said, but I was really wondering if the retreat center worked in the same capacity; the thought of having to lug containers of water to the retreat center would be a definite deal-breaker.

I was surprised to see a newer looking building made of the usual 2 X 4's on the left side of the quadrant. Its entire façade had been varnished and smoothed giving it a hard glossy look, clean and unused, like it had never been opened or even unlocked. Facing it from the opposite side of the yard, I followed Hyacinth's lead and took a few steps back with her, tilted my head back to look where she was looking. In the center of the newer building's roof I saw a metal cross and knew this was the retreat chapel.

We stepped on the front porch and turned around to face the hogans. Hyacinth explained the layout for the road was for the convenience of the retreatants. It ran by each cabin for easy loading and unloading luggage by quests and that each of the hogans was built with a skylight dome in the center of the roof like authentic hogans letting the bad spirits out while keeping the good spirits in. But in the hogans, the sky holes here are covered with hard clear plastic, while Navajo hogans are not. Indian sky holes let the smoke from their cooking out as well as heating them. "A hole in the roof in our hogans is not a good idea in the winter," she said, laughing. "Traditional Navajo dwellings have entrances facing east to welcome the sun; our hogans were designed to fit the curvature of the road."

Hyacinth turned around and unlocked the door of the building on the porch that was in need of another coat of redwood paint. As little as I knew about retreat work, I thought a retreat should at least look presentable, starting with having the road clear for guests. If I did decide to work here, clearing the road would be the first place to start.

Leading the way into a hallway we passed two offices. The front office was her office and the second was extra and was used for administration needs. The back part of the building was used as a convent where she stayed, and she walked me to a larger room known as a community room that had a television.

"You'll be staying in the Brother Sun hogan. Each hogan has been named after a different line in a poem written by our founder, St. Francis. We have a Brother Wind hogan, a Brother Sun hogan, a Sister Moon hogan, and a Brother Fire hogan. And I almost forgot the largest hogan on the end is named Sister Mother Earth," pointing to it. We didn't think people would want to stay in a Sister Death hogan, so it was left out. "I hope you won't mind being separated from the main house, but you'll be comfortable."

I wasn't worried about comfort, I was thinking about safety and how I was going to be sleeping over there alone. "Does it have a phone?" I asked hopefully, but my question was unheard, or ignored, by someone who had never had such a ridiculous thought cross her mind in her life.

"Here is the kitchen," as she ushered me into a spacious work area that was as clean as an operating room. I really *could* eat off this spotless floor.

"Credit Sr. Celeste, the other Franciscan Sister assigned in Gallup with me. She's French and does an excellent job of it. She does all the cooking when we have a retreat on, but during the week she supervises a home for girls in town. Sometimes she starts a meal at the home and puts on the finishing touches here. 'Meals *a 'la car*', she likes to kid."

Butcher block counters attached to long stainless steel serving counters, coffee makers, toasters and a large hood over the stove, what I would expect to find in a restaurant kitchen.

"This is a good kitchen," I told her, like I knew what I was talking about, checking to see if it met with my approval. When we passed two large sinks, I leaned over and nonchalantly turned on the cold water and to my relief water slowed out. 'Thank God' gushed through my mind like the cold water on my fingers. Having to lug water in would be a real deal breaker.

Hyacinth patted me on the back. "Oh don't worry, we have running water *now*. But there have been times when the temperature drops and the pipes freeze and if it happens during a retreat, Celeste and I, on rare cases, have been forced to boil snow." We'll hope we'll never have to go through anything like that again."

Artic blasts, bitter cold, frostbite, all sounded exciting while standing in the warmth of a kitchen.

Sr. Hyacinth walked to the other side of the kitchen and then backed out of my way, waiting till I went under her arm so I could face the next part of her tour. In dramatic fashion, she flung open a door and said, "Here is the conference room."

I felt my eyebrows involuntarily raise and my mouth went slack like I had unhinged my jaw. If it wasn't Cinderella's garden out in front, this palatial room could have been her ballroom. As I walked into the room I'm convinced an orchestra was escorting me into the most beautiful room I ever saw! I let Sister lead me under three long redwood arches that extended widthwise from window to window and that was just the beginning, the rest of the room was just as striking completely finished in redwood. This room, designed with its natural wood décor, was magnificent.

I was astounded this beautiful room existed in the middle of car washes, hogans and bull riding competitions! But here it was, to say I was beside myself was an understatement; I felt like running around the room feeling the wood on the walls, caressing it lovingly, to make sure it was real.

There was something just as visibly pleasing at the other end of the room too. A huge fireplace and hearth had been pieced together with rocks from the surrounding hillsides. The mixture of overlapping rocks was a tribute to the art of masonry standing out in grey and white rockery. An off-white couch had been placed in front of the hearth. Any objections I was harboring about living in Gallup dissolved with the ice in the drinks I saw myself sipping in front of the rock fireplace. Suddenly melting snow for water once in a while didn't seem like a big deal.

A crucifix with corpse big enough to be seen by an entire dining room filled with retreatants hung in the center on the fireplace. Flanking the chimney were two large windows made of many smaller square windows, evenly divided on both sides.

Hyacinth led me under the graceful arches walking the length of the dining room toward the bright glare of light at the other end passing round walnut-finished dining tables with low-backed chairs pulled close to each table. This pleasing room was the working hub of the Retreat Center.

When we reached the end of the room we stood in front of the divided windows. Hyacinth stopped next to the massive fireplace and I stepped from behind her. I raised my eyes to follow her gaze and did a double take. Below, beyond the highway running in front of the hill, was a great expanse of reservation land that went on endlessly, the late afternoon sun emblazoning the landscape in golden incandescence, outlining the clouds in bright gilded edges. This view worked better than a drug to ease my anxiousness and resolved any remaining indecisiveness I had.

Something in the distance below caught my eye. A car had stopped on the highway below and a woman had gotten out and was beating her hands against her thighs. From the high point I was able to see something running at top speed across the field toward her from another direction and for a second I was afraid for her; collision was inevitable. But instead of getting back in the car to protect herself, she opened her arms wide in welcome and I was surprised to recognize the advancing assailant as the same straggly dog I had seen wandering the hillside this morning. Jumping and frolicking followed as the dog danced happily around the woman in unfettered delight.

There were times in my life I'm certain I've drawn situations to myself by the overall way I was feeling and I was convinced I had brought this reunion between pet and owner into my vision; both of us had found a home.

CHAPTER
3

It wasn't fair being jerked out of my sleep the next morning by the shrill shouting of a woman. Disoriented, I rolled out of bed and nearly into a wall.

Ruby! Come back here," a woman's voice scolded. "You know better than to open the door when the car is still moving!"

Looking around at my new surroundings, it gradually dawned on me I wasn't in my bed at home. It took a few seconds before I realized the cries were being made by an irate woman outside.

Struggling to my feet, I threw on my clothes and went to peek out the front window. The shouts were coming from someone sitting in the front seat of a white truck. I watched as the door opened and a nun woman got out. In my grogginess I could see it wasn't Sr. Hyacinth but it could have been her clone. She was wearing a black habit and a black veil with a strip of white across the top of her head. A cross was hanging around her neck; she was a smaller version of Hyacinth. True to her word, Hyacinth had arranged for Celeste to check on me. As I looked, I could see several heads in the back of the pick-up too.

Still physically and emotionally drained from my train ride, I opened the front door of my hogan a crack and tried to sneak out. It was too late, I had been spotted. I watched what appeared to be a human canon ball, zoom across the yard in the form of a little girl, hands thrust deep in her pockets, heading straight for me, totally ignoring the threatening voice coming from the pick-up.

Pulling up directly in front of me, the girl asked bluntly, "Who are you?"

"Anne," I said back to her.

"What are you doing here?" the girl spoke out again without a hint of inhibition.

"Pulling out weeds," I pointed out, making my answers as short as her questions.

"What for?" she burst, confused why a stranger would be cleaning the yard of the Retreat Center.

"Don't you think there are too many?" I said, nodding my head in the direction of the mass of weeds between hogans and the overgrowth covering the walkways.

"I guess you're right," the dark haired little girl approved, happy to have made conversation before she would be told to stop bothering me.

"What's your name?" it was my turn to ask.

"Ruby, I live with Sr. Celeste. She has a group home. I'm a special case," she said proudly.

"Good for you," I answered, not wanting to say anything that might upset this precocious, head-strong little girl. I wondered if all Navajo children were so sure of themselves.

All we chatted I noticed there was something different about her looks but it was hard to pinpoint. She wasn't deformed, she was just different but it fit her forward demeanor. Everything about her was small; she had small slightly crossed dark eyes and a little nose with a wide bridge above thin lips. Even if she didn't have a Navajo accent, she still would have been hard to understand. She was unclear what she was trying to communicate and easily reached her frustration level trying.

The other girls had jumped out of the back of the truck and had caught up with Ruby.

"Yah-te-hey," an older girl said as she walked up to us. She was eating something out of a white paper bag and in-between swallows, she said, "I'm Joyce, I live with Ruby."

"Hi, I'm Anne, a volunteer," introducing myself.

Joyce was a teenager wearing jeans and plaid shirt. Noticing that I was watching her eating to make conversation offered the bag to me asking,"Want one?"

The question was innocent enough. Whatever was in there, I'd try. What harm could there be in tasting a strange food? Besides, I didn't want to look like a lightweight on our very first meeting. I enjoy all types of food and after all, this kid was nibbling on one. If she could eat whatever it was, I was certain I could too. Was I wrong! Reaching in, I was surprised when I didn't feel the powdery outside of a donut but the pod of some kind of fruit. It looked interesting so I bite off a piece. I couldn't even keep it in my mouth because as soon as pieces took hold, the villainous pepper erupted in angry snaps over every part of my mouth, lips, gums, tongue, with each seed igniting a fire of its own to the friendly delight of the watching Navajo girls who had gathered around me, doubled over with laughter.

"Water!" I squeaked, fanning my mouth."Water!" I gasped, really playing it up so the girls would get the most mileage out of their practical joke, one they had undoubtedly pulled on every new newcomer like a rite of passage.

"Hello," I heard from the approaching footsteps walking up from the truck. "I'm Sr. Celeste," the heavily accented French voice directed. "I came up to see if you needed anything."

"I need water!" I demanded smiling, but not spitting it out.

"Here, drink this," the woman said, handing me a can of soda.

Waiting several seconds for my voice to return, I said, "That was *some* welcome!"

"They did bring something else to welcome you," handing me a contraption of some sort.

"It's a dream catcher, one of the girls blurted out pointing at the gift. It catches the bad dreams and lets the good ones pass through."

Through watering eyes I choked out, "Thanks on both accounts," taking another swig, and turned toward the French accent and saw a blurry clone of Sr. Hyacinth in black habit and veil, only smaller.

Holding the feathery gift out in front of me, I inspected the soft, light extensions on the welcoming gift at close range. I had never seen anything like it; amber feathers with brown edges and a circle of webbed yarn in the middle.

"Hang it near your pillow and it will let only good dreams pass through," the younger voice boasted.

"I'll be sure to hang it by my bed then," I said, making the girl smile. "Thanks!"

"Yah-te-hey," the Sister said in a formal tone. That's the Navajo greeting for hello. I tried to catch you before they did. The chilies are hot. They're called ristras and they give spice to New Mexico's food."

"You're not kidding! I've *never* tasted anything so hot," bringing on another burst of laughter from the girls.

"They are *really* hot!" It was beyond me how something so hot I could taste good to them and I cut my teeth on hot sauce and was used to spicy food. Because the girls were long-time connoisseurs, I was convinced they didn't *have* any taste buds left as I repeatedly pulled in long cooling breaths through my mouth. Thinking I had been the object of some good-natured teasing, I was glad I hadn't backed down from their offer. I wondered how many other initiates to New Mexico had been the recipients of their trial by fire or if I was the only one naïve enough to actually put a piece to in their mouth and chew?

The Sister turned her attention toward Ruby and before Ruby said anything, the girl shouted, "I'm not doing anything wrong."

"I see you've met Ruby," and turning to the rest of the girls encircling me, said in a French accent, "This is Valerie, Daniel, Molly, Virginia, and Jessica; and of course, Ruby. These are my girls."

"*Yah-te-hey*," they responded in unison in Navajo, each one greeting me a shy smile as her name was called.

Apologizing for Ruby's pushy behavior, Sr. Celeste announced in front of Ruby, "She's a fetal alcohol syndrome baby, a condition caused by the mother drinking while pregnant," making Ruby to grin from ear to ear as if she had won a contest. Without a hint of self-consciousness, Ruby visibly swelled when her special contribution to the home was declared.

"I turned sixteen this week," Ruby gushed, announcing this benchmark in her life with pride.

"Wow," I said, genuinely surprised at how young she looked, about thirteen.

"Girls, this is Anne," Sr. Celeste broke in. "She's a volunteer and will be helping Sr. Hyacinth at the Retreat. I was just telling her about Ruby and how her condition was totally preventable."

By their reactions, Ruby's plight was old news to them; my working as a volunteer is what they found hard to believe.

"A volunteer?" they asked in unison. "You're working here for free?"

"That's right," I croaked, the feeling on my lips returning along with the gradual opening of my air ways.

I stood in the middle of the group, hunched over, panting like a dog.

"We stopped by to check on you. Hyacinth was worried you might be frightened staying here by yourself."

"Me, frightened? What's there to be scared about staying in an empty retreat by myself surrounded by the spirits of saints and guardian angels to protect me," and remembering where I was, added, "and warriors to protect me?"

"Well, we just stopped by to be sure and the girls wanted to meet you. But if you're sure you're…," Celeste asked again, looking at her watch.

"I'm fine and there is plenty of food in the refrigerator," and aware I would be feeling the effects of our meeting long after they were gone, looking at the girls, I said, "You've left me with more than enough."

Sister asked if I wanted to join them on a trip into town but I declined, I'd already seen the town. It was the countryside I was anxious to explore. Nothing was pressing at the retreat, no guests staying in the hogans and no visitors ambling about; there was absolutely no one around. This was the perfect time to go on a leisurely sightseeing hike by myself, when the place was deserted. It sounded like a good idea at the time for some innocent fun and as long as I promised myself to be careful, where was the harm?

There were a couple of buildings at the top of the property that belonged to the local parish I hadn't investigated yet, but they were so close, I could check them out them out any time I needed to investigate the surroundings before deciding whether I wanted to volunteer here or not, and like I said, I had already seen the town. I needed to make the most of the time I had left during my decision making week.

I waited until Celeste's car was out of sight and almost before the dust settled, I was off and running. It felt good having time to myself, I could finally breathe. Getting to know the retreat director and meeting her Franciscan partner and her teenage dependents, no matter how friendly they were, was still work having to *handle* myself by watching what I was saying and the way I was acting.

I glanced at the empty grounds and unoccupied buildings. If I didn't know better, I would have thought I had stumbled into a ghost town. I imagined seeing movements out of the corners of my eyes, ghosts of old timers searching familiar haunts. And for a second, I felt the desolate feeling that comes from being far from home. Shaking it off, I ignored the wind rolling tumbleweed across the yard and the forlorn sound of a lone bird launching itself high in the air in an obvious rush to vacate the premises.

Outside the retreat grounds I walked to the edge of the hill behind my hogan and stopped to look at the white fluffy clouds in a background of deep blue. A feeling of reverence came over me as I was engulfed in the physical peace of an endless New Mexico sky and stood in readiness at the top of the hillside looking down, ears cocked and eyes staring at the steep descent of the gradient in preparation for sliding. I cautioned myself not to take unnecessary risks as I prepared to shalom all the way to the bottom of the hill.

Little by little I slid on the incline like a skier traversing a mountain, the tongue of my white tennis shoes filling with red dirt instead of snow as I angled downward, stopping and starting with some difficulty. With a panting heart, I came safely to a stop reaching the bottom unscathed, only picking up pebbles in one shoe.

The crusty reddish brown land was easy to walk on in shoes that were now the same color of the hill. Walking on a terrain full of dry withered weeds dotted with rust colored rocks, I thought how the best thing about sightseeing was in not knowing what you will experience: a lone bellow from a steer on the next hill, seeing an eye-catching hue on the horizon, or finding an artifact from an earlier age. More than once I've had to do a double-take at what I've found or what has found me.

Clear of the hogans, I started walking in earnest. Moving in a slow, steady pace, felt like I was in a walking meditation where the language of the body slows the language of the mind. Taking slow deliberate steps was an easy way of sorting through new experiences and unfamiliar people of the past few days as I acclimated to my unfamiliar surroundings.

Nearly tripping over a hefty size branch on the path I recalled how canes were branches once. The image of the plain wooden cane I used for a brief time came back to me after my severe bout with M.S. There were all kinds of walking sticks I discovered besides wooden: beautiful pieces of folk-art decorated with carvings of snakes that lend themselves to the stick's form, chrome ones, decorative, exotic, even collapsible. It brought back unpleasant memories of how the disease had weakened the strength in my legs. Releasing pent up anger aimed at the disease, it felt good to rear back and send the branch in the path flying, kicking it as hard as I could. I wanted to walk away from memories like these and anything else that reminded me of M.S. Canes, to me, were more of a hindrance than a help: Cause of death— *Contusion to cranium tripping over her walking stick.* The last thing I needed was something else in my way I could stumble over.

Reaching thicker ground cover, a warning crossed my mind; this is just the kind of place snakes like to hide. I looked at what was protecting my feet and saw tennis shoes and thin socks; together they barely kept my feet warm and regretted not wearing my garden boots, the same ones I used as protection against snakes in the monastery. I pictured the crumpled and hard boots standing useless in the closet. They were nothing like the comfortable looking pair of knee-high moccasins I saw Indians wearing but at least mine were high enough to keep snakes from biting my ankles, carefully placing my feet over a patch of dense foliage.

I continued walking with the knowledge I should have been more prepared against attacks from low-striking critters. I have never owned a snake-bite kit but at least I could have brought a knife for opening a bite and sucking out venom. And feeling a pebble rubbing a spot raw on my heel as a painful reminder, bringing a band aid or two to use as cushioning would have made my walk more comfortable.

I came upon a very large desert cactus covered with numerous open red flowers. Describing the color as plain red didn't do it justice as I looked at the continuous sequence of purple going from violet to mauve with every flower in-between a slightly different hue from the last.

The flowers were embedded in needlelike spines that didn't allow me to get close enough to detect a scent. I held my palm just out of its touch, wanting to find out for myself if the spines were as sharp as they looked. I teased the plant repeatedly by putting my hand near its porcupine covering when I was suddenly violently poked, and watched stupidly as a bead of blood formed on my finger that convinced me I wouldn't want to accidentally fall in its clutches. I had to admire a survival ploy that used a sequin of red flowers to attract birds together with a sharp defense to keep the species growing for eons.

Wiping the blood on my jeans, I wondered if the cactus was poisonous and ran through my knowledge of what to do in the event of accidental poisoning, but other than opening the wound, sucking out the poison and spitting, the only other medical treatment I remembered was to induce vomiting. I held out my hands that I used like rudders sliding down the hill but neither of them was clean enough to cut into, put to my lips and draw out the poison or stick down my throat. Scrunching up my nose at the thought, I promised to be more careful.

Circling the leafless plant, I had the uneasy feeling it was trying to evolve me there on the spot, attempting to turn the pink blush on my cheeks from the sun a deeper shade of red, luring me by its beauty in an effort to get my face to match the rest of the flowers. I didn't like the uneasy feeling of a plant surreptitiously trying to take over my body, so even though it was a breathtaking find and something I had never seen before or since, I made tracks out of there fast, walking away from my ultimate desert discovery.

As a woman walking alone, I am always on the alert. So when I heard a rustling in the weeds ahead I could feel adrenaline shoot through me like it was rocket fuel. I needed to find out what caused the rustling before I went any farther. The most logical explanation, it probably was a snake; it was the word *probably* that bothered me and I needed to know for sure.

Staying low I crept closer looking for a good place to peer through without being detected. There weren't many bushes around but there were a few and I was able to split a tall dry weed with my hands and quietly open a clear view. And there, in an undergrowth of loose branches and twigs, I saw the tips of two fuzzy ears. Momentarily, a body appeared. The pointy ears were attached to a kitten. Was I relieved to know it was only a cute tan colored kitten! But what was a kitten doing way out here other than looking confused, lost and very much alone? Separated from the rest of the litter, how could it survive out here in the wild? What was it living on? At this young age, it wouldn't have learned how to play cat and mouse yet and it wouldn't be fast enough anyway to expertly pounce on a field mouse or lizard. Leaving it here would mean certain death as it wouldn't be able to fend for itself.

That's when I had a brilliant idea! Since I'll be staying at a place that had a prayer by a famous friar reputed to be a lover of animals, the founder of their Order, no less, posted in each of the cabins, I felt it would be an act of kindness and my duty to take it home and care for the poor wayward creature. St. Francis would be proud! I avoided thinking what Sr. Hyacinth would say.

Ihave always been partial to kittens, especially ones as cute as this with its prominent ears and short tail. I had the brilliant idea of taking it back with me to live in my hogan, and for the next half hour we must have looked like a Laurel and Hardy comedy routine with me trying to catch it with awkward grabs and missed lunges with no luck. Clearly it did not want to be caught. I leapt at it over bushes, sidestepped assorted cactus and followed it through low chaparral. Its little body was almost a perfect blend in the weeds, camouflaging its darting in and out of the patches of brown scrub I couldn't keep up with the blur. Kneeling down, jumping up, trying to head the skittish creature off at every turn was no use, the compact flurry of pent up energy was frightened to death and running for the first of its nine lives.

Grabbing an opportunity of calm, I cautiously advanced until it was almost within my reach when suddenly a flash of heat pounding insight ran through me. I don't have many of what I would call insightful flashes, but this one hit me like a sledgehammer and stopped me in my tracks. This was not a house cat, a *Felis cactus* or even a *F. domesticus*, this was a bobcat! And where an offspring was, the watchful eyes of the full grown parent were sure to be prowling around here too! When I realized this, I felt all the blood drain from my face feeling the mother's cold, calculating eyes staring at me from a hiding spot somewhere out in the desert!

At that moment, two things about cats came back to me; *Jacobson's organ* (an organ in the roof of their mouth that allows them to taste what they smell) and how cats were ambush hunters by nature (lying in wait to make surprise attacks!) This second bit of cat trivia I remembered didn't make me feel any better; lying in wait, creeping up, and pouncing, these images came to me, not one at a time, but in animated shorts; alive, attacking and ferocious!

Now I was literally afraid to move. Ever so slowly I straightened up and made two sweeps with my eyes around me, one to the left and one to the right; nothing fast, just slow side looks round about, hoping against hope my vision wouldn't land on anything licking its chops in preparation for feeding.

Not knowing what would be considered aggressive posturing to a wild bobcat, I kept thinking, *easy does it* as I slowly backed away, not wanting to make any sudden movements.

I continued my slow retreat in a non-assertive backward slouch for what seemed like an eternity. Then putting one foot heading the opposite way from the other, in one quick spinning move I was able to turn around and face the other direction and started walking. After a while my walking broke into a loose trot, and with my heart fluttering with dread, my worry broke into a high speed acceleration that I didn't think even a puma could match.

I found myself walking faster and faster while thinking about my averted close call and what *could* have happened. Now with every step I heard *how stupid could I have been* resounding in my head realizing I had cheated death once again because it hadn't picked up my two strong scents, that of my deodorant or that of my trembling fear which had broken out as a salty perspiration over my body, which in my calculation, was more of a dead give-a-away.

A stab of hope quickened my step when I realized I had I saw the familiar stack of logs in the walls of the hogans on top of the hill and finally relaxed. I was able to breathe freer still after I had climbed the hill and looked out over in the direction of the bobcat. Uttering a murmured thankfulness, this was one sightseeing day I was glad was over.

Sr. Celeste and the girls were back and they were carrying food items into the retreat kitchen and it didn't take long for the girls to spot me as I walked into the front yard. It felt good to be back safely at home seeing the familiar faces and friendly smiles of the group home girls in the yard.

The next moment I was surrounded by excited girls being followed closely behind by Sr. Celeste, all of whom were frantically telling me about their day all at once, the girls going on about a sale at a *Trading Company*, Sr. Celeste making sure I knew of the shameful cost of soaring meat prices at the market; Sister commending my decision of staying behind and taking advantage of the peaceful retreat surroundings.

The girl's detailed summaries of the day suddenly quieted when little Ruby asked the question that must have been on everyone's mind, after turning down an exciting trip into Gallup for excitement, what did I do all day?

With their inquisitive eyes searching my face, I quickly thought back over the events of the day; how I risked life and limb scrambling down the back hill, avoided being poisoned by a cactus (no sign of itching or a rash yet) and how I had outrun a mother bobcat leaving it to eat my dust, instead of me, then scrambling my way back up the hill again.

That was the moment a piece of chile decided to work free from a tooth to release its stinging sharpness on my tongue along with memories of this morning's fiery onslaught, making the rest of the threatening events of the day pale in significance. With the audience of curious juniors and an interested adult standing in rapt attention around me, I knew out of everything I had done that day, the most difficult and challenging of them all had been worth it; wiping my eyes, I had earned their respect, even if it was one seed at a time.

CHAPTER
4

The next morning without hearing the chortling of Hyacinth, the playful romping of the girls, the reprimanding presence of Celeste, or retreatants wandering about the Center muttering prayers to break the silence, it was a good knowing I had the entire place to myself. I sat up in bed and listened to the quiet. Being newly diagnosed, quiet was just what I needed to give my speaking muscles a chance to rest and heal.

Becoming accustomed to solitude is an adjustment in itself, but coupled with having so much leisure time, it was intimidating. It put me in mind of the curler lady, a homeless woman I knew growing up who walked about town with green, quarter-size, plastic curlers in her hair. I never saw her without the curlers. She didn't try to hide them under a scarf or a cap making me wonder what or who had interrupted her as she readied herself for the day that was so disturbing she was never quite right again. She seemed complacent enough when I passed her sitting on park benches, visiting service stations or crossing streets; other than her weird hair fixation, she was completely rational. She wasn't a danger to herself or others and I would never call her crazy, but I questioned the mental stability behind her odd behavior. Madness surfaces in a variety of ways and being here alone with my thoughts, I wondered how long it would take before I started talking to myself.

I dressed quickly and pulled on socks and shoes. Sitting at the kitchen table watching the seconds disappear on the stove clock, I asked myself the same question every person who goes on a contemplative retreat must ask when faced with the prospect of filling time—what do I do now?

It was logical for me to about hermits and what they did to fill their ascetic solitude. It didn't take long before I thought of Thomas Merton, hermit and Trappist monk. I had a good idea what he did all day, write. The more I thought of him, the more things about his life came to me, especially an episode that didn't actually involve him; it was after his death but it was connected to the memory of him and his hermitage.

Merton lived as a hermit later in life in a cabin in the back woods of Kentucky on his monastery's property. After his accidental death by electrocution in 1968 in Bangkok, a freelance writer wanted to see what it was like to be a hermit like Merton. He wanted to relive Merton's life as closely as possible wanting to experience everything Thomas did so he asked permission from Merton's Abbot in Gethsemani, to let him stay in Merton's hermitage. One afternoon a storm developed and lightning hit at the same time the visitor was using the Merton's electric typewriter and the visitor was severely shocked, uncannily reminiscent how Merton's electrocution.

The visitor got what he came for, any closer he would have experienced Merton's final breath too. Now if the visitor had been a true contemplative, he would have stopped typing to stand at the door and watch the rain as it splattered on the leaves in the forest. In Merton's own words in The Sign of Jonas: "As long as it's going to rain, I'm going to listen."

I walked to the hallway and looked through the sky-hole; not a cloud in the sky, it wouldn't be raining anytime soon and a sign I should start landscaping the yard. I went outside and walked through the overgrown walkways and cacti with tumbleweed stuck in their spines. When I reached the top of the property, I stood at the hairpin turn and looked at the sorry state of the yard. I told myself the night before the yard would look better in the morning, but after a good night's sleep, it looked worse. There was so much to do, the labor involved was overwhelming and remembered a comment Hyacinth made when I first arrived, "Frankly, I don't know how the parish let it get to this state." I could see her point, then again, Gallup isn't known as a spiritual hub of the West, and why it took so long for a prospective religious community to decide whether they should take on such a risky venture located in the poorest diocese in the U.S. Assuming the financial obligation of running a retreat center in a place where the majority of the people didn't even speak English, I understood why the yard looked the way it did. What religious organization had the personnel strong-willed and far-sighted enough to believe they could turn the center around and hold out through the hard times? I was beginning to understand first-hand what the words pioneering spirits stood for.

Even after my walk yesterday, I was anxious to get started on the yard. A spiritual place like St. Francis retreat needs to be a place to make you want to pause and reflect in the beauty of a well maintained yard. But, I didn't want to haphazardly clip here and saw there, I wanted to bring a botanical alchemy to the yard and transform its wild energy into a benevolent energy more suitable for a retreat center. Desperate matters called for desperate actions. It called for extreme measures to transform the hill into a perfect spiritual spot; it called for feng-shui. I was sure the traditional Chinese art and science of living in harmony with the environment was what the yard needed. Based on the Taoist vision that believes the land is alive and filled with energy, this ancient art of interconnectedness was a concept I could easily get behind.

It made sense that to have perfect harmony and peace of mind, the grounds must reflect the same orderly tranquility. I firmly believed that once the grounds were in balance, the retreatants' energies would follow. Hyacinth would never discern my intentions from the way the yard looked, all she would think was that the yard had been straightened and cleaned. I would re-energize the yard so we would be living in its happy effects right under her nose.

A spiritual place like this should look organized. I saw clearly how it should be with the dirt walkways cleared and the borders defined. Mentally, I sketched in paths to curve around plants eliminating the jarring effect of the dagger-like pathways leading directly to the office and hogans. I'd replace the paths with bending walkways to give off softer energy. As far as Hyacinth was concerned, the yard probably just looked better, not balanced due to feng shui. She wouldn't know I used feng-shui to fill the court with forces of yin-yang bringing it into balance. She would be overjoyed seeing how much better it looked and not because, in essence, I had cleaned its energy too to help bring retreatants to harmony and tranquility.

I didn't think Hyacinth would go for hanging lanterns around the yard but she might invest in a small statue of Buddha sitting in a full lotus position in the bushes to bring a contemplative awareness to the yard, or possibly a statue of a Native American Chief sitting with his legs crossed holding a Peace pipe; both figures represented a strong life force.

Invigorated by my spiritual plan, I went to work on what would make the biggest difference the fastest. I slipped my hands into work gloves, picked up a rake from the porch breaking a wed of cobwebs, and began clearing the jangled mess of lifeless, limp plants gathering them into a pile to be tossed over a back hill.

I was testing my physical endurance, when I was picking up branches, I was examining my balance. With every task I was testing my muscles unobserved. And there was no job too menial to me because I was overjoyed just to be walking! When my raking muscles tired, I picked up a saw and went to work on the juniper and manzanita shrubs. One by one I cut the dead branches felling them in deadened tumbles like watching paratroopers dropping to the ground, their red berries landing on my old garden boots like drops of blood.

There was little I could do about the energy of the linear road at the top of our hill joining the circular road without a bulldozer even though the straightness of this road suggested turmoil, confrontation, disputes and battles. There was even less I could do about where the hogans had been placed: adjacent to the circular road, forced to receive unsettled energy from ongoing incoming and outgoing retreat traffic. And because the hogans were irregular octagonally shaped, I questioned whether they were all in or out of balance. It made sense buildings with irregular shapes would hinder the flow of energy and cause it to flow irregularly. The challenge for me was what, if anything, I could do to neutralize the bad energy filling the yard.

The rest of the week I looked for something I could put in the yard that would offset any leftover negativity of former occupants. Maybe an Indian artifact hidden among the cactus or a strategically placed angel in the juniper, or a small sign like the sign in the kitchen—God Bless St. Francis Retreat positioned somewhere in the yard to counterbalance the energy. It was tricky finding anything to counterbalance the energy in the yard, but I was certain there was something, but what? Maybe burning a yin/yang symbol on a piece of dead manzanita would work? I did bring my soldering iron with me…

Working hard on the yard made time go by quickly. I became accustomed to being by myself and noticed a deepening within like I was on a retreat myself. At the end of the week, I felt like a real hermit and less threatened and even began eating in the large dining room to enjoy the view over the reservation. I wouldn't call it fasting, but I did eat sparingly; Merton would be pleased.

In a short time I saw big improvements by eliminating clutter first. This created a favorable way for the yard influence retreatants. Anything that was unnecessary, I discarded. I wanted the energy of the retreat to flow unimpeded along the walkways, around trees, shrubs and rocks. I was sure this unobstructed environment would free the flow of energy for retreatants, as well as the retreat staff.

There had only been two phone calls during the entire week but this was to be expected in a place recently taken over by another order and under new management; the news was just starting to get around.

Toward the end of the week, late in the day, I heard the advancing sound of a truck working its way up the hill and put down the rake and listened. There it was again and growing louder by the second. With a cloud of dust, a whiff of exhaust fumes and a loud voice, no doubt about it, Hyacinth had returned! And she was hauling a large white object in the back of the truck.

She pulled the pick-up truck into the retreat and parked, yelling through the window, "Wait till you see what my brother left the retreat!" pointing to the back of the truck.

I ran to see. She had only been away seven days but it was long enough for me to forget her frequent smatterings of laughter, her hearty laughter and gladsome guffaws.

I didn't know Sr. Hyacinth very well at this point. She could have brought back anything—a large ceramic wood nymph, a bird bath attached to a figure of Francis, or maybe a sign, the retreat needed a sign identifying or property as Catholic retreat Center. I stood near the back of the truck and contemplated the options.

A large bundle in the truck had been wrapped in furniture pads for the transit. It was exciting unveiling the object amid a backdrop of Hyacinth's laughter and I was glad I had chosen this retreat center for my volunteer assignment and live among easy going Franciscans.

The second I saw the tall statue standing rigidly erect in the back of the pickup, I involuntarily yelled, "Jesus!" not in a profane way but in surprise. It really was a larger than life size statue of Jesus, its arm sticking out to the sides like they were built-in perches for birds.

I was stunned. It was as if Hyacinth had been reading my mind all week! What better object could there be to ward off negative influences at a Catholic retreat center than a statue of Jesus? I had been looking for something to draw negativity out of the yard the entire week and here it is delivered at my feet like she had picked up my brain waves.

She said her brother left it to the retreat. "I thought it would look good here in front so people will make no mistake they were entering a Catholic retreat center.

A statue is almost as good as a sign I conceded.

"Anne! Wait till you see it up close!" she yelled, excitedly.

"It weighs a ton, so wherever we decide to drop it, it has to stay. One other thing is, when it was loaded, two fingers on the right hand were knocked off." And without hesitating, she turned to me and asked, "Anne, do you think you could fix it?"

Anxious to have it repaired, Hyacinth took out the two fingers from her pocket and said, "One little finger and one regular finger, intact," handing the grotesque looking digits to me. The fingers had been snapped off at the knuckles but I was happy to see they still had the outlines of fingernails at least.

"I can't believe I am saying this, but as a matter of fact, I think I can," surprising myself as I pictured my hands in a lumpy mixture of plaster of Paris making glass mosaics in the monastery.

Sr. Hyacinth backed the truck in and stopped to the left of the big tree in front, got out and walked to the back to let the tailgate down. I climbed up into the bed. Taking the statue by the shoulders, we waddled it end of the truck bed, opened a furniture pad and placed it on the end of the gate and slowly let the statue slide down to its permanent resting place. Jumping down, we pulled off all the protective pads and stood momentarily sizing up the unobstructed likeness of Jesus.

"Just look at it," Hyacinth urged, with stars in her eyes. "Isn't it beautiful?" her eyes taking on a dream-like quality like she was imagining the majestic statue in Rio de Janeiro standing at the entrance.

I didn't know that much about statuary, but I thought this artist's rendition of Jesus was a good one. Tasteful and simple, it was just the right whiteness in its unpainted state to pull off a porcelain-like purity that was so white it looked like it was giving off an aura.

"I like it. It will add a lively effect to the yard," I told her, making a mental note to stick my head out of my hogan tonight to see if it glowed in the dark.

Looking at its open arms I thought it couldn't help but pull people in. It's just what the yard needs to encourage people to come on retreat and leave their everyday anxieties down the hill."

She smiled in agreement.

Motioning with her hand and I followed her to the front of the property so we could get the full impact by pretending to be retreatants walking in seeing it for the first time. It was an impressive figure even minus the two fingers standing fast; arms open wide, hailing all passers-by with its radioactive hue.

After close scrutiny, she exclaimed, "I know what it's missing. It doesn't have any eyes!"

I had noticed it too; staring straight ahead unblinkingly, gave the impression it was sizing up its new location. I knew what she meant it didn't have any color in its eyes.

"Anne, when you're attaching the fingers, do you think you can put in some color in the eyes as well?"

"I don't think…" I said weakly, my protestations were unheard, lost as they were in her gift for all humanity.

The next day Hyacinth took me to an unfinished basement beneath the chapel I could use as a shop. A stationary table had been wedged into the dirt floor for stability and the rest of the unfinished room was a sloping mound of earth where renovating had stopped. Cobwebs hung from the wooden framework of the roof like icicles glistening in the light now the door had been pulled open, and an unopened bag of plaster of Paris was waiting for me next to the table for my project. Cans of paint were stored against the far wall.

I questioned her judgment in letting an inexperienced person, someone who she had personally known for about one day total, reattach heavy cement fingers to a raised hand on a statue. I agreed, on one condition, that I wouldn't be held responsible for any psychological damage incurred by a retreatant who happened to find two lifelike dirty fingers washed up in the garden somewhere after a heavy rain.

It was creative work and it was fun, challenging, but fun. Standing on a wooden box, I fit the two fingers into the hand of the statue smearing Plaster of Paris around the knuckles and painstakingly cleaned the outlines of fingernails. The eyes were more difficult. Remembering the eyes on the children of Fatima didn't help because they were in ecstasy after seeing the vision of Mary and not many people are physically able to look up and back so unnaturally. The tall white figure standing prominently with its arms extended was imposing enough without adding pupils that could make people stare and point.

The steady blank stare on the statue made me think of the opposite, and what nystagmus, a condition associated with M.S. had done to my own eyes making them impossible to control their jumpy eye movements. One thing was for sure, the nausea and vomiting I felt along with it was nothing like the overpowering joy brought on by spiritual ecstasy.

The washed out and faded pupils on the statue brought back a change in the way I saw colors too when I had the acute attack; optic neuritis. Another distinguishable M.S occurrence that makes color imperceptibly dim for a week (or two) but, to my great relief, colors return just as slowly. Which explains my wearing alizarin crimson with phalo blue even though it was a color no-no; I literally couldn't see they clashed. But at the moment I was free of these conditions and while I was cleaning the statue's eyes, it was difficult not to feel an overwhelming thankfulness.

I went to the workroom to pick a color for the pupils. Searching the cans of paint along a wall I went with Seductive Sable because seduction comes in all forms and since I was using the statue to draw bad energy from the yard, somehow it fit.

When I applied the dark brown to the pupils, as gingerly as I brushed the muted brown on, my attempts didn't look right. It was only by accident I picked up a brush with a drop of paint thinner that made the pupils immediately look right. From its head to its toes, it was perfect, finished at last and let it dry in the sun.

I summoned Sr. Hyacinth to view the final product and we stood in the pine air, evaluating it with a critical eye. The moment of truth had arrived.

"You can't even tell which fingers you put on," she said, inspecting my work at close range. "And those eyes, I love what you did with the eyes. They seem to look right through you. You know what would be nice though?" she coaxed. "Let's bring one of the little benches on the porch over and put it in front so people will really feel the presence of Jesus even if it's only His shade."

"Let's get it" I said, jumping up, relieved even at this close range my handiwork met with her approval. We walked to the porch and took hold of an end of a bench, staggered with it to the statue and set it under the branches of the oak tree. I was happy the job was done and was really glad Hyacinth was untrained and unqualified in the art department so she wouldn't be able to know what a crude and inexpert repair job I did. To distract her I kept pointing out different plants in the revitalized yard, "Look at the star cactus, I think it grew another rib while you were away. See what a little water did for that old man cactus? It nearly doubled its hairy spines."

We sat in the shade for some time regarding the statue philosophically under from the watchful gaze of the statue of Jesus. After a while, with the promise of good things to come, in a hopeful tone she said, "There's no telling what will come from this!"

I knew she was talking about the physical state of the yard and not her awakening awareness due to the subtle changes in the landscape, because when it comes to articulating the unseen, not many people are able to put spiritual feelings into words. I wasn't about to mention how the steady flow of energy from the yard's transformation was bound to have a positive effect on the spiritual well-being as well as the internal health of retreatants and staff alike. I'd let her make her own connection between the straightened and orderly state of the yard and the new sense of peace at the retreat, that by maintaining balance in the immediate organic environment surrounding the retreat, balance was imparted to everyone in the vicinity. Nor was I going to bring up how by separating the twisted and tangled greenery, it freed magnetic energy to radiate in all directions about the yard; when I cultivated the plants, I had cultivated the energy in creation too.

Yes, I thought with conviction, Hyacinth was right; there's no telling what will come from this!

And in her next breath said, "Oh, I forgot to tell you, one of the phone calls I returned was from Sr. Edith, a member of my own community. She received permission to work at the retreat with us. I know you're going to like her, she's an artist."

CHAPTER
5

Looking ahead, I could optimistically say it was a case of so far, so good. The director, Sr. Hyacinth, seemed to like me and so did her religious associate Sr. Celeste, stationed at the group home. The Navajo girls in her supervision were like kids everywhere; my tongue was still smarting in places to remind me of their visit. I knew I would enjoy their periodic visits to the retreat when they came to help and had hung the amber feathered dream catcher Sr. Celeste and the girls gave me as a welcoming present by the head of my bed. I thought I'd met everybody associated with St. Francis Retreat. That's when we heard the honk.

Without having to look, Hyacinth said, "That's Sr. Carol," as she got up from behind her desk and looked out the blinds. "She's a missionary from the neighboring parish. You wanted to see the reservation. Here's your chance. Go ahead, you'll have fun."

"Missionary Sister?" I wondered out loud. "I thought *all* Franciscans were missionaries."

"Yes, Celeste and I are missionaries too, you're right. But there are missionaries and then there are *missionaries.* Sr. Carol is not from our Order although we work alongside her at times. She has a real zeal for her work, you'll see. She typifies missionaries everywhere who go where they're needed and do whatever is needed. She is selfless and hard-working."

The last thing I heard Sr. Hyacinth say as I got up to go to a reservation with a total stranger was, "She's a real live wire, and you'll like her. Carol visits people in need by filling their bodies with physical sustenance while filling their souls at times with spiritual food in the form of God's word."

Sr. Carol slid her 4-wheel drive mud-splattered Bronco to a halt in front of the retreat porch. She was sitting behind the wheel of the Ford and it occurred to me that in her line of work of visiting the poor and attending the needy over remote reservation land, unlike her city counterparts who only went off-roading when they accidentally back over a flower bed, Carol actually *needed* a four-wheel-drive vehicle.

"Yah-te-hey Anne!" she shouted from the driver's side window. "Hyacinth said you wanted to go out to the reservation? I'm Sr. Carol, by the way."

"Yah te hey, Sister," I said back to her, although any resemblance to a Sister was solely in the mind of the beholder; no veil, no habit, no scapula (sleeveless outer garment hanging from the shoulders had been replaced with a miniature version worn like a necklace under garments). The only visible sign she was a member of any apostolic ministry was a small gold cross on the collar of her white blouse but you had to look hard to see it.

It was late afternoon when she threw the vehicle into reverse and said loudly, "Prepare ye the way of the Lord!" as she pointed us in the direction of the entrance and waited much like a bull pawing at the ground in readiness.

Although I had no first hand experience of the reckless driving skills of religious, a myth exists like an urban legend I suspected had grown out of one isolated incident exaggerated by second hand reports that had been widely circulated. I never paid any attention to them and disregarded them as hearsay and rumors but sometime in my life I had been warned. Sr. Carol looked like an able-bodied person; what could happen with an older, God-pushing nun driving? I didn't see any major damage to the body of the Bronco and took it as a good sign so I pulled the door closed tight behind me and heard it fasten shut with the finality of a prison door.

The first indication I was going to have a difficult ride when I moved in beside her was and searched around for a seatbelt and there weren't any; Sister Carol was riding unrestrained, free-wheeling like one of the feathers dangling from the rear view mirror.

Carol fit the description of a missionary like the inlay on her pocket knife. Of medium height with a wiry build; this plucky seventyish nun was as feisty as the devil and I was quickly under the impression she had the habit of giving to Peter what may have belonged to Paul when no one was looking, giving her the reputation of being devilishly angelic I found out, depending on who you talked to and where their affiliation lay, with Peter or with Paul. She belonged to the parish that built the church next to the retreat center near the top of our hill. It had a very unusual roof in the shape of an umbrella, a very large wooden umbrella, and I wondered if the parishioners were inclined to call on God for good weather. "It *is* a beautiful church," she boasted, "and full of beautiful artwork."

I told her I was looking forward to visiting it and she seemed to be visibly pleased but I was really thinking, how could there be art, way out here? I never expected to find a conference room at the retreat that looked like a ski chalet either, so I really was looking forward to visiting it.

"A visit to a church will do you good," she coerced, seeing me as novice potential. And making the most of a captive audience, her persuasive arguments as God's emissary began.

"Vocations today have gone the way of the world. Chopping wood for fires has been replaced with short walks to the thermostat to move the indicator up. Self-initiative in individuals has dipped as low as April temperatures in the desert. I can almost hear the rush to easier lifestyles in cushioned air soles, but when everything is handed to you on a silver platter it's hard to expect the opposite. I see this softness as laziness. Novices today enter with good intentions but head for the door in no time when the going gets tough anxious to put their gold rings back on and head for a manicurist. The last line heard on their way out: *it was too hard.*"

"It's always been the task of missionaries to bring spiritual and physical sustenance to oppressed people," she continued explaining.

Half listening, I thought, so what if she was trying to bring me round to her side. I can take a little Bible thumping, especially if it gets me inside the reservation.

Hanging from the rear view mirror was a ring made out of bark that had feathers dangling from it with two broken arrows intersecting the center. The abstract design was made of beads and string that were interlaced throughout in a meaningful fashion. At the bottom of the wobbling mobile were a miniature drum and a tiny leather pouch.

Hoping to change the subject I started fingering one of the feathers to look at it more closely. She explained, "It's a replica of a Medicine Wheel, a symbol of peace and tranquility used to ward off evil spirits. I use it to ward off bad drivers."

"Does it work?" I asked.

"So far," she said, giving a quick glance up to heaven. Adding, "But part of the peace pipe fell off last week," letting me know there could be cause for concern.

Half joking and half serious, I asked, "Do you think that's an omen a piece of the car was going to fall off next like a tire, do you?" Being New Mexico, I was beginning to wonder just how much stock I should put in these symbols. I could see the cynical expression on an officer's face if we told him a piece of a Medicine Wheel had fallen off so we should have known something was going happen. Considering we were in the land of enchantment, he may have agreed with me and not even flinched.

Sister pointed at it explaining, "These four sections with the arrows represent the four sacred directions. But if we think like a Navajo, there are really six; east, west, north, south, and up and down." I was beginning to realize how much more advanced Navajo thinking was from my own.

We were driving on a smooth paved road of the main highway at the bottom of the retreat hill traveling away from town. It was only a couple minutes before Sr. Carol slowed and turned right. We never passed a sign letting us know, Reservation Next Right with an arrow.

I don't know how she knew *where* to turn because the land all looked the same, patches of weeds and dirt, then more patches of weeds, but she could tell which turn off led to the reservation and we went off the main highway on a road. (I use the term *road* in the broadest sense; it was evident someone had driven this way before because the weeds were crushed).

I was very surprised I didn't see any signs notifying us we had crossed onto the reservation; no informative signs reading: ***Welcome to 26,000 square miles of Navajo Reservation, Elevation: 6,000, Population 7,000, 'A Timeless Community'***. I expected to see something more dramatic like a Thunderbird, the well-known symbol for happiness, carved in a fence post, or even a spear sticking out of a mound of dirt at the entrance might be all that was needed to signal the start of reservation land. But the only indication was the paved highway was now a dirt road full of bumps, holes, and rocks. I was disappointed to see Indian reservations **looked** the same as other land so a visitor would have to know *beforehand* they were passing over a boundary line and were now on federal land.

There were no road signs posted whatsoever; not even speed limits. I especially missed seeing signs warning, **DIP AHEAD**, or cautioning **ROUGH, ROUGHER** and **IMPASSABLE** marking the surface accordingly would not be amiss. All the while, Carol had been concentrating on the road trying to identify landmarks and an occasional familiar homestead to help keep her going the right way, with me bouncing around the cab like a lottery ball.

After an hour of turning this way and with no miscues, I asked her how she knew where she was going and she told me, "When you've been over these roads as often as I have, you remember." As a passenger, I steadied myself by holding on to the dashboard, the door and the bench seat, anything that was buckled own. It was past dusk when she found the turnoff. And even if she was steadying herself by holding the steering wheel, the jolting roads didn't faze her in the least; Sr. Carol was as rugged as the Southwest itself.

We pulled in front of Leonard's dark hogan and turned off the engine. Our headlights had shown there wasn't a door to knock on, it was off its hinges and leaning against a barrel on the side of the hogan. Doors I learned acted like thermostats; taken off in the summer and reattached in the winter. Anything or anyone could have wandered in. It was an eerie feeling standing in the dim light trying to adjust our eyes to an interior of a dwelling that was darker still.

Peering through the window from the Bronco into the hogan we were to see someone or something sitting quietly inside, but we couldn't be sure. It was dark and absolutely motionless. Muttering softly between us, we decided it looked like a hunched over figure and without the engine running, the deafening silence seemed to confirm the figure was dead. I looked at Carol without speaking, and saw her quietly open her car door, so I did the same. Little by little I transferred my weight to my right foot and slid from the car, keeping one eye on the vacant door and one eye on Sr. Carol, who was miles away on the other side of the car. I wanted to get back in the car, lock the door and leave this crypt behind. Instead, I swallowed hard and watched Sr. Carol inch her way toward the hogan. It was as quiet as a cemetery and it took all my courage just to stand there in the dark holding onto my open car door for security, in case I had to suddenly leap back inside.

At that moment a chicken flew out the hogan door, squawking and flapping, flying for its life. My heart stopped beating and I could tell I wasn't breathing. From somewhere in the room came a voice, "Is that you, Sr. Carol?"

"Good Lord, Leonard, you 'bout scared us to death! What in the world are you doing sitting in the dark like that? Where is your lamp, and I'll light it for you," as we were about to enter the dark interior of his hogan.

"No, I will," he said, striking a wooden match against something lying on the floor beside his armchair without getting up. "I was sitting here watching the sun go down." He leaned over the lantern and the room brightened with light as the wick caught the match.

As my eyes adjusted to the dark, I let go of the car and moved behind Carol now that I could see more clearly. I stepped toward the hogan keeping Carol in front of me and I took a sniff of the strong odor of kerosene as we went inside the hogan. A man was bending over adjusting a wick of a lantern and I had my first glimpse of Leonard.

He had the dark tan and deep laugh lines around his eyes typical of a Native American revealing how he had taken severe punishment from the intense, dry, New Mexico sun. I was aware Native Americans are unable to grow facial hair but his rugged face had a strong jaw that didn't need to be hidden behind a mustache or beard. His age could have been anywhere from 50-100, in the flickering shadows thrown by the lantern it was impossible to tell. He was sitting in a sagging armchair resting squat in dirt like it was growing there. His immobility may have been due to rheumatism which would increase my estimation of his age, or his not getting up could have been just sleepiness. In any case, it made guessing his age difficult.

I was introduced out of courtesy but I held about as much interest for Leonard as if I were vacuum salesman for his dirt floor. With the lantern flickering light around us, we watched as the awakened chicken backed its way to its nest again and began pecking at the straw; sufficient cleaning for someone who may or may not have a door depending on the season.

Carol and I sat on wooden chairs in a haze of twilight shadows cast by the lantern. Facing the lamp, Leonard stretched out his stiff legs to the woodstove, content just to sit and listen to Sr. Carol talk. I looked around at the mixture of dented pots and pans on the shelf along the wall, to the water barrel on the floor he was using as a wood stove next to a cot with a gray blanket straightened across it near the woodstove, to a little pile of cut wood within reaching distance and was overcome by the force of his circumstances. The strong impression of a scavenging wolf running through a forest of pine came to mind just trying to exist.

Small talk was not one of Leonard's strengths as I listened to Sr. Carol and Leonard exchange community news, Carol doing most of the talking. I admired his lack of small talk as he leaned back in his old and worn armchair. This simple one room hogan, with an old rusty pipe sticking up through a hole of the rough timber roof, acted liked his hermitage and I felt envious of his contemplative nature. In an un-dramatic way, Leonard had achieved detachment and peace; he didn't need to turn on a light, he was living in the light of his own consciousness.

It was usual for Sr. Carol to leave a couple of bags of groceries on her visits to isolated people who were miles from a store before she left. With good wishes, we finally said goodnight and left Leonard as we had found him, sitting motionless in his big chair in total presence, now less moribund to me after getting to know him.

Calling Yah-te-hey from our car windows, we waved goodbye leaving him to his quiet existence. Carol stepped on the gas and our vehicle bolted ahead but not before I turned to get one last look at Leonard. I watched as the light in his hogan grew dimmer and dimmer and knew he was adjusting the wick. The last image I had was of a completely dark hogan and knew he had extinguished the wick in the oil.

Turning around to face the long road home, we heard the unmistakable loud cry of a wolf from somewhere from behind the hogan that was too close to ignore. I looked at Carol and saw her eyes widen in at its close proximity to us and she immediately stepped on the gas; we were both in a hurry to get home now. Maybe the cry loosened a primordial memory in her, and with it was a strong belief that fear can be controlled with a gas pedal, but as the car sped into motion I knew I was about to find out whether the old tale about a nun's lack of ability to drive was true. Rocking this way and that, I thought about the severity and duration of the rough ride ahead and how a bumpy ride couldn't be good for M.S. Resigning myself to my fate I hung on for dear life.

After gaining air hurtling a good size hole, I remembered people with M.S. should be careful not to upset their balance, and what a time to remember, when I was in the clutches of a mad motorist and there was nothing I could do. The next second we were streaking down an incline in the dark when fortunately something else about M.S came to me, *how patients having attacks involving vision problems usually recover fully.*

Squaring my shoulders, I put my faith in that one optimistic sentence and hoped it was true. Nevertheless, I still wondered what would come from all this bouncing and tossing about. It was bound to have a deleterious effect somewhere in my body; maybe it would knock my eyes back into nystagmus again and cause my eyes to jump repeatedly? The worst outcome of the ride might be and I shuddered as I thought, was if it brought on another bout of nausea, anything but that.

To my dismay, the sound of the lone wolf moving through the countryside had awakened a need in Sister to save my immortal soul and the next thing I knew she began to unleash a series of spiritual sayings before it was too late that included hornet's nests, gnashing of teeth and the necessity to atone for my sins. Realizing I was a captive audience in the seat beside her and not wanting to blow a golden opportunity of saving me from my hedonistic lifestyle, she began unleashing a series of warnings and impending chastisements doomed for the earth if we, as sinners, didn't straighten up and become remorseful. "The justice of God will fall like a thunderbolt," quoting the stigmatist Sr. Aiello.

Undoubtedly, learning the earth was to experience episodes of darkness and firestorms during three days of darkness wasn't the best topic for conversation when we were in a place that didn't have street lights. Looking down the road ahead, with our headlights bouncing off the darkness, I had the uncomfortable feeling the three days had already begun.

"Steady as she goes," Sr. Carol said, reaching a hand across to steady me as I felt my head lightly hit the roof when we rebounded off a mound of dirt.

"I'm all right," I reassured, hoping my vision would be too. It really wasn't her fault, I knew, she had no idea that I was struggling not to be sick. Between her thunderbolts, the impending '1800 thunderstorms' and my personal struggle to avoid car sickness, I was doing everything to hold myself together and wondered how much more I could take. I had the distinct impression she made for the reservation every chance she had so she could drive off the city's regular paved roads and go off-roading.

Seeing me as another soul to save, Sr. Carol didn't want to waste valuable road time, she kept up the pace of frightening judgments and prophecies: "Fight ye children of light; combat, ye small band that can see!" quoting Our lady of LaSalette.

Even though at no time did I feel we were ever *really* out of control, by the time we finally shot up the hill to the

Retreat Center, between the harrowing ride worrying if my soul already been corrupted and my ever present concern about the state of my health, when I was finally dropped off in front of the Brother Sun hogan, I wanted to get out and kiss the ground.

Opening the car door I stepped down and turned my face away from the low wattage outside light by my hogan door because I didn't want Carol to see I had turned green, not from the ride, but from worry. I was physically and emotionally drained, my legs were wobbly and I felt like I was still vibrating from the ride. Carol, on the other hand, had right on her side and her indignation to fortify her purpose was still raring to go. No doubt about it though, being a Sister or not, she could drive!

Now I had proof, concrete evidence about the driving capabilities of vowed individuals and developed a theory; because religious people live in communities are not allowed to own things like cars and don't have certificates of ownership in their names and use *community* cars, it's easier to be rough with something that isn't your own. On a deeper level, they see community cars having about as much worth as our mortal shells; both are rentals to be used for a brief time and returned. It was plausible.

She gave me a final "Yah to hey", punched the accelerator and was gone.

I answered back with a feeble, "Yah te hey" but by then she had almost crested the hill. I looked across the dark yard, at the shaded and silent retreat buildings and knew Sr. Hyacinth had gone to bed long ago. Fumbling for my key, I opened the door and was right back in Leonard's hogan remembering the pungent odor of kerosene and how the light danced on his features as we huddled together around a wood stove with grossly distorted faces. I pictured him now falling back easily in his frayed armchair as he listened indifferently to Carol's news of a world outside his hogan, the latest news bulletins meant nothing to him.

There had been something remarkable finding him sitting alone in the dark appreciating the quiet. It gave the impression that even though every day was the same as the next for him, he was one person who appreciated the silence of an unspoken word and unspoken voice while sitting in is comfortable chair listening to the hissing of the wood stove.

My hogan was cool as slipped on my pajamas. I was having a hard time shaking off the impact of my last look back as we drove away, of Leonard sitting by himself in a dim interior waiting for the dark night to engulf his one room hogan. It was a scene I'd like to remember always and one I hoped would pierce my sleep tonight in a dream… that is, if the dream catcher let it pass as a good dream, because as dreams go, it was bound to be a doozy.

CHAPTER
6

As soon as I pulled the curtain to one side in my bedroom bright morning light flooded in followed by current of cool outside air. I pictured Leonard wrapped in his faded gray blanket motionless, still sound asleep at this early hour and knew the morning air would rouse him and he would stumble, shivering and chilled to the pile of split wood beside his stove where he would reach with stiff arthritic hands to stoke the woodstove to start another day and wondered what he planned on doing today. I knew what he *should* do; put his door back on.

But this was my city-mind thinking. I was beginning to understand there is timelessness in New Mexico that causes people act in a slow, unhurried manner. I felt it too, although the deadline to give Hyacinth my decision about whether I wanted to volunteer here was pressuring me to make a decision and disrupting this slower mindset. Two years was a long time to be stuck in a place didn't turn out as trouble-free as I hoped. The skeleton staff of Sisters seemed nice enough, the location promised adventurous trips to locales not often visited, and the Indians were a unique group of people I'd find anywhere. Why couldn't I decide? It was as if I was waiting for a visible sign or some kind of divine intervention to take away the last of my nagging doubts. Moving to Gallup was a major life change to be sure. I would feel better if I had something concrete to let me know this was the right place for me to work as a volunteer and was the right decision.

I dressed quickly and crushed my way through the weeds to the main house for breakfast. Picking a box of cereal from the pantry, I joined Sr. Hyacinth who was sitting in the small dining room spreading jam on a piece of toast as I sat at my place.

"You must eat something more substantial than cereal if you want to keep up with Sr. Carol," she said, kidding. "How was your trip to the reservation?"

"I couldn't have asked to meet a more interesting character," I said.

"Sr. Carol told me she was planning on taking you to see old Leonard," she said, smiling as she remembered him. "He really is an odd type of shut-in; a real hermit."

"I was talking about Sr. Carol," correcting her. "But

Leonard certainly was a curious character too," I said quickly, telling her how he had scared us at first by sitting in the dark like a mummy. "Did you know he lets chickens wander in and out of his hogan?" I asked, excitedly telling how he had no door, electricity, phone, or heater, like I was imparting new details that were new to her.

"Gallup is a land of contrasts you'll find. There are over 200 millionaires living here while the rest of the people like Leonard live in grim conditions with no electricity, heat, water or phone."

"He doesn't seem to mind," I said, hoping we hadn't embarrassed him by the way we dropped in unexpectedly.

"Most people Carol visits are without phones so dropping in can't be helped; generally it's the only way and we have to."

I kept quiet about Carol's frantic driving if I had any hopes of visiting the reservation with her again so I didn't say anything to alarm Sr. Hyacinth about her flying over mounds of dirt, white-knuckle turns or Carol's speed on the straight-a-ways known as any available flat land. I moved the conversation instead to my immediate plans that involved no driving all; visiting the parish church next door.

With more exploring to do, there was little time for eating and I finished quickly. I pulled the door of the kitchen closed behind me and looked to my right from the retreat porch and could only see part of St. Jerome's roof from where I was standing. The church was within walking distance; a gradual walk uphill, but uphill nonetheless. At this altitude, *any* walking made breathing a chore and I took a deep breath and filled my lungs with crisp, sharp air you only find at 7,000 feet. After the harrowing ride the night before, a quiet visit to a church was just what I needed where I could sit and pray in peace on a fixed, stationary pew.

I listened to the loud sound my steps made crushing the sand in the quiet as I approached the entrance of the church. Standing at the bottom of thick wooden beams wedged into the side of the hill I thought if there was a rack of votive candles inside, I would light one to help me with my decision.

The climb was only seven over-sized steps but I was already winded from the slightly uphill walk across the yard at this altitude. Taking large gulps of air as I climbed, I stood at the top in front of two large wooden exterior doors and another set of typical storm doors used in cold climates to keep in the heat.

I pulled open the first heavy door and gently pushed through the second set until I was in the back of the church. My eyes blinked more from surprise more than from adjusting to the interior light. Rubbing my eyes, I couldn't believe what I was seeing, two gigantic floor-to-ceiling stained glass windows; one of St. Benedict and one of Our Lady of Guadalupe. I knew both figures intimately from having spent months painstakingly piecing each likeness together for glass mosaics while in the monastery in Arizona, only I measured my glass pieces by the inch, not by the foot. The two figures embodied a very important time in my life and when I had pushed open the doors to this church it was as if I had pushed open doors to my karma.

Seeing the same figures I had crafted out of bits of glass here before me was such a coincidence I stood in the empty church and just stared. I couldn't take my eyes off the beautiful panels of colorful glass, at the same stars on the garment of the woman, the same book of *Rules* in the hands of the monk; finding the two glass Saints felt like I had found two lost friends. I even imagined the smell of the warm, noxious fumes of the solder wafting over me as I fit in another piece of glass, the remembrance was that strong.

From that point on, I felt an immediate kinship to the retreat, to Hyacinth and to New Mexico. It was as if destiny had placed them here for a reason. The only way my decision could have been any clearer would have been if God Himself had called out to me, *Yes, you belong here*!

After the initial shock wore off I glanced around at the rest of the church and spotted another work of art to my left that was as bold as the windows. A plaque on the wall plainly identified the abstract work as a representation of the lion that had befriended St. Jerome, and went on to tell how after the saint pulled several thorns from its paw and doctored it, when the paw healed, the lion was as tame as a lamb and followed Jerome around from that point on.

The huge wood carving was spotted with dark textured knotholes, twisted limbs and uneven crevices winding around the truck in a villainous strangulation. The piece of gnarled mesquite was at least six feet tall and had been placed in the meeting room like the animal described on the plaque. Now that I knew what it was I could make out the pouncing posture, the ferocious head and wild mane, the vicious teeth, and swaying tail. The lion was still guarding his namesake.

The chiseled piece had been carved out of a thorny piece of mesquite, and from the little experience I had woodworking, scraping, sanding and staining branches to use as bases for artwork; I could appreciate the amount of effort it took to finish such a large sculpture. The entire piece had been covered in a heavy coat of shiny lacquer, reassuring the observer of its domesticated temper.

Not a moment to lose now, I bolted back out the inside set of doors and flung open the second set of double doors and jumped down the steps two at a time and ran down the hill to the retreat office. Bursting in on Sr. Hyacinth sitting behind her desk, I told her I was ready to make a two year commitment to live in Gallup and work as a volunteer at St. Francis Retreat.

"I thought *something* must have happened to you in church, the way you were running down the hill. That's great! That's what I was hoping, I'm glad you decided to stay on. Here, have a congratulatory mint," pushing a rounded dish full of them toward me.

I picked out a mint.

As I sat across from her, it looked like she was unconsciously preparing for my long term arrival already by straightening papers on her desk pad, sharpening pencils, moving a figurine of Mary to the middle of the desk, choosing a book out of a line of books being held together with bookends, reading the title, putting it back in line again.

Realizing her staff had just increased by one meant her workload had been cut and this came out in a variety of ways—the way she loosened the leather belt around her waist, untwisted the folds in her scapula and smoothed the black material across her lap before sitting back in the wooden chair to consider the possibilities.

I excitedly told her how when I was in monastery, I spent the months working on glass mosaics and I couldn't believe it but when I walked into the parish church, like a sign from God, the very same figures were here at the retreat. I told her I was confident I had made the right decision and I was looking forward to volunteering at St. Francis Retreat.

"Of course, you know what this means, don't you?" I asked, hoping she'd remain calm.

She looked at me with a quizzical look, afraid to ask.

"It means another road trip."

CHAPTER
7

It has always interested me how I think nothing of pushing my body; the sixteen or so hours sitting in the same cramped position, the stress and fear of losing my way, the very real danger associated with driving alone, all dissolved in the face of having my car with me so I could check out the land beyond the perimeter of the retreat property.

With one phone call to the depot, just that easy, Sister had me booked on an afternoon train scheduled to leave the station the next day at 2:00, saving me the cost of one votive candle. I was glad I didn't need to waste a petition to help with my decision, because although I try not to think this way, the petition I send up to heaven on the steady stream of smoke from a votive candle, reminded me of the imaginary smoke rubbed from a genie's bottle and I felt much better knowing I would be coming back to Gallup with all my petitions intact. With two years to go, something told me I'd need all the help I could get.

I felt an abrupt jolt and a glide forward, and like a python the train edged its way forward on the track. After spending a week in Gallup, some would call my going back to L.A. a cowardly act. Others would call my backtracking a hindering of forward progress, while still others would say it was plain idiotic. But this is what I planned all along; to check out the town and visit the retreat center to determine whether I could get along with the staff. If I was okay with all this

I would go back to L.A and drive my car back. As to the sanity of this plan, any objections to the contrary that surfaced were quickly dismissed by one very important fact: having my car with me meant I could go anywhere I wanted. Another encouraging push by the train in a westerly direction made me feel it was completely in charge of my situation and in complete agreement with my decision.

I could tell I was nervous about having to make the long drive back by myself by the way I was folding and refolding the map of California stretched across my lap. Tracing the route with my finger I saw no complicated freeway changes, roundabouts or zigzagging switchbacks to prevent me from driving straight through. Calculating the mileage from Gallup to L.A. as roughly 850 miles, I told myself the return trip would be like driving to the mall 20 times, if the mall was 50 miles away and somehow it made it feel less threatening. I estimated the drive time as only eight hours, wind and fog permitting and barring any unforeseen circumstances such as road closures or difficult maze-like detours, I told myself it wasn't going to be a bad drive back at all.

Our train moved up the track to where the pallid green frog was selling nerve pills. Its message spoke to me again with the same advice telling me *not to be nervous,* that prompted me to remember the words of my monastic retreat director, Fr. Walchars, to come back to me with a force:*God doesn't move the mountain; He gives you the strength and power to climb it.* Driving through a desert was a gargantuan mountain to me and my moan was lost in the noise of the engine.

I tried to remain calm. In an effort to assuage my panic I pushed back memories of my parent's desert breakdowns that had always been 1) in cars without air-conditioners 2) in cars that had been pushed to the boiling point trying to make good time and 3) and happened on a budget that didn't allow for breakdowns.

I forced out images of hissing radiators shooting geysers of scalding hot water over our car, onto the windshield and into my father's face. I blocked out the times we had to wait in the hot sun for radiators to cool before adding more of our dwindling supply of drinking water.

Smiling, I relaxed as I pictured my own car filled to overflowing with green coolant ready and waiting in the driveway at home.

I forced back nerve-racking memories of how a sudden desert rain storm caught our station wagon by surprise and the right windshield wiper blade wouldn't swing back, obscuring the right side of the road. I tried not to think of how dangerous it had been driving with rain pouring into us like a waterfall or how the person in the passenger seat had to reach around and push the blade back each time it needed to retract, leaving stringy strands of mop-like hair across the drenched face of the pusher. How unfortunate it was we didn't have a stick or ruler to push the blade back with because I was having a difficult time putting aside the distinct image of a cucumber moving back and forth, back and forth in front of my eyes, the only item of measurable length in the car.

I was trying hard to remain peaceful but with thoughts of the past materializing in my mind, it wasn't easy. I ignored memories of the flat tire our family had on a highway outside of Blythe in 100 degree heat and not seeing another car for what seemed like hours. And when we prodded our thumping lop-sided car to a run-down gas station, I remember how horrified I was when I opened the door of the restroom and saw hundreds of strange looking desert bugs clinging to everything. It took some fast guaranteeing on my part, but I convinced myself when I drove back this time, I would only stop at clean and modern looking, sanitary rest stops.

I looked from the train and saw Sr. Hyacinth standing in her calf-length black habit and I thought as I always do, it takes a lot of guts to wear a habit in public. It was easy for onlookers to mistakenly think the habit was being worn for effect; either the wearer was trying to get attention, or they were showing others how religious they are, missing the point entirely: reminding people of the presence of God.

I was glad the seat next to me was empty. Straightening out a crease, I followed the entire projected course again, flattening the paper as I followed the freeway with my finger along our route that looked straightforward enough; all I had to do was head east. I didn't see any dizzying heights better fit for llamas than cars, or indications showing the disruption and slowing caused by toll roads. I would be driving a Mustang and as long as the horses pulled together, I planned on driving straight through. Some would think this was unnecessary. Stopping for any reason gives the car a chance of not restarting; it's best to keep moving and not give trouble an opening.

I wouldn't let myself think of tire going flat and the battery not turning over or the fan belt snapping like an old rubber band; it wouldn't take much to disengage an engine, then with a sputtering and chugging, I would be stranded in the intense heat in the Mohave Desert shooing away vultures. I had spent the past week at the retreat convincing myself I had nothing to worry about concerning the long drive back, but I was still unconvinced.

Watching her wave brought up how different Franciscans were from Cistercian Sisters. Cistercians travel incognito, changing flowing cowls to regular street clothes to not attract attention. Sr. Hyacinth looked like she was starting a race as she good-naturedly flapped her arms waving goodbye; and with the roar of the engine warming up, in my mind I heard, "And they're off!" and observed the shrinking figure of Sr. Hyacinth as I moved away. Working with a community that was so outgoing and open, promised to be an adventure in itself.

Because it hadn't been that long since I left the monastery, everything had a monastic significance for me. Seeing Hyacinth in her religious trousseau waving goodbye to me, reminded me of the words of a Desert Father: *The cowl is a sign of innocence; the scapula a sign of the cross; the belt a sign of courage'. Let us then conduct ourselves in a manner consonant with our habit, wearing all parts of it with zeal, so that we do not appear to be wearing an alien garment.* Having heard the passage a number of times in monastery the words came easily to me. Even the ordinary act of watching Hyacinth wave goodbye brought a passage to mind from *The Rule of St. Benedict*, "Monks sent on a trip shall not neglect the Divine Office" and recalled how as Cistercians we were obliged to recite the Divine Office wherever we were; if we running errands and was time to recite the Office we pulled the car over and recited it privately. I remember with fondness the times we pulled into a park and watched the ducks floating gracefully on the lake while we prayed. And in an incredible stroke of luck, I remember how we happened to be visiting a parish church in Tucson when the organist began practicing Bach's *Jesu, Joy of Man's Desiring* in the loft above us and how the angelic sounds of the organ filled the empty church. A lunge from the *Southwest Chief* brought me heavy-hearted back to the present.

I waved one last time to Hyacinth before looking back at the route map spread across my legs and forced myself to think of my upcoming visit. I would tell my family it was only going to be a short visit. Long enough to tell them I was still among the living and what the retreat was like, that it had a conference room like ski chalet built completely out of redwood which made the entire room turn red at twilight, and how the retreat was directly across from an actual reservation. And yes, I did meet a real live Indian named Leonard, and no, he wasn't wearing a head band full of feathers. I would describe an Indian's version of a hogan with no electricity or water first *then* describe the revamped Retreat version that had these *modern conveniences*.

I'd brush aside the fact that my hogan was a few hundred yards from the main buildings. There was no need to worry; it was close enough for my screams to be heard. I would assure my mother my health could take working at the retreat so there really was no need to feel apprehensive. (I'd leave the bobcat episode out entirely.)

I would tell them I'd come back to pick up my car and I was lucky, even though this was Christmastime, they were not to worry, it was turning out to be a mild winter and the roads were sure to be without snow; I was too excited to think about Christmas anyway. And after all, I was used to spending Christmas away from home having lived two years in the Arizona monastery, the memory of practicing the carol, *Carol of the Bells* still fresh in my mind.

I imagined the astonished looks on their faces when I would tell them some Indians believe by taking their picture, some believe you are taking a piece of their soul, so please don't expect to see an album full of Indians when I returned for good. But after being exposed to the endless beauty of New Mexico, I felt it important to have my camera so I would have a permanent record of my incredible stay in New Mexico.

It is a long ride. I stepped from the train and set foot on my home turf but it wasn't until I smelled the salt in the air from the ocean that I knew I was really home.

My brief two day stay was filled with a happy excitement of what it was going to be like living in the southwest. My time home was also overshadowed with the knowledge I'd have to drive back through Arizona's deserts alone. And although I tried not to think about it, the drive back was weighing on my mind. Over and over I pictured traveling along the Cottonwood Cliffs, over Bill William's Mountain and through the Petrified Forest National Park. I could truthfully say I cut short my stay home just so I could get the drive back to Gallup over with.

Looking at the darkened house in the early hour it saddened me to be leaving my real home. It wasn't until I was outside the city limits that I became aware of the real direction in which I was traveling— away from the city where I had to hurry up to slow down with traffic, and I was going into the quiet and calm of the desert. As I imagined living in the slower pace and natural rhythm of New Mexico, I had the unmistakable feeling because I was going beyond words; I was going really going home to my self.

Settling into the car seat next to my camera case, I took off the top of the canteen on the seat beside me and checked for the umpteenth time to see if it was full. Confident neither I nor the car were going to die of thirst on some empty desert highway, I turned on the key and was relieved to hear the engine start up on the first try, but when I turned on the radio, instead of music, I heard the soothing voice of my former retreat director, Fr. Walchars reminding me *God doesn't move the mountain; He gives you the strength and power to climb it.* His words were like a booster rocket helping with my re-entry into the new and different energy of New Mexico by steadying my heart reflected in the slowing of my acceleration.

The trip was interminably long as expected but thankfully mechanically uneventful, picture-perfect, in fact. I was still basking in the fact that I was really going to live among Indians, learn their spiritual ways, soak up as much local color as I could; I had made the right decision.

With a dusty and grimy face from the road, I finally drove into St. Francis Retreat and parked next to Bro. Sun hogan and stepped on the emergency brake like it was an exclamation mark signifying I had returned for good! Sr. Hyacinth was happy to see me; in fact, from her enthusiastic reception I think she thought she'd never see me again. It made me wonder how many other volunteers had turned and run in the other direction after seeing the town. I almost did.

CHAPTER
8

I would have expected to see a forgotten passenger biting her nails in worry, but not Sr. Edith. The first duty Sr. Hyacinth and I took care of to begin the new year was pick up another Sister at the train station. We found her patiently waiting on a bench in the train depot reading a book and sipping a drink, totally oblivious to the fact Hyacinth and we were over a half hour late. She was casually drinking coffee out of a paper cup when we walked up and the way Sr. Edith was holding her little finger in the air led me to believe she was drinking some rare blend of tea rather than coffee prepared in a machine.

When she saw Hyacinth approaching, Edith gathered her belongings to her side, graciously stood and held out her arms to give Hyacinth, her old friend, a warm hug in greeting.

Edith was a delicate and dainty featured nun who was an artist and it was easy imagining her as a beatnik in her pre-nun days, smoking and drinking and hanging out in night clubs listening to jazz. Her black veil did little to keep long strands of wispy grey hair from flying in the air like a wild Bohemian and I had to suppress the urge to reach over and straighten her crooked veil. After I got to know her, this perpetually unbalanced look may have been the way she wanted to wear it; it didn't seem to matter to her. I smiled when I was introduced to this tall, thin Sister and caught myself before asking what she was wanted to drink when I ordered the next round.

The three of us walked to the Center's white car with Hyacinth explaining how she thought Edith would be a good addition to our staff which now consisted of three. Four, if you counted Sr. Celeste as part-time cook. I regarded Edith happily because it was good for Hyacinth to have other Franciscan community members around; one volunteer with a Cistercian background on staff was just not a proper religious community.

Edith seemed genuinely happy to be here and took time recently learning about Indian art, curios and customs. She was especially attracted to Indian spirituality answering my question why she had volunteered to help at this particular retreat center. As we drove through own, she stared so intently out the window at the town it made me wonder if she was having second thoughts. Learning about Indian spirituality was different than actually living in the Old West; book learning was fine but this was reality.

When we crested the hill and Sr. Edith saw the retreat center for the first time, she oh'ed and awed like I had done, surprised at the unusual shapes of the hogans, the size of the large conference room, at the chapel, and how spread out it all was. We pulled in and stopped. The moment we stepped out of the car onto retreat property, there was a different feeling, a palpable holy silence.

But there was something else, the slight sound of scraping. We didn't see a car or truck on the property, nothing to alert us of any company. There was no car, truck or horse on the property so the stranger must have walked in we figured. Our eyes eventually fell on a short man leaning against the tree, cleaning the heels of his boots with a stick. He was wearing jeans and a faded red plaid shirt and a brown cowboy hat was hanging on a branch above him.

The man's bent posture bolted upright on hearing the sound of our heavy footsteps plodding across the yard toward him. I saw him throw the cleaning stick off to the side now that introductions were imminent.

"Yah te hey," Hyacinth greeted him. She introduced herself as the director and asked who he was and if he was in the habit of cleaning his boots on someone else's property.

I was surprised by his response. "Yah te hey," Sister. They call me Franklin," in clear English. "I look over land for work; this looked like good road."

"How can you say that bumpy, second-rate road is good?" Sister asked puzzled.

"Any road that brings work is good; it is full of hope."

Dwarfed by Hyacinth's height and girth, I noticed his posture straightening as he was talking to her.

I guessed he was about fifty, age being determined by personality and vitality rather than looks. Guessing a Navajo's age was tricky; crippled and toothless could be signs of a rough life and not necessarily to age. So far, my guesses were way off. This time was no exception; Franklin said he was thirty but I had the feeling it was a rough estimate for him too.

I knew alcohol was a serious problem for Indians, and Gallup was no exception because when Franklin wandered into the retreat looking for work and a square meal, the first thing Hyacinth said, "If you're here looking for work, we can use a man with a strong back and a truthful spirit. There is only one rule; you may not bring alcohol to the retreat."

"I won't. I haven't touched a drop in over a month," he volunteered with pride.

"Good. If you want to work here, keep it that way," she barked, her tone was one of exasperation. "I'll have none of that at the retreat."

"I promise not to take alcohol. I will be like the eagle soaring high over the need for spirit water. I will be brave and rise high to the place of strength and power. I promise to be strong and work hard." And with dignity and pride he extended his hands displaying the effects of hard labor with reverence. "I am good worker." If calluses and cuts were an indication, he was.

"Good, be here tomorrow at 9:00 and I'll have work for you." Taking another look at his hands, Sister added, "Bring gloves if you have them. Yah-te-hey," she said as good bye and walked back to the office.

Sr. Edith, taken with this show of Indian spirit and initiative, pressed him further, trying to find some common ground with the stranger. "Did you walk here with the *Great Spirit?*" emphasizing the words to impress their importance.

"Yeah," he answered flatly. Then after a second, so as not to worry her he continued. "But I got my truck parked over on the next hill," throwing a thumb out in its direction.

I looked over and caught the of look of humor in Sr. Edith's eyes, both of us trying to keep smiles from spreading across our faces at this unique blend of traditional belief and modern ways and said, "Welcome to Gallup Sr. Edith, welcome to Gallup!"

The next morning I found Franklin waiting on the bench under the tree. I walked over and was greeted with a *Yah te hey*, that I returned and sat next to him. Immediately I was aware of birds above us chattering nonstop to each another as birds do.

"The birds tell me today is happy day," he began, making me attune my ears to the chirping.

"You can tell that from their twittering?"

"They are excited about this happy day; listen."

I stopped and listened more intently. "You're right. They *do* sound happy," if all the clear, bird chirps were a sign of happiness to come.

We heard the office door open down the slope behind us and the unmistakable gait of Sr. Hyacinth marching towards us drowning out the sound of the birds. Looking around at her, Franklin said, "I told you birds say this is a happy day; her hands hold gloves for me." I realized then when a person is hungry and has work lined for the day, it makes the day happy.

I knew what Hyacinth wanted us to do. She clued me at breakfast that before she started booking groups in earnest she wanted to have paths put in the yard so retreatants wouldn't have to walk in dirt or mud. I couldn't see how heavy cement trucks could make it up the steep dirt driveway to pour the cement when she told me she had already selected the rocks she wanted to use, and now that we had Franklin, she hoped we could arrange pathways to connect the buildings in the retreat.

I thought, rocks are rocks; why did you need to select them? Franklin started to get up but she motioned to him to stay seated and stood in front of us.

"*Yah te hey*," she said, smiling. "I'm glad to see you here Franklin, I have a big job planned. Between the two of you, do you think you'll be able to do it?"

I looked at Franklin. "Sure we can do it, can't we, Franklin?" picturing a pile of dirty brown rocks.

"The wind guided me here to do work for God," he said confidently. "I will do it."

"That's great!" Sister said, pleased her plans for the retreat were falling into place. "I hoped we could give retreatants something better to walk on than dirt, especially when it snows."

The rumble of a truck cut short her directions. Standing up, her cheeks flushed with emotion, she announced, "They're here! Franklin, your arrival was good timing," handing him the pair of new work gloves, then walked up the slope to meet its arrival.

It wasn't just one pickup truck full of plain rocks filled with commonplace rocks I was imagining. *Three* dump trucks drove in and each one was filled with plum-pink colored rocks, cubic yards of the stuff, dumping their load around the circular drive at three different places.

Hyacinth swung into action doing what she did best; take charge. Giving commands, her arms pointing this way and that, her shouting increased in decibels as she tried to drown out the mechanized lifting of the truck beds that were jerking and shifting, trying to slide the rocks off the back of the truck beds. Then all was quiet. The drivers hopped up and fastened their open flaps back in place and with a wave of arms and a calls of *Yah te hey* to Sister, they were gone and we listened to the empty trucks shake, rattle and roll all the way down our bumpy grade to the highway.

When the dust settled, Franklin and I walked to the closest pile and each picked up a rock, turning it over in our hands. We thought it was an odd color for rocks. It felt like a piece of volcanic lava, porous and abrasive, (I wouldn't want to fall on it). "No wonder Sister brought gloves for you," I told him. And it was weighty, like I was holding a fishing weight.

Walking over to Hyacinth, I said, "Nice rocks," who by the heavenly look on her face, was already picturing pale pink paths connecting every building in the retreat.

"Won't be wonderful? Instead of mud and snow for the retreatants to walk on, they'll have stone paths all around the center!" The promise of new walkways was blotting out the labor required for such a monumental task.

"You're right, it will look great." But I was really thinking, 'when we finish the walkways it will finish the feng-shui of the yard too and this in turn will transfer the feeling of completeness to the retreatants.'

"I couldn't agree with you more, Sister," I said.

So my first duty working at a retreat was going to be designing paths, how anticlimactic. I had hoped it would have been something with more of a spiritual nature, but when I thought about it, it *was* spiritual; I was beautifying the grounds surrounding the retreat, making them inviting to visitors that may have left a lawn of their own that needs cutting or hedges that need trimming; I wanted to take them away from all that. It had to be beautiful. I knew this task meant more to me than to others because I would be cautiously testing my physical endurance while I worked seeing how far back I was on the road to recovery after the M.S episode I was. No job was menial to me. With every task I was testing my muscles unobserved.

This was the start of weeks of working beside Franklin giving me a golden opportunity to learn about Navajo ways. He would shovel the pink quarry rocks into the wheelbarrow and empty it where I wanted, and I dragged a rake over it spreading the pink lava on the paths as evenly as I could.

Leonard on the reservation hardly said a word; Franklin didn't stop talking. He filled me in on the ways of the Navajo while I filled in the paths and it was a terrific way of learning about the Navajo culture. It was uncanny how listening to Franklin made time go by. No sooner would we start in the morning, than it was time to put the tools away. Franklin was a good worker. I never once had to urge him on, in fact, it was the other way around and I couldn't keep up with him. There was only one time when Sr. Celeste introduced the girls to him briefly that he was distracted for a while, watching Ruby flit from place to place and he turned to me with the comment, "She is a butterfly! She never stays in one place." The nickname stuck; from that time on whenever he saw her, he would lift his hand, smile and greet her with, "Yay te hey, Butterfly!"

Franklin was always waiting for me on the bench at the start of each new day and true to his word, he was always sober. He ended every day without fail by urging, "If you want to learn about the Navajo, come to parade."

And at the end of very day I would tell him, "We'll see, Franklin." I wasn't much of a parade watcher. I was having a hard time working up enthusiasm for hunching on a curb for hours in chilly weather watching amateur floats. (I kept it to myself how I had slept overnight in a sleeping bag waiting for the most well-known of parades to begin, the Rose Parade, so the bar was set pretty high. I had a feeling if I went into downtown Gallup to watch his parade, I would be trapped and have to feign interest for hours and the prospect wasn't very appealing).

"Where does this pile go?" he'd ask.

"Over by that flat rock to flush out any snakes under it," I would direct him.

"It will be better if you please take this load. It's bad luck for Navajos to kill snakes. I never kill snakes."

"I think the opposite; it will bring bad luck if I *don't.*

"Okay."

"Where would you like this pile?"

"Over by that old pine tree," I would instruct.

"Let me look at that tree," walking to it. "This tree is sick" he said, relieved. "The black is fungus, not marks from scorch."

I fingered the tree lightly saying, "Don't worry, Franklin, lightening never strikes the same place twice, if that's what's bothering you."

"Navajos always stay away from trees that have lightening scars."

"More bad luck?" He looked at me with a face that read, *Isn't it obvious?* I continued pulling and raking, smoothing the pink stones.

Our time together passed like this. I learned the Navajo people referred to themselves as the *Dineh*, 'the people'. They had to follow a narrow path through a world swarming with supernatural beings. Powerless creatures such as humans could survive only by learning to live in harmony with these forces."

"This is the last of pile number two. Where, over by that hogan?" his voice strained as he tried to keep the wheelbarrow from branching off into a rut.

Dumping the load, he sat down in the dirt facing the front door of the hogan to catch his breath. "That is a good way" he said, pointing at the hogan. "The door of a hogan must face east to meet the rising sun."

I told him I had already learned this from Sr. Hyacinth when I first arrived.

"But did she tell why?"

"No, I don't think she did," I said, trying to recall.

"It is to make sure the first thing the family living in the hogan does is greet Father Sun."

"Did she tell that behind the front door is a fire stick which protects the family from evil spirits?"

"No, I'm *positive* she didn't tell me that. I would have remembered hearing about a fire stick!" And told him about the branch I kept by my bed to ward off intruders."

"See, you have Navajo spirit," he flattered.

"Say what you will, I'm not moving it behind the door; it's staying right where it is by my bed!"

Franklin told me how the Navajo religion did not believe souls of the dead belonged to an afterlife, but rather they believed the evil part of a dead person stayed on earth in the form of *chindi*, spirits that returned to the place where the person died to haunt the living. And standing upright, he warned in all seriousness, "One should avoid *chindi* at all costs!"

"I plan to," I said, but knowing how strongly he believed in the spirit world gave me an uneasy feeling.

It was uncanny how fast time past being with Franklin. No sooner would we start work in the morning, than it was time to put the tools away again as if my perceptions had been distorted in some way. He didn't initiate a subject, only when I questioned him his answers took me on fascinating journeys as he spoke reverently of Navajo ways, rituals and teachings. Whether I could tell folklore from fairytales wasn't important to me, I listened to his explanations *till the going down of the sun,* as he liked to say.

I couldn't decide if it was the subject matter that was changing my thinking or if it was what Franklin represented to me, a classic old-world Navajo with strong belief in the spirit world but I knew I should give his ideas a chance before dismissing them. Up until this point I had been listening to his stories with uncertainty and considered his tall tales half truths but tall tales all the same. Whereas Franklin believed they were completely true. It wasn't until I began considering them from a perspective of a Navajo hearing these stories most of their lives, that the possibility opened there was something intrinsically valuable in them.

"You really should see the parade," he started again. I politely resisted, but it was getting harder and harder to come up with excuses to avoid going.

Sr. Edith would occasionally sit on the porch to watch us work. We would both call "*Yah te hey*" to her to acknowledge her, glad she felt comfortable just to sit and watch without having to dash here and there. She had been given an office next to Hyacinth's and there was no question of her artistic talent from the displays of her original artwork soon hanging in her office; entering her office felt like entering a museum. As the artist in our group, she was put in charge of advertising the retreats, a natural fit. She created artistic flyers for upcoming retreats and had business acumen required for placing blurbs in local papers that covered an area the size of New Jersey. Her colorful notices went a long way with people who couldn't read or speak much English. Using hand drawn pictures depicting familiar places brought people's attention to weekends that would have been otherwise disregarded, people signed up from far and wide.

She was very enthusiastic about her new position. She took great care in detailing, conscientiously adding this and erasing that on her designs. I wouldn't call her a perfectionist, just very observant to detail, except for the crooked way she wore her veil off to the side; one way a non-conformist in a religious community could set herself apart without too much notice. I liked her and was glad she chose Gallup she had decided Gallup to work in the twilight of her religious career.

We found she was especially adept at drawing inserts to go along with short adverts in the weekly church bulletins; no clip-art for her: the **Ministers to the Sick** group meeting the first Sunday of the month should expect more than a simple Rx by their name, where limping figures on crutches were more her style. Her time spent coming up with clever lead-ins was well worth it, picking up attendance for a retreat that was lagging in numbers due to dry, usually intellectual, subject matter.

After a while it dawned on me, she wasn't just watching us work, she was *sketching* us, and I prayed my face wasn't going to end up on some religious trade magazine bringing in new vocations with the caption, **This Could Be You!** I shuddered at the thought.

"You know, there is a Tribal parade being held soon," Franklin coaxed. "If you really want to know more about Navajo culture, you should come to our parade."

"I'll ask Sr. Hyacinth," I said, out of politeness, wondering what I could possibly pick up by attending a parade in Gallup.

"You will learn many things," he replied, reading my mind.

What could a small town like Gallup possibly have that could teach me anything, I hesitated, but kept an open mind.

The next day I couldn't wait for Franklin to arrive so I could tell him the good news. Sr. Celeste was taking the girls to the parade so I would be able to tag along and see it too. This wouldn't be the first time Sr. Celeste had attended a parade in Gallup, it was an usual outing for all of them because she thought it was important for the group home girls to connect with their past. Maybe it was the same for Franklin too; he needed to connect with his past. But other then seeing the usual floats and hearing school marching bands belting out off-key renditions of John Philip Sousa's piece, I couldn't imagine why he was so anxious for me to see it.

He seemed pleased when I told him, but as I was learning, Navajos aren't exuberant when it comes to showing emotions. He did smile a little though.

While I was learning about the ways of a new culture, I was also learning about my new boss, Sr. Hyacinth, and how besides being a good business woman, she liked to surprise people, like springing Sr. Edith on me. I had learned Hyacinth had a strong will that wouldn't back down but could back *you* down; I was sure her red-colored cheeks had something to do with this, giving the impression she was holding her temper and could blow at any moment, it was better not to chance it, and as I observed her in her dealings with people over the months, she was usually right anyway.

Hearing the whine of an engine making a fast track up the hill, at first I thought it was an Indian coming up to fill a water barrel. But when I didn't hear the familiar clanging of an empty container in the back of the truck, I knew we had company. Happy to have a break, I stopped and saw it was Sr. Hyacinth and she wasn't alone. Franklin and I put down our tools, wiped off our hands on our jeans and walked over to the porch.

She had two passengers: one was barely able to see over the dashboard, and the other barely had enough clearance for her head. All three were wearing black veils! She opened the driver's side door and called to us, "What good is a retreat center without a full time cook?" We looked at each other dumbly and said nothing. "Exactly! We need a cook! While you have been working on completing the yard, I have been working at finding a permanent full-time retreat cook. Meet Srs. Godwina and Evangelista, our new retreat cooks," she introduced as they got out of the car.

Hyacinth led the way to the porch. "I bet you thought these were Sisters from another parish, didn't you?" she teased, looking at me eagerly. "They're not from a neighboring parish up the road, they're novices from our *own* community out of state," pleased her community had approved the extra help, forestalling the exhaustion that often comes making do on a skeleton staff.

Hyacinth hadn't said anything about the Sisters arrival to prepare me, a trait I was learning to accept and I was at a loss for words. That's when the tall one spoke up and introduced herself. "Hello, I'm Sr. Godwina, Godwin for short," glad she hadn't gone with the shorter version still.

Godwina stood looking down over us all and I made a point to see what kind of heels she had on, but they were shoes St. Francis himself might have worn; flat, dusty, leather sandals. Judging from her slightly hooked nose, together with her height, she unavoidably reminded me of an owl, wise and reflective, watching us from her roost on high. She was twenty-some years old and it didn't take long before my brainy impressions of her were justified.

"Gallup; longitude 108.74 degrees West, latitude 35.528 degrees North," she said eruditely. "I always wondered if the geometrical relationship with the earth and sun had a role in making New Mexico a land of enchantment."

She made the statement in such a confident manner, it gave me the feeling she thought the rest of us unhesitatingly agreed with her. We stood there bewildered, trying to make sense out of her comment or trying to figure out if we were east or west of the prime meridian; or both.

And I'm Sr. Evangelista," the shorter Sister piped in shaking my hand in a cheerful greeting. I looked at her realizing her name was longer than she was tall. She had a smattering of dark freckles across the bridge of her nose and was wearing sturdy light colored oxfords to match her stout legs. I've never known a cook who didn't taste their own food.

"Wait till you try my corn bread," Evangelista urged. "The trick is to make several shallow, diagonal slices across the top with a single edge razor blade to keep the crusts from cracking," nodding her head with conviction.

She really knows her breads, I thought, picturing the kitchen littered with baking sheets and paper muffin liners, and imagining all the new aromas.

"I'm more known for my pastries; cakes, turnovers, scones, and fritters," she corrected, smiling. "And don't forget my blueberry pies, they really are delicious, if I say so myself."

I always felt lucky, and this confirmed it; I could see she fancied herself a baker and my taste buds were already at attention. In fact, it wouldn't have surprised me if she had been placed here solely on her reputation of being a pastry chef, that is, if Hyacinth had anything to do with it.

"We can use all the help we can get," I said with encouragement. Both Sisters looked in their twenties, but that's where similarities ended, physically they were opposites; one was tall and lean, the other short and stout; a real Mutt and Jeff combination.

"This is Anne, the volunteer I was telling you about," Hyacinth interjected. "And this is Franklin," nodding toward him, as he continued to look at the ground. "He's helping Anne in the yard."

"*Yah te hey*" he said meekly, looking at the potted cactus by the door.

"I have some good news," Hyacinth informed us. "These two Sisters are from our motherhouse and have volunteered to work at the retreat. They will live here at the retreat and be our permanent cooks!"

At this, Franklin's head went up, able to see light in the situation, and asked, "Would you like to see a parade?"

I winced. It was one thing to pester me in private about attending the parade but these two new Sisters haven't even had a chance to put their belongings away.

Hyacinth surprised me. "You know, that's not a bad idea," she said, like a light had turned on. "What better way to introduce the new Sisters, Sr. Edith too, to Gallup than to let them see the citizens marching through the streets tomorrow? Good thinking, Franklin."

He shuffled his feet and walked back to the yard. His work there was finished.

Turning to the new arrivals, Hyacinth said, "You two will be staying in the extra bedrooms in the retreat which we can now officially call a convent. Grab your suitcases and come with me and I'll show you to your rooms. We'll have coffee and cake as a snack afterwards. It will be nice to have Sisters to say the Office with for a change in the chapel."

I could almost hear the wheels and cogs turning in her brain, set in motion at a frenzied pace thinking of possibilities for the center. In her eyes, the working opportunities were endless.

"Yah-te-hey, like *aloha*, also means good bye too," I explained as I walked back to join Franklin.

"Well, you must be pleased," I said to him. "We are all going to the parade tomorrow; me, the girls and all the Sisters!" Now I *was* starting to get excited.

"You wait and see. You will like it.

"You know, Franklin, I know I will too," smiling at him. But in my mind, I was less enthusiastic and was worried. It was one thing to exert energy working in cold weather, but quite another to stand on a street corner for hours watching a slow moving parade go by in chilly weather. I had my health to consider. I kept saying to myself, *hang on your hat*; *you're going to see a parade*!

During the past week I had monitored my health by the physical work I was doing; spreading rocks, shoveling rocks, transferring rock, hustling about and I felt no ill effects. I looked and acted so healthy no one would ever suspect I had M.S. But now looking at the sky, there was another cause to worry. The day was growing colder. I thought back; I knew *heat* had a detrimental effect in some M.S. patients (even a hot bath worsened symptoms like arm movements in a number of sufferers). What did the *cold* do? The highest incidence of M.S. in the world is in Scotland, and Scotland has bitterly cold winters. How would it affect me? I didn't mention my concerns to anybody; how else was I going to know how far I could push my body but by being a human barometer; if I collapsed in the street due to cold temperatures, I would definitely know to stay out of the cold, *next* time.

The next day when I woke up I was surprised I didn't hear the blare of trumpets announcing, *ta ta ta Da*, Parade Day! I pulled my thermals on under my jeans and pulled a dark toned sweater over my head, then wrapped a dark green coat with sheepskin lining around me buttoned up to the neck. I put on black mittens to keep my fingers from being exposed to frostbite and last, but not least, I pulled on my old red knit ski hat over my ears.

With Hyacinth and the three Sisters honking to hurry me, I double-checked my pocket to be sure the nausea pills were stuffed in. After all these preparations, I was ready to brave the elements; and oh yes, to see the parade.

Drifting in from every direction was a good cross section of Gallup's populous lining the parade route and I wondered if every Navajo there had prepared a small bag of medicine with part of a liver from an animal or corn pollen, like Franklin talked about, to protect them among strangers. I sympathized. I understood how bringing something from home could make a person feel secure, running my hand over my pocket feeling for my container of pills. Where was Franklin, anyway?

Sr. Celeste and the five group home girls had a front row position across the street, Ruby already waving her arms off at me making sure I saw her. Small Sr. Evangelista had claimed a front spot as well, a natural fit height-wise and it looked like her first assignment was helping Celeste keep a watchful eye on the girls, mindful no one would be accidentally pushed into the street during the parade, especially little Ruby.

Sr. Hyacinth stood with Edith. The new Sister was bundled in a blanket next to me along the curb opposite the girls on the other side, with tall Sr. Godwina standing behind us. All the Franciscans were wearing their mid-knee black Franciscan habits, and I thought as I always do, how much nerve it takes to wear a habit in public, constantly making heads turn to stare at them like they were floats themselves.

Everyone kept looking down the street in preparation for the start of the parade hoping to see movement from the oncoming step-by-step procession. But the spectators were just as interesting to watch as the parade, almost more so. Standing along the street were grandmothers as remnants of the distant past, some with scarves wrapped under their heads and necks, others displaying hair buns knotted in the back set elegantly in silver combs, watching patiently with their families. Everyone seemed to know everyone else. On the whole, the crowd was subdued and reserved. I didn't hear one wise-crack, one snide comment or one boisterous remark throughout the entire parade.

I was continually waving back to Ruby as the friendly thing to do and noticed her wandering into the parade route time and time again, and being pulled back by Sr. Evangelista just as often; a true butterfly; Franklin was right. When somebody screamed, **"HERE THEY COME! THEY'RE COMING,** I finally saw Franklin. He was looking down the road like everyone else. We caught eyes for a second and waved to each other before turning back to watch the start of the parade. I was relieved to see he had made it there, but even more relieved he spotted me among the milling crowd, evidence establishing my whereabouts here so I could incontestably swear I was present at the parade.

When Franklin spotted Ruby across the street, he called out, "Hey, Butterfly," and lifted his hand in acknowledgment making her smile. I was glad he had acknowledged her; an older person paying special attention to her would make her feel special.

Oohs and ahhs started from the crowd. First up, were the school bands with cheerleaders leading the way twirling batons with only a few minor mishandlings slowing the parade in its tracks as a baton flew into the crowd, located, and returned to the twirler. In a town the size of Gallup, there weren't many high schools so that portion of the parade was over rather quickly, all but residual soreness caused from the clean bonks the misguided rod left on a few spectators.

Next were men carrying banners announcing the name of the group they preceded, Heart of the West, and in small lettering, blood wanted, donate today; and, *Thanks for Putting Your Feet in Our Hands*-Dr. Whitehorn's Podiatry Center.

There were educational foundations and several Indian sponsored programs, and signs displaying names of mission schools and one battered women's program together with 'needy family' organizations and many alcohol counseling centers. These groups were comprised mostly of women and judging from the happy-go-lucky, carefree way they were walking they seemed overjoyed to have been included in the parade at all.

There was a banner reading—*For Wood Stove Installation and Home Repair call Manny at...* And for comic relief instead of clowns, there was a small work crew of Navajo men dressed in old work trousers with hammers and other tools dangling from work belts having a good ol' time waving and smiling at all their friends. They carried no sign at all.

Next were horses decked with buffed saddles, and harnesses adorned with polished silver, turquoise and malachite fittings ridden by Navajo men just as decked out as the horses with large turquoise rings, every one of them was sitting tall in the saddle. I had to admit, they were impressive. And just when I thought this could be Anytown USA, I noticed long braids coming from under their cowboy hats when they passed, reminded me this was Indian country. Brand new ropes, wound in neat circles, were hanging around the saddle horns against recently curried mounts, adding to the parade's fanciful spirit. In a western town like Gallup, equestrian talent and horsemanship was greatly appreciated and I could tell these riders were a crowd favorite.

No one had mentioned the next group of quiet riders. They were a different class of riders. Slowly the people watching stood up out of courteous respect when a small group of older Navajo men came into view. All talking subsided as the men solemnly walked by and was replaced by a gradual and building applause; it was a dramatic moment as the remaining Navajo Code Talkers proudly moved through with little fanfare other than our growing applause. Wearing light yellow shirts decorated with war emblems, they walked with all the nobility of crown princes carrying themselves with dignity, pride and honor holding their heads high under soft brimless rust colored hats for the vital contributions they made during W.W.II. Serving as marines using their native tongue, enemies found the Navajo language with its varying voice tones, too difficult to understand.

Watching Franklin from across the street clapping enthusiastically, I knew this was the reason he wanted me to see the parade, because when the Code Talkers left their mark on the world, he must have felt it was his mark as well. I suppose patriotism was all Franklin had left.

The Parade made me happy: the sky stayed friendly and I'd learned some remarkable Navaho history. I was filled with indebtedness for the contribution the brave Code Talkers made and had reached a deeper level of appreciation and gratitude and walked back to the car transformed by this by this rising new consciousness.

Waving goodbye to the familiar stooped figure of Franklin looking at me from across the street, he was still wearing the same old jeans, cowboy boots and hat, but something had changed about him. I now saw him as part of something so noble and honored, almost regal; his posture was straight and he looked taller than ever as he stepped sure-footed through the onlookers that were parting for him, a veteran, in deference. The respect he now embodied made him stand out like a beacon urging me to take one last look. Turning, I watched him disappear into the crowd: a true patriot.

CHAPTER
9

The breeze, full of expectation, swirled its way around the shrubbery moving quietly along the walkways in this picture-perfect tableau of peace. Up until now our enthusiastic group of retreat workers hadn't had a chance to show off their expertise in their field and the air was heavy with an anticipation you could feel.

I imagined the entire weekend in my head many times. I saw an attractive yard reflecting a prayerful and orderly atmosphere, footpaths cleared like country lanes for meditational walks, a caring and responsive staff willing to assist in the inner journeys of retreatants; the entire weekend was designed to take retreatants away from their everyday world.

Today was Friday, the day when our first sizable retreat began. Hyacinth had even hired a housekeeper who was supposed to start on this retreat. Gloria was a dark haired, dark skinned person who apparently hadn't been in the country very long. I didn't know how much use someone would be who could only recognize two words, *Fernando Valenzuala*, but at least we had that between us. I found this out the hard way she couldn't speak English. After telling her at length I was from Los Angeles and missed living near the ocean, and her blank look of no recognition didn't change along with an ingratiatingly wide smile, I knew that there had been *no comprendo*. It wasn't until I happened to mention the baseball player's name that her face lit up and a genuine smile spread over her mouth. Now we were on familiar ground.

Sr. Hyacinth and the rest of the Franciscan Sisters, of which I was now a part, had transferred to Gallup from a large retreat center and from a community that made their living actively hosting retreats. They knew how important it was for people to spend time alone with the inner self. St. Francis Retreat could use people who were trained in the bare bones of retreat work, *I* was the one who needed to learn and get up to speed. In the Cistercian monastery I was with for two years, we had individual retreatants use the guest house and sometimes I would see them walking back and forth to the chapel; that was the extent of my retreat experience. I wanted to be more prepared so after dinner I waited until the retreat office was empty to peruse the reference shelf. Finding an *Encyclopedia of Religion*, under Retreats, I read:

Retreats may be defined as a limited period of isolation during which an individual, either alone or as part of a small group, withdraws from the regular routine of daily life. During this period retreatants interrupt their ordinary routine, break off regular social relationships, and (except for those who are already or the like) withdraw into a solitary place or to a special building set apart for such purposes. This isolation as well as the interruption of social intercourse and ordinary life, is adopted as a condition that enables individual retreatants to establish contact with the divinity or with the world of the spirits.

Hence, retreats often involve the use of various ascetical means, such as fasting, abstinence, prayer, meditation, and techniques aimed at inducing a revelatory dream, trance, or ecstasy."

As good a pantomimist as I was, I didn't think I could relay this to Gloria, the new housekeeper; this was something she'd have to pick it up on her own.

I was certain our Center was the perfect reserve for quiet prayer. It overlooked the city of Gallup and the chapel had been built on the side of the hill for the impressive view. Sr. Hyacinth had taken me to see it when it was dark so I could get the full effect and be able to see the lights of Gallup in the distance. As soon as I walked in I was struck by the twinkling lights from the city below flooding the large floor-to-ceiling windows like someone had opened a jewelry box and I could reach out and run my fingers along the strings of lights like they were pearls. From this angle Gallup appeared to be the most ideal community on earth. I knew if no insights were forthcoming during the retreat the shortfall wouldn't be due to the chapel, unless the spectacular view was too distracting.

I pictured the dining room filled with the happy sounds of hungry diners looking forward to, if not epicurean delights, then at least enjoyable, pleasing ones. I saw relieved mothers glad to be freed from cooking and clean-up, and visualized men with unquenchable appetites, turning the retreat weekend into an all-you-can-eat marathon and hoped Srs. Evangelista and Godwina had prepared enough food to enable quests to go back for seconds if they wanted, making a mental note to see which quests looked liked they would take two bites of a cherry pie and put the fork down, and who looked like they could eat two whole cherry pies.

I scanned the guest roster for the weekend; three vegetarians in a total count of forty retreatants. Did this mean cooking three separate dishes for each of them at every meal time, and how much? Who can judge appetites? I realized then what a stressful job cooks have in planning, ordering, and actually cooking and was glad I didn't have the responsibility. How do the cooks know how much food to prepare, I questioned uneasily, and was glad I wouldn't be held accountable for guesstimating people's hunger. From then on, I never took the cook's job for granted because I realized what a precarious and stressful occupation it is, because if the food is terrible, it is a reflection on the overall retreat. But if every bite puts the retreatants' palate in a blissful out-of-body-experience, they'll leave fulfilled, enlightened from head to toe and will give a favorable review of the weekend. "What a great weekend!" might not have anything to with the subject of the conference talks, chances are it was a comment about the last meal. But if the food was awful, "I didn't get anything out of the retreat," could be regarding a blueberry pie they found uneatable. Such is the influential power food has over a retreat, the cook serving up a spiritual bill of fare.

"Need time alone?" Sr. Edith's simple blurb read to advertise the upcoming weekend in the local paper. I wondered if this was the best selling point for the retreat; everywhere I looked there was wide open space. Edith was still being motivated by city thinking where private space is a valued commodity. Realizing her mistake depicting an Indian sitting on a horse overlooking a valley surrounded by miles of empty deserts, offering a quiet place at the retreat didn't have much appeal. She saw her drawing was overkill and remarked, "Parishioners around here may have too much alone time; I'll know for next me."

Hyacinth explained to her how Gallup's faithful liked the old-fashioned kind of retreats, pointing out the retreats at St. Francis were geared toward the more traditional themes of prayer, fasting and Scripture, you know, the important things. Overhearing her once on the phone, I was reminded members in this diocese weren't the most affluent of people. "No one will be turned away for lack of funds," I heard her say, explaining to the caller the Retreat Center wasn't here to make money but to give retreatants time to spend with God and assured the caller the retreat would consider a person's individual needs. Hearing this didn't surprise me but made me wonder how many times she had been paid with live chickens, fresh corn or handmade pots.

Before the weekend began I gave one last check of the Center; at the orderly yard with the new footpaths, at the chapel set with the correct color vestment for the liturgical season hanging at the front of the closet in the sacristy. There were boxes of new hosts, and enough incense to asphyxiate the entire town of Gallup; boxes of matches easily lasting to the end of the decade, and last, a monstrance (a receptacle for displaying the consecrated Host) in case the priest was in the mood to hold a meditation. The staff was poised and waiting too, everything was ready for our first sizable retreat and all was peace and tranquility.

That's when I heard an unfamiliar voice behind me.

"Hello there, I'm Mrs. Snelling" interrupting my review of things to be done list. She was hours early! In one fell swoop she had disrupted my time schedule for the rest of the morning. But because she was my first actual retreatant, I couldn't help feeling pleased.

"I wanted to get some quiet time in before the rest of the crowd arrived." And while I could see her point, it was a startling surprise, like someone had thrown a gutter ball and all I could do was watch it roll down the channel, ending with the clunk of her suitcase on the walkway.

Turning to face her, I babbled something like, "Welcome. I'm Anne. Let's go to the office to see what room you're in."

Mrs. Snelling was a large woman wearing a brightly colored flowery print dress. She was constantly looking around and knew this must be her first visit to this retreat center, all the more reason for me to make a good impression.

I showed her to the office thinking, "What am I supposed to do when a retreatant arrives early? The Priest/facilitator hasn't even arrived yet!" But because she was my very first retreatant, her early arrival didn't bother me, she was the first in what I hoped would be a long line of retreatants I'd have the opportunity of serving so she was special to me; my retreat career was off and running. She did teach me two valuable lessons: to *expect* retreatants to arrive hours before the retreat started as the *norm*, and that a retreat worker should be as *accommodating* as possible, no matter what.

I introduced Mrs. Snelling to Hyacinth who signed her in and gave the woman a brief welcome, handed her a room key and a printed itinerary for the weekend. Hyacinth made sure she knew where the chapel was so the woman could occupy her time in prayer without needing us to keep her busy in some way. "I'm here to pray," the lady said happily.

I escorted her across the yard and showed her which hogan she was in and thought: one down, 39 to go, happy the weekend was underway nonetheless.

More and more retreatants descended on the Center throughout the afternoon with their nervous energy, talking and laughing. Hyacinth asked several times if I'd seen Fr. Delaney, the priest in charge of giving the retreat, who was unpredictably late.

As time went on and I showed more and more people to their rooms, with daylight beginning to fade and still no priest for facilitator yet, Sr. Hyacinth began to pace in the hallway dropping crumbs in front of the picture of the pope as she nibbled in nervousness. She opened the conference hall and asked Sr. Evangelista to put out platters of her homemade goods next to the coffee urn in the hopes retreatants wouldn't notice the retreat was long past due to start. Sister Evangelista was only too happy to show us how she had mastered high altitude baking and served fluffy and light almond croissants with a sweet glaze.

What happens when the priest, facilitator or the person in charge of giving the entire retreat, is a no—show? The retreat is cancelled by the coordinator, Sr. Hyacinth in this case, the people are turned away disappointed, all the extra food is given away before it spoils and the staff has a hard time making eye contact with the departing guests; bad word of mouth for any retreat center.

"That does it," Hyacinth said, suddenly enlightened. "Do you know what we need, what every retreat house needs?"

Watching her pace up and down the hallway, somehow I was afraid to ask. The last time she asked this question we ended up with two more cooks. "What?" I asked in uncertainty. I didn't want any more surprises.

"We need a priest! A full time priest living here on the property! If there was a priest in residence, we wouldn't have to rely on outside clergy showing up. Tomorrow I'm calling the Bishop!"

Everything was easier now she had come to this resolution. She wouldn't have to worry about standing in front of a large group of people explaining why the retreat was cancelled ever again. All we needed was to get through this one retreat.

Our troubles were over when we saw a black car pull to the office and knew the priest had arrived. Hyacinth was spared the trouble of having to explain why the retreat was cancelled and their money would be refunded.

Hustling Father Delaney into the conference hall, he put his notes on the podium, he loosened his white collar, took a sip of water from the glass set on the podium, wiped his brow with the back of his hand, and his long awaited lecture on how to remain peaceful and calm began.

Another late arrival, a retreatant this time, after I pointed out her end hogan, found me again and complained, "There's a strange odor in my bedroom. I think something died," she choked out.

Now what? I thought, shrinking back. "I'm sure you're mistaken," I apologized, stalling for time. The middle aged woman took me to the last hogan, stood out of the way in front so I could assess the situation for myself. Covering her nose with one hand, she flung the door open with the other.

"See," she sputtered.

Sure enough, no mistaking that foul odor and it was definitely coming from inside her room.

Ushering her out the door in a hurry, I apologized profusely; assuring her the hogan didn't smell like this yesterday and gave her a room in the new building because she'd had enough of an authentic hogan for one day. Worst of all because the retreatant had gotten here late, by the time I had settled her into another room, father's talk for that evening was nearly over.

I went back to see what had wandered in the hogan and didn't make it out alive. Sniffing around the rooms, it wasn't hard to find. A dead squirrel, tangled and stiff was stuck in the coiled metal springs underneath one of the beds. I tugged at the bony carcass with a piece of old newspaper, and extricated the tree-dwelling rodent by wrapping it between the prices of rump-roast and chuck steak. I opened all the windows in the room and sprayed a deodorizer for the time being, thinking how Gloria wasn't going to like disinfecting and cleaning in there as one of her first retreat duties on Monday.

When the weekend was over, the Sisters and I mingled with the departing crowd to pick up comments about the weekend. The Sisters received an enormous amount of thanks, gathering reviews abundant with praise ranging from *spiritually uplifting*; *a truly enlightening weekend*, to one person remarking how she could feel a general sense of positive energy at the retreat; that was a real morale booster for me. They loved Fr. Delaney, and thought his lectures were insightful and inspiring.

And Father, ranking the retreatants, said they were an open and receptive audience. The food was delicious, attested by the number of recipes the cooks handed out. The accommodations were delightful, "a veritable escape," one guest remarked. "And *wasn't it exciting staying in a hogan?*" I overheard from another.

The retreatants raved about the weekend and went away happy, feeling they got their money's worth which put Sr. Hyacinth in a happy mood for days. The priest left happy too, confident he'd made a powerful connection with the group and hoped the rapport he established would last long enough for them to sign up for another weekend retreat. The cooks were well-pleased but embarrassed when they were brought out of the kitchen and to the dining room and given a round of applause, making me wonder if Evangelista and Godwina would ever have the nerve to put a tip jar on the counter for future retreats reading, *Don't applaud; just throw money*. But most of all, I was happy discovering I loved being a spiritual concierge.

The only one who had a general distaste for the weekend was Gloria when we found there was one more word we both recognized, adios.

CHAPTER
10

The following Monday started with Sr. Hyacinth teasing, "You'll never guess what I did," a roguish personality showing in her healthy demeanor shaking as she laughed.

Getting to know this impulsive director, my first thought was it could be anything from choosing new paint for her office to buying a treadmill to ordering a pair of walking shoes, all requisite items.

With her hand at the side of her mouth confidentially like she was letting me in on some sort of trade secret, she said "I just made an appointment with Bishop Struther. I told him in no uncertain terms St. Francis Retreat needed a full-time priest!"

I got the feeling that passing a problem on to the upper echelon of religious hierarchy wasn't all that kosher, a lowly Sister bothering a high ranking Bishop, but if anyone had the chutzpah to so it, something told me it was Hyacinth!

I pictured the elderly cleric tottering to the other side of the room as she pushed her idea at him full force; there weren't many who could refuse Hyacinth's determined requests.

"I'll tell the Bishop if we had a priest in residence, the prospective retreat groups wouldn't have to scrounge around the diocese hoping to find a priest that wasn't busy on particular dates. We could have a priest right on the property available 24 hours a day!" In her excited tone, any practical objections I brought up would go unheeded, like laundry facilities, meals, kitchen privileges, and items you wouldn't think to bring up until they presented themselves as problems and then it's too late so I agreed with her.

She continued, "I'll tell him flat out we needed a priest who is fit and has a strong moral character to match… and no stranger to the ways out here, besides we need a priest to say daily Mass for us anyway, now that members of my community have joined us and that will eliminate our daily walks to the parish church." I could feel the tension drain from her as she rehearsed what she was going to say to the Bishop with me.

No one could say no to Hyacinth's persuasive arguments it seemed, not even the Bishop. An appointment was set up at the chancellery in town and like she had placed an order from a catalogue, four days later a clergyman arrived driving a tan sedan. As he pulled into the retreat yard, I happen to see a felt hat under the window in the back, like the kind fishermen wear, as the car coasted by me. My curiosity was now set but I waited until I heard the emergency brake tread down, the car door slam shut followed by the sound of footsteps walking to the office, knocking, the office door opening then closing before I stepped into the visible wake of dust left by the car's passing.

Convinced that the owner was inside the retreat office being distracted, I inched my way toward it treating it like some wayward creature that had washed in like seaweed on our shore. The closer I came, the more I felt a smile spreading across my face. Were those buttons I saw pinned all over the hat in back or were they floating lures, decoys designed to entice denizens of the deep? I had to know.

Hoping the colorful headdress wasn't used in a *passing the hat* portion of a traveling show, I disguised my approach by taking calculated giant steps over the partially completed rock paths like I was a stone skipping over a lake top. I didn't want to be caught snooping but that was exactly what I was doing, I didn't want to be caught doing it. I had to know what this stranger had pinned to the hat.

Keeping a watchful eye on the office door in case it should suddenly open, I moved closer, becoming a little braver with each step, keeping a look out for witnesses, if only a squirrel. I was knee deep in curiosity and sinking fast. This snooping gave me the same feeling of guilt I used to get giving a quick tug on my father's fishing line when he wasn't looking; it wasn't right but I did it anyway.

Making sure the coast was clear I sidled up to the car to hurriedly inspect my catch before my nerves got the better of me and would be compelled to release it from sight. Nonchalantly looking over I saw a small red ice chest in the center of the bench seat. This made me happy; what self-respecting fisherman would be caught in the middle of a lake without sandwiches and drinks? It was a good sign. Next to the ice chest was a ball of clothes tossed in without regard to the crumpled look. Another good sign; spending all day in a boat, cutting bait and untangling lines was messy business and told me the wearer wasn't overly-concerned about his personal appearance; the owner of this car was no tea-drinking Englishman who held up his pinkie whenever he sipped his favorite tea.

What I saw resting on the back shelf made me do a double-take. Lying on the ledge was a purple hat all right, but what I saw as the car rolled through the yard were *lures*, not buttons. All different kinds that had been carefully knotted and tied ranging from feathers of different colors: orange with black stripes, purple with blue stripes, green with black stripes, all brandishing shiny barbed hooks. As I looked fixedly at the hat, I noticed one lure sporting two hooks set back to back, making it look like an anchor. It was full of thick bristles of feathers that had been painted silver camouflaging dark hooks. I knew this had to be his *lucky* lure. I walked away well pleased.

Hearing a clicking sound made by the office doorknob, I turned and made myself walk directly toward the opening door and into whoever was coming out head on, proving I had nothing to hide.

"This is Fr. Lighterman. He's a Jesuit," Sr. Hyacinth introduced. "He's our new resident chaplain. The Bishop stationed him here after Father spent two years as acting chaplain in a school for Indians outside of Gallup. I guess there's a certain progression, retreatants learn about spiritual matters."

I was getting used to Hyacinth surprises by this time. But with a name like Lighterman and owner of a fisherman's hat, I expected to meet, in keeping with his name, a slender, fit figure of a man; a real sportsman. Was I surprised when he stepped in front of Hyacinth! I had never seen a belly this size on a person before man or woman! It was the perfect mesh between man and sport; what other activity could he spend hours thinking about which recipe to try, feeling his mouth water like a cat every time a fish jumped. It was a natural fit. I didn't know anything about Jesuits so I made it a point to go back to the reference shelf in the Office and look for information when I could.

"Father will be saying daily Mass for us in the retreat chapel and he'll join us for the Office as well," Hyacinth

informed me before showing him to his room. As they walked away I saw they were about the same height and noticed strands of grey hair throughout Father's thinning hair.

"You'll be in one of the front bedrooms on the side of the chapel," Hyacinth pointed out. "It's in the new building and doesn't have anybody else in it, so you'll have the whole building to yourself but if we have a large retreat and the hogans are occupied, extra occupants will have to go in the extra bedrooms. I'll give you the grand tour tomorrow but now I'll let you unpack, pointing to the outside light above the door. When you're finished, come back to the office and then you can meet the rest of the Sisters over dinner.

I watched as he pulled the car around and opened the trunk. I wasn't disappointed; inside I saw a jumble of poles, nets, fishing boxes, and a couple old knives with scales embedded in the handles that had seen their share of fish gutting.

"That's quite a mess you have in there" I said, hoping he'd want to talk about fishing.

He responded in all seriousness saying, "This is where I store my gentleness of spirit and serenity of mind. Good man, that Washington Irving." I knew what the subject would be during dinner.

For our first official meal, I rang the large bell outside to call everyone together, except Franklin who lived off the premises. I pulled at the short rope swinging the heavy metal bell from side and loud rings sounded that I was sure could be heard in downtown

Gallup. Everyone took the hint and one by one veiled Sisters appeared heading toward the kitchen and the inviting aromas.

We gathered in the small dining room table off the side of the kitchen. I looked at the staff that had been added in the short time I was here; Hyacinth had done a good job, two cooks who were novices, one professed Sister who was an artist, a Navajo handyman and a priest.

We were now a large group: Fr. Lighterman as a priest sat at the head of the table; Sr. Hyacinth, director/businesswoman sat at the other end; Sr. Edith, artist in charge of advertising; Sr. Godwina, dinner cook; Sr. Evangelista, breakfast and lunch cook; desserts her specialty; and me, a secular concierge. In absentia was Sr. Celeste as a back-up cook. Sitting at the dining table with everyone, it felt good to be in on the ground floor of a retreat center just starting up.

Fr. Lighterman stood and gave a short blessing and we all bowed our heads. His presence here had one big advantage; it was nice having someone responsible for saying grace at each meal instead of taking turn.

His blessing was meaningful and we sat, pulling our chairs close to the table in thoughtfulness.

When he went to sit down, a fact occurred to him looking at the close proximity of the table and the size of his large belly and the impossibility of it fitting. Undaunted, with his index finger he drew a rounded arc with his finger and told us this was where the table should be cut so his stomach could fit in nicely. It was a good ice-breaker and we all laughed.

He told us again he was a Jesuit, an order of men founded by St. Ignatius of Loyola, and filled us in on his training and experience that lead up to being stationed at the retreat. He was proud to be a Jesuit, I could tell, and as if it meant a great deal to him, told us the Latin version of their motto—*Ad Majorem Dei Gloriam.* For the unenlightened like me, he gave the translation, *To the Greater Glory of God* telling us it was the object of Jesuits to spread the message of the Church by preaching and teaching. He had years of study and admitted visiting the Holy Land twice.

To some Catholics, Jesuits are the elite order in the Catholic Church. So after dinner I went to the office and read from Funk & Wagnalls Standard Reference Encyclopedia and was sure of it: The time of preparation required of a candidate for membership is considerably longer than that required for the secular Priesthood or for membership in other religious orders: after two years of seclusion and prayers as a novice, the candidate takes simple vows of poverty, chastity, and obedience, and becomes a *scholastic*; he then speeds two years of study in review of classical subjects, and three years studying philosophy, mathematics, and the physical sciences; five years of teaching in Jesuit colleges follow, and, after four years' of theology and another year of retirement and prayer, the candidate takes solemn vows and is ordained a priest, becoming a *professed*. In addition to the usual vows of poverty, chastity, and obedience, the professed take a vow to go wherever the pope may send them, and a vow renouncing all ecclesiastical honors.

With all his training and years of study, he still knew it was important to take time out and spend time alone and reflect; in other words, fish! Hearing this, my opinion of him grew.

It wasn't hard working lakes and rivers into the conversation. When a faraway look came over his face as he recalled a time he reeled in a big one, he said, "The stories I could tell you!"

Then I took my turn. "Oh, but Father, I have the story to end all stories and if I hadn't seen it with my eyes, I wouldn't have believed it," I said with as much conviction my voice could convey. The last thing I wanted was to have Fr. Lighterman's first impression of me being a show-off, or a braggart, even if my unbelievable story was true.

I don't know if Father's mood was cheered by the prospect of having an audience actually willing to listen to his fishing exploits, or watching Sr. Evangelista cut into a chocolate cake for our dessert, but he wasted no time narrating the times he had met his match describing in great detail the weight, length and color of each sizable catch, how long it took each one to land, and what type of bait or lure he used, ending with the inevitable 'one that got away' story in every fisherman's repertoire.

His stories were all well and good, but very predictable, even for a priest who made a living thinking up interesting homilies to keep churchgoers coming back week after week. Somewhere around his third fish however, I began picturing him with his cane pole wedged in tightly between his stomach and the side of a row boat. He was reeling in a dented can of tuna fish, holding the metal container up and watching the water drip, drip, drip from the container, gratified he at least snagged *something* that had to do with gills, fins and scales.

"More cake anybody?" I heard Sr. Hyacinth's voice jolting me back. I stretched and shifted to a more comfortable position in the hard back chair.

"Don't mind if I do, Father said, passing his plate. "How can *talking* give me such an appetite?" he questioned out loud like he was genuinely mystified. "Have you ever heard wilder stories than these?"

Sorry I had to upstage him, I said, "As a matter of fact, Father, I have a better story about the one that got away."

"Just a minute," he said, his brow wrinkling. "It only counts if you took the hook out of its mouth," like he was an authority from the *Fish & Game Department.*

His comment sounded like a challenge but it didn't take much prodding to get me to tell about the time my brother lost his lucky pole. Growing up with two brothers and a father who liked to fish, my sisters and I had our share of getting our lines wet either in the ocean or in fresh water lakes using little red salmon eggs or pieces of cheese, depending.

One summer my brother and I, a person who takes fishing for sport seriously, after reading how good fishing was supposed to be in Oregon, decided to drive up and see for ourselves. Of course, Jim had his lucky fishing pole one he had painstakingly wrapped himself coiling identifying strands of colored line on the outer covering, in the back of the truck. Whenever he'd talk about landing 'the big one,' which was quite often, I would end his thought with "God willing," because I knew we could use all the help we could get.

At one point he turned to me and said bluntly, "God has nothing to do with whether I catch a big fish or not, it's skill."

When we arrived at the lake, we stopped at a rustic bait & tackle store and bought a container of worms, but not just any worms, these were big, fat well-fed Oregon worms; they were they were *all* big. I poked around in the paper container stuffed with dirt and worms looking for a little one, with no luck, they were all big, juicy worms and I couldn't bring myself to bait my hook. My brother gladly obliged from time to time.

Thankfully, motorboats were prohibited on the lake and after paddling around trolling for some while with no luck, we decided to pull up on land and try to fish from the shore.

Casting out, Jim secured his pole at the end of our moored row boat before coming over to bait my hook with the biggest worm I have ever seen. In the middle of his fiddling with a worm for me, we heard a splash and looked at each other with wide-open eyes. We both knew what had happened. In a flash, Jim went running up and over the embankment with me close behind and confirmed his worst fear, "There goes my lucky pole!"

I couldn't bring myself to say anything. What do you say to someone doing you a favor that ended up costing his entire rig? We stood there in silence looking at the ripples. There was nothing left, no lure, no reel, no pole. It had gone to a watery grave, done in by a large Oregon fish.

We were still standing on the bank in shock looking out at the calm water when suddenly a huge fish jumped in the middle of the lake, leaping high in the air, flopping and twisting. It made me feel even more dejected thinking Jim *could have had a fish like that* if I hadn't asked him to bait my hook… and then suddenly, the fish jumped again, then again, almost in the same spot.

"That's my fish!" Jim shouted with indignation, and then the lake fell quiet.

"That was my fish, I *know* it was!" he yelled, as we stood dejectedly on the bank looking at the all too quiet lake that was now filled with a heavy silence of what might have been.

Then out of the blue we heard another loud splash but this time it was coming from a *different* location in the lake, and this fish too was jumping over and over in the same place. As disheartened as I felt at that moment, I couldn't help admiring what a big beautiful rainbow trout it was, its greenish blue color glistening with water held fast just out of reach by a deus ex machina taunting us by holding it just out of reach.

We ran to the other side back over the embankment towards the new splash site. Standing there, putting two and two together, Jim figured the fish was dragging his pole around the lake while it was trying to free itself but the pole kept getting caught, forcing it to jump.

"I'm going in!" Jim yelled, ripping off his tennis shoes.

"You're kidding?!" I yelled back. "That's snow on those peaks around us; you know how cold icy lake water is? Besides, you said these are cut-throat trout. They have teeth!"

"I know," he shivered, already standing up to his knees in the lake.

Without hesitation, he let himself sink into the freezing water to his waist, to his neck, and in one final exertion, he slipped under the water, popping up periodically in different locations, gasping for air from the coldness. Plunging in again, he swam farther out and again came up for air. I watched him do this repeatedly but on about the fifth try, he popped out of the water yelling, "I can see it! I see it! It's caught on a big log!" And taking a big gulp of air to fill his lungs to capacity, he dove to the pole and freed it, and burst out of the water holding it above his head like a trophy, feeling his way, backtracking toward the shore the entire time.

Once his bare feet found stable footing on the rocks and stones along the bank, he started reeling it in.

"What are you doing that for?" I shouted.

"The fish is still on the line!" he yelled back excitedly.

"It still has the hook in it mouth?" I screamed, unable to believe after all the jumping and swimming then jumping again, it still had the hook stuck in its jaw.

"Yeah, but it looks exhausted from dragging the pole around the lake and doesn't have much fight left. I'll have to reel it in as gently as I can to try not to pull the out the hook."

"You can try," I said, but I didn't have much hope.

With his body drenched from his dive glistening in the sun, he patiently and methodically wound the handle of the reel pulling the fish in closer and closer.

"Here, take my pole," he demanded, putting it in my hands.

"What?" I shouted in a loud voice; "What for?"

"So I can grab the line and *pull* it in!"

I watched dumbfounded as Jim felt for the hard ring of the eyelet at the end of the pole and followed the line out as far as he could. I stood by watching him literally pulling the line in, yards of the straightened line gathering on the water in an unraveled jumble.

Then we spotted the huge fish. It was a beautiful rainbow trout! During all this time Jim had continued his backward walking tugging at the line until he finally had the fish close to shore. It was flopping wildly and as we watched it thrashing about in two inches of water, now that we knew he had landed it, we looked at each other and started to laugh, not at the doomed fish but at the unbelievable way Jim brought it in. And once we started laughing, we couldn't stop.

"Not many people would dive into freezing water after a fish!" I declared.

"I know," he said through chattering teeth. "The worst part was in not knowing what was down there! There could have been anything hiding in there, rusted car frames, snakes; why there could have leeches in there for all I know!" he shivered.

"I was more concerned you'd be caught on a branch or something and *couldn't* come up and I wasn't about to dive in after you!" I said, laughing in relief. The entire episode was *so* unreal, if I had spotted a grinning Cheshire cat sitting in a tree watching, it wouldn't have surprised me.

Now for the remainder of the trip, every time we looked at each other, we shook our heads in disbelief and said, "*I* don't *believe it! I don't believe what just happened!*"

I brought out my camera and snapped pictures to record the momentous event: Jim in his trunks, dripping wet, proudly holding the colorful trout showing it from various angles, over his head, laying it on the ground next to a beer for prospective, and one or two close ups of where it had been snagged in its side.

Back at the bait shop, we felt very distinguished to find Jim's fish weighed a whopping 14 1/2 lbs. and was the largest trout ever pulled from the lake! Admirers crowded around but we didn't mention *how* it was caught only that it was one that *didn't* get away. Jim shared his good fortune by dividing the fillets with a couple of mountain men who looked like they could use a good meal, while I tacked up one of the pictures of Jim holding his record trout along with its specs on the back of the door with all the other pictures of anglers and fish, that is probably still there today.

At one point during the long ride home, Jim turned to me and said, "We're making good time, we should be home before you know it." And looking over at me as an afterthought, added… "God willing."

It came to me then, what better way was there to let a fisherman feel the sacred presence of the Divine than when his fingers were wrapped around the bloody entrails of a recently gutted fish?

Sr. Hyacinth didn't know what to make of my fishing story and said absently, "Thanks for sharing it," speaking for all the Sisters.

Not being an angler I knew she wouldn't appreciate any fishing story. But although Fr. Lighterman was, it was impossible to tell what he about it from his noncommittal opinion of it afterwards. He simply said, "Good story, good story," like I had just delivered a weather report. I was hoping for something more personal, at least, "That's *some* fishing story!" But from his vague comment, I couldn't tell what he *really* thought until…

Bright and early the next morning, it was time for Father's first Mass in the retreat chapel. There were no retreatants so we were a small group, four Franciscan nuns and me. Everything was going fine; the candles were lighted, the holy water founts were filled, I had marked the pages for the readings, the key to the tabernacle was in place; I could relax.

Out of all the topics Father could have picked for his homily, he chose to talk about a Spanish senorita in the seventeenth century who had been caught stealing. For her punishment she was to be publicly stoned in the town's bull ring. As she was being pummeled with rocks, with her final breath she had the wherewithal to reach down to her skirt and cover her legs when she fell, right before she died. I would have thought his homily would have then been on modesty, decorum or even shyness. Instead, for the next twenty minutes Father lectured on mendacity, untruthfulness and deception, touching a little on each of them at some point during his sermon.

I never was sure if his homily was directed at me or was just an uncomfortable coincidence. But as his disapproving eyes bore down on me from the pulpit, in my heart, I finally knew what he thought of my fishing story… and me.

CHAPTER
11

It was mid-afternoon and it seemed like all hell had broken out in the yard; bushy brown squirrels were scampering about in quick light runs, redheaded woodpeckers were pecking repeatedly at dried trunks of trees, and birds were stretching their vocal chords in miniature arias all over the yard. I tried being as perceptive as Franklin to see what was behind all the commotion but my interpretive skills weren't as honed as Franklin's yet.

Rubbing the rust off the heavy clapper on the bell in the yard, I appreciated how sounds have the ability to affect my mood: the hypnotic-like effect the gentle clinking of a chain against a pole, or the faint rustling of leaves, free and loose, is a movable feast for the ears. But there were few sounds more evocative than a solitary car moving on a highway at night creating the change in pitch, known as the Doppler Effect, I find so captivating and love to listen to its almost forlorn, hopeless sound as I lie in bed contemplating the driver alone like me, traveling on a deserted highway at night, both of us sharing this moment of sound; the pleasing sounds of a train whistle moving on the outskirts of Gallup, a close rival.

I guided the clapper to the side and let go but it wasn't a chime I heard, but the sound of a car speeding up the drive to the retreat. Its fast pace slowed as it negotiated the hair-pin turn at the top of our drive, but any engine barreling up out hill without the sound of empty water barrels banging against the sides in the back of the vehicle, could only mean one thing. With a short skid, the vehicle stopped, I should have known, it was our closest neighbor, missionary Sr. Carol. I would know what the frenetic signs of nature this morning meant for her next visit. When the dust settled, I heard the familiar loud voice confirming it, "Yah te hey, Anne! Want to go to the Reservation?"

Waiting for the air to clear around her dirty yellow Bronco, I approached the creaking vehicle as it rested in a swirl of gritty dust and called back, "Sure! Let me tell Hyacinth and then I'll go with you."

Knowing this might be the last time my feet would be on firm ground for some time, I felt for the nausea pill I carried at all times, and by the time I reached the office, I'd already swallowed it; I'd learned how to swallow pills quickly some time ago, but I had Carol to thank for perfecting my knack of doing so without water.

With the encouragement of Sr. Hyacinth urging me to experience as much as I could, I hopped in the all-terrain vehicle and took off with this Bible thumping, Scripture quoting, Amen-ending missionary Sister. She was as dedicated as they come but riding with her was a white-knuckle ride but it was also solid evidence older people could take the turns with the youngest of them.

After a short five minute ride on the highway, we slowed and turned right on a dirt road, the entry to the Reservation. I wished again there was some sort of demarcation letting people know they were entering a reservation, if not a regular sign, maybe a pair of moccasins on one side of the entrance and a couple arrows in a post on the other letting outsiders know they were on tribal land. By leaving the entrance unmarked, showed how they weren't keen on making their presence known and people had to know they were on Indian land.

Traveling with this docile looking evangelical Sister was no doubt fun, even if she had taken it upon herself to convert all the heathenish, irreligious, uncivilized persons she met, and who I suspected, had me at the top of her list. This one woman envoy set out with good works, sacraments, and Gospel teachings to carry out appointed salvation by faith. If I could stomach the preaching, trips to the Reservation were worth it, as she went about saving my soul with all the zeal of an encyclopedia salesman. No wonder I heard a trumpet blast in my mind heralding her entrance when she drove up.

When Carol drove, she used three gears: first, third, and get out of the way. Without hesitating she turned this way and that until I was completely lost. I marveled at her keen sense of direction on intersecting dirt roads that had no signs marking streets, no name-plates identifying families, and no speed limits posted, which Carol no doubt appreciated. Wending her way deeper and deeper into the Reservation, over fields and gulches, I noticed with growing concern, we hadn't passed one gas station in case we had car trouble or if we needed directions. I didn't think she would have stopped to ask for directions anyway; she struck me as the type that would drive in circles for hours rather than admit being lost.

Reservations have vast amounts of land and looked like a gigantic flat field with hogans spaced generously apart with every homestead looking like the last, especially since they all faced in the same direction—east.

A trip to the Reservation was a humbling experience for me. By crossing into the realm of Indians, I had crossed into a different belief system that included fetishes, sweat lodges and sand paintings and the mystical feelings were palpable. As if to offset these mysterious feelings keeping me grounded, were a number of hogans with vegetables growing out of their roofs—corn, squash, tomatoes— and the spiritual feelings were replaced with a number of practical questions; first, how did they get all the dirt up there? When they watered the vegetables, didn't the water drip through the logs in the roof and down into the living area? And, wasn't it inconvenient to climb on the roof every time they wanted a tomato?

As the Bronco shuddered and shook on the dirt roads I realized we didn't have one close call. Sr. Carol knew where she was going and how to get there and in the days before seat belts were mandatory, the hardest part was staying in the seat. I had to hold onto the door handhold or brace myself against the dashboard and sometimes against the roof, but I mainly held on to the edges of my open window. No mistaking it though, she could drive!

The land was dry and covered with scattered, low-lying weeds. And because water was at a premium, there were no trees and lawns. I didn't see any businesses along the way, and I understood why Sr. Carol was delivering supplies to a family who had lost the support of their bread winner after he had been kicked in the ribs by a mule.

While Sister Carol's physical eyes were riveted on the road, her inner eyes concentrated on my forgotten soul throwing out a epithet at times, "**How straight is the** gate **and how narrow the way that leadeth unto eternal life!**" To my horror, I noticed the more she was filled with religious fervor the more she pushed on the accelerator. When she finished with, "**There are few that find it!**" the tires suddenly caught after sliding around a corner and we almost flew headfirst into life everlasting there and then. As the car straightened, I vowed to do better in life.

I suppose I could have let her know we were both on the same side fighting the good fight and that I knew all about the *slippery slope*, but my experience in dealing with eager religious who were ready, willing and able to impart their accumulated wisdom told me it was pointless, nothing I could have said would ever change her opinion of me; I would always be a God-forsaken little waif who needed the simplest Scripture passages explained. Which might be true, other than knowing a passage was from the Old Testament or the New, when it came to knowing what chapter and which verse, I had to look it up every time. I could stand to hear an occasional shout of **Hosanna** or **God Help Us All**, welling up from her zeal, there was no harm in that.

By the grace of God, Carol found the right hogan. The front door had been taken completely off so the hogan was wide open when we pulled in. Looking from the car, the light was dim inside but I could see a wood stove in the center with a metal pail on top and beds were lining the far wall with the injured party in, too sore to move but Helena, the wife, came out to greet us.

I climbed from the car stretching my limbs. And with Helena directing us and helping herself, the three of us carried cardboard boxes full of supplies containing corn, rice and beans, flour, sugar, red and green chilies, sunflower seeds among other food items to the entry where we left them neatly stacked near the front door. Carol said a few words to Helena who responded in Navajo; I could tell she wasn't as fluent in English as Leonard had been but she did know enough English to thank us. That was the extent of our visit. Carol wished her well, we got back in the Bronco, I waved good bye and we went on our way.

I looked over at Sr. Carol and watched as she readied herself for the drive home by straightening the rear view mirror, reaching around to the window to flick a bug from her field of vision, and readjusted the position of the outside mirror. I wouldn't have been surprised if she pulled out a pair of leather driving gloves from under the seat. Gunning the engine, we were off.

I waved to Helena and watched as she brought her hand out from under the folds of her brown jumper and shyly waved back. She waited until we drove off the property before walking inside the dark hogan. Our whole visit had been about ten minutes but we left with the knowledge we'd helped a family in need and waves of benevolence poured over us as we looked at each other and smiled on the drive home and for a fleeting moment thought how it would be nice to be a missionary. I looked back at the hogan and saw smoke rising from a rusty pipe sticking out of a hole in the roof and it gave me a good feeling thinking the wispy condensation of smell floating over the hogan was from the food we'd left.

"Good driving, Sister," I encouraged, hoping she'd take my meaning and slow down a little, but as our car bottomed out over a shoulder, I knew my compliment hadn't been taken seriously. Up until this point, I had repressed the need to ask her to pull over and leave my queasy feelings on the side of the road, and I wasn't about to ask her now that we were almost home. She wasn't trying to scare me. I think she just liked to drive fast. If I could just keep my stomach under control, I'd be safely at the retreat in my firmly fixed hogan made of heavy cement and hefty logs.

As it always does, the ride seemed shorter on the way home with no expectations and I was glad to see the turnoff leading to the steady ground of the Retreat Center and be out of harms way. My relief was short-lived however. When we drove within yards of the driveway Carol called out, "Dear God!" pointing to a straw figure at the base of the drive.

"What is it?" I asked.

"Looks like someone was upset," Carol answered, suddenly brisk. It's a figure burned in effigy."

Carol slowed and pulled alongside, but didn't get out. I could tell Sr. Carol wasn't in a hurry to investigate it and she pulled away and continued on up the hill saying, "Quick, Let's get out of here in case anybody is watching."

"Good idea!" I agreed. She couldn't leave fast enough for me. It gave me a creepy feeling knowing someone with evil intentions was close to our retreat and the disgruntled person was somewhere in out vicinity.

Carol explained, "It happens out here, not often, but it happens," as we pulled into the retreat.

"The straw dummy represents an undesirable person, or out here, it could represent an unwanted spirit as well, in an effort to banish the unwelcome element from someone life, there's no telling."

"I can't believe what I saw, it was so… backward," I told her truthfully.

"Did you notice how the edges were singed on the hands and feet? They were trying to burn something out of their lives and it could be anything. I remember something like this happening a few times, but remember I've been here over twenty years. Let's hope that's all they'll do."

When we passed the statue of Jesus at the top of the hill Sr. Carol insisted in a serious tone, "Make sure you tell Hyacinth about this. She may have seen it already if she ran errands in town today but make *sure* you tell her."

"Don't worry," I said, and climbed down from the Bronco.

Even if we had the strange welcoming, it was good to be home and let the pine air fill my lungs. I stood and watched as Sr. Carol once again pounced on the accelerator sending the car lurching forward up on the way to her parish.

Maybe the model name on her car had something to do with it but there was a moment when I watched her riding into the sunset, an impression came to me of her flapping a cowboy hat against the side of the vehicle to make it go faster. Considering Doppler's principle was affecting my hearing when I heard her call out one last spiritual epithet; I'm sure it must have been "*Hallelujah*," but it sounded an awful lot like, "*Ye ha*!" and gave her the benefit of the doubt.

I stepped up on the porch and opened the office door to the Retreat and went inside thinking about the distorted figure of straw propped up against our hill.

"How was your trip to the Reservation?" I heard Hyacinth call from her desk. "Did you see anything interesting?"

"As a matter of fact, we did run across something *very* interesting," I sat across from her on the motionless wooden office chair and stared for a second. "It was definitely one of the weirdest things I've ever seen but it wasn't on the Reservation, and it was right here at the base of our driveway."

"What's that?" Hyacinth asked, suddenly attentive, taking off her reading glasses.

I explained, "Someone dropped off a dummy that had been stuffed with straw at the base of our entrance. Sr. Carol said it was a figure burned in effigy because the edges were singed; shoulders, neck, feet and hands. It's dreadful looking."

"Are you *sure*?"

"No kidding, there is an entire body made out of straw: head, arms, and legs, with tight little bundles of hay stuck in for hands and feet; quite disturbing actually. Wire is holding the bulky figure together," I told her excitedly. "There is a bag on top used for a head with eyes and the nose drawn on."

"Was Carol sure that's what it was? Maybe someone's advertising a garage sale and put it out to advertise," she questioned, hoping it was something insignificant as something pointing to a *garage sale*. "Do you think Carol could have been mistaken?"

"No, you can't mistake something as hideous as that," I said without doubt. "Wait till the new Sisters hear about this. Hope it doesn't make them change their minds," trying to mask the excitement in my voice.

"Oh yes, I'll have to alert the Sisters to be on watch. If they're going to live out here, they have to know things like this happen at times. Speaking of which, I need to tell Fr. Lighterman about Mr. Effigy too, to be on the safe side."

"Good idea. Do you think an angry Indian put it there?"

"No, it's not their style. More than likely it was intended for someone else living up the road; maybe a rancher," reminding me we weren't the only people living along this road. "But since this is the only entrance, in all likelihood it was meant for someone else. It could be any number of reasons why it was put there. There's no way of telling; maybe a fence was strung too close to somebody's property, maybe a goat got lose and wandered in a neighbor's vegetable garden. It might be anything."

Level-headed, sensible Sr. Hyacinth could have easily been a successful diplomat in another lifetime.

I laughed nervously and I told her, "I'd forgotten we weren't the only ones using this road." I felt much better knowing we might not have been the ones responsible for infuriating someone. It still gave me the willies though.

"Well, it can't stay there," Hyacinth stated with finality. "Tomorrow morning we'll go and get the truck from the group home and throw the thing in back and get it out of here." Nothing disturbed Hyacinth.

It gave me an uneasy feeling knowing someone was sneaking around at night close to our center, and pictured a gruff, an unshaven sort slinking from hogan to hogan by the light of the moon.

Her words made me feel reasonably confident the straw figure was intended for somebody else and helped restore some of my peace of mind but it was uncanny how one malicious act tainted my whole outlook.

Early the next day Hyacinth and I drove to town to pick up the truck at the group home. We saw that the dummy was still propped up against the side of our hill on the edge of the drive but at least no one had added anything to it during the night. Knowing the responsible party hadn't been doing more mischief was a relief in itself and we raced into Gallup on this little wave of optimism, then slightly breathless we raced back up the grade to remove the grotesque image.

She pulled the white truck as close as she could to the stuffed figure and we hopped out. It was unsettling knowing an angry person had gone to all the trouble to make it and had been creeping around our property under cover of night. Worse yet, was now imagining watchful eyes riveted on us because we had the audacity to disturb it.

We tried to avoid touching the burnt ends of charred straw that smudged anything it touched and flung it in the truck and drove up to the retreat grounds. With Hyacinth in her habit and me in my jeans, we pulled at the pieces of dry straw like we were drawing and quartering it until there was nothing left but the paper bag used for a head and pieces of wire. Hyacinth held onto what was left of the head and I grabbed what was left of the ankles, we swung the rest of somebody's indignation off the back of the truck.

Hearing Hyacinth mutter *"good riddance"* as she slapped her hands together, I knew we were both relieved the ugly incident was now only a memory. Still standing in the truck stunned, I mentioned to her how fortunate it was directors overseeing Retreat Centers in urban areas are not forced to deal with rural, voodoo-like, practices like this.

"I'll take effigies over gangs any day," she replied confidently.

But as we climbed down off truck, I thought how Retreat Centers in cities were usually situated on multi-million dollar properties in suburbia in the most beautiful surroundings imaginable patrolled by private police; they didn't have to worry about gangs. I jumped off too, latched the tailgate and walked away.

In the weeks following, no one 'fessed up' to it and we didn't hear one possible explanation from anyone, including a number of unlikely scenarios from retreatants so we considered the matter closed. But every time I walked down the back hill I made it a special point to go way around the scattered parts of the body until the day it had blown completely away.

CHAPTER
12

Working in a place run on a skeleton staff made me feel like I was back in the monastery routinely praying for postulants that would among other benefits, add to the work force. Priests and nuns are hard workers there is no mistaking, how did Merton put it, *with an exaggerated reverence for work*, and one could get caught up in the feeling of duty and forget the real reason why we were arranging the tables in the first place, to give people time apart to rest, relax and pray.

We had our share of down time with nothing to do too, and we earned it. After months of working on non-stop retreats, even being accommodating was a chore. In-between the retreats we could use our time off any way we wanted and each of us had varying interests and different ideas of how to fill this spare time. Fr. Lighterman went fishing on lakes in the area—Bluewater and Nutrina and he probably had a secret spot somewhere he kept to himself. Sr. Hyacinth, being extended between the group home and the retreat as she was, usually spent any extra time at the home helping Sr. Celeste, whereas Sr. Edith liked to go into town to attend Masses said by different priests for a change of perspective and familiarize herself with different congregations and spread the word about our upcoming retreats.

We all had different ideas how to spend an afternoon. Testing a recipe wasn't for me, but Sr. Evangelista wanted to try a recipe for

Navajo Fry Bread at little Ruby's insistence one afternoon. Mixing cups of flour, sugar and salt, the petite Sister added melted grease and worked the soft mass of dough into patties with Ruby at her side begging to let her make the patties look "*as round as the moon*". Even though the mixture turned out the way it was supposed to, Evangelista was disappointed to find it was an acquired taste.

At times we played cards in the community room; rummy, Uno or setting up the Scrabble board for an occasional game. We could watch television but because we were in the country, reception was sketchy so we didn't spend much time in front of the set. Then there was the day Evangelista burst in excited with news about her day…

"They called it a Pow-Wow," she exclaimed breathless. "I went to a ceremony celebrating Indian ancestors; at least that's what the girls at the home told me."

Poor Evangelista, I thought, recalling the chili incident when I first arrived and hoped they hadn't talked her into doing something she really didn't want to do. "Sister, kids, no matter what culture, will tell you anything to get you to go along. The girls at the home have probably gone to a number of Pow-Wows." I'd heard these festivals were a way to help keep the traditional ways of Indians alive and assumed Hyacinth and Celeste would have urged the girls to attend these educational outings.

I never went to one because I felt they were private affairs suitable for Indians only and I'd feel out of place, although what would be more out of place than someone wearing a long black habit? I wondered how Evangelista reacted to the crush of the clannish crowd mingling wall-to-wall in unity. It didn't seem far-fetched that a broad shouldered Indian smeared with ceremonial paint would have sidled up to her letting her know in no uncertain terms she was intruding on the brotherhood of the tribe and she better not start any funny business. That's what I imagined and that's why I never went. To someone brand new to the Southwest like Evangelista, the gathering must have been a true culture shock.

"What was it like?" I asked, genuinely interested. I'd heard the Plains Indians danced to keep in time with Mother Earth and that if even one eagle feather drops to the ground during a Pow-Wow, they clear the area where the feather was found and a ceremony is performed right then singing special songs while it's picked up and asked her if anything like that happen.

"No, there were no feathers involved except on some costumes, as far I could tell. A Navajo Pow-Wow is like one big tribal party where everyone knows everyone else. There were booths selling souvenirs, crafts, supplies and food. Ruby kept pestering me for change for cherry drinks every two minutes."

"Was there dancing?"

"Are you kidding? There was continuous dancing, everybody danced."

"Did you dance?" I could picture her moving in and out among the bare chests of men.

She turned to me with raised eyes and moved her dark framed glasses to the end of her nose and looked at me with a *you've got to be kidding* look and said, "No, no, I didn't go inside the dance area but the girls did. And they were hard to keep track of too, dancing in, dancing out. I kept losing them. And then there was the singing; I think it was one long song mixed with the beat of the drums. "What were the dancers wearing?"

"That's another thing. Everyone was in traditional Navajo dress, long colorful fringes, feathers, really striking outfits, and here I was in my black habit and veil not blending in very well at all."

"That must mean there was music?"

"Music; was there music?" she almost screamed, her eyes growing big and bugging out so far I thought the pounding obbligato had actually affected her nerves. "Drums are the pulse of the Pow-Wow and they never stopped! Anne, we were at the Pow-Wow for nearly five hours and I don't think there was a second that didn't have drums beating! **Boom Boom Boom**! It was loud, I tell you. I think I may have suffered permanent hearing loss!"

"I see," I commiserated with her, watching as she placed her palm against her right ear tapping it gently testing it.

"**Boom Boom Boom**," she imitated again. "If they were trying to wake ancestral spirits, I think they succeeded. **Boom Boom Boom**," she sounded, tugging gently on an ear making sure the lobe was still intact.

"All of it, the pounding beat of the drums, the music, the singing and dancing made it feel like the culture had come to life, like I was in another time."

"But you were. In this day and age not many people can say they attended real Indian Pow-Wow," I congratulated.

"Did you know that drums are very important and there is even drum etiquette? Musicians are not supposed to casually leave the drum and it never should be left by itself," the day's exciting events brimming out of her.

"The girls really enjoyed it, I could tell. Even before it ended, they were after me to bring them back again. Letting them connect with their past made it all worth it. I can still hear the drums," she repeated.

"I see," I said again, letting her get it out of her system. It must have been a relief to be back in the quiet at the Retreat.

She stopped for a moment, then said, "You know the whole Pow-Wow really was an impressive Navajo experience you shouldn't miss," suddenly building it up. "It's a once in a lifetime opportunity, you really shouldn't miss it."

"I know, but you said…"

"There's another one in three days. Sr. Celeste and I are taking the girls again. You can go with us if you want," she said, egging me on.

She must have noticed the dumbfounded expression on my face and knew I needed more convincing. So reaching into one of the deep pockets in her habit, she pulled out a small white object with red hearts decorating it and dangled the woven object under my nose like a bribe, saying with a twisted smile, "Look, you can buy a basket!"

Sr. Godwina's filled her time off in another way, with a love interest. An opportunity came up to her to fill in at an ongoing Bible class that enrolled a handful of children, Navajo and others. The program's staff was always shorthanded because there didn't seem to be much interest in getting cleaned up just to learn about God's Word on a nice spring day and the attendance fluctuated from week to week. Classes were conducted in a small parish building not too far from the retreat. Sr. Godwina decided helping children understand Biblical passages and Catholic beliefs wouldn't be too difficult and something she had training in, so she volunteered to meet with the children once a week.

For weeks Sr. Godwina discussed and explained passages of Scripture and helped and encouraged the few children who thought it was important enough to make the effort to show up. Everything was going along fine. Sr. Godwina even enlisted Sr. Evangelista to go and try her hand at instructing too; Evangelista patiently offered her expertise to those having trouble with the language skills of English, a second language. I went a few of these sessions to help too, but because I wasn't part of *any* community and wasn't wearing a headdress, I wasn't pressured into service compared to Srs. Godwina and Evangelista who were *real* nuns in their black habits and veils.

Sr. Godwina was tall and lithe and one little boy developed a crush on her. But it wasn't really him she was refusing; his pre-adolescent mind couldn't understand her indifference with a popular action figure of the time, Conan the Barbarian. He would bring crayon drawings of a muscle-bound He-Men he'd spent hours on to impress her. She was inundated with these drawings and even if the pictures weren't exact replicas of Conan, they were good and you could tell he spent a lot of time coloring them. Accompanying his artwork came the descriptions Conan's feats of daring and improbable exploits, all of which she listened to patiently.

I could never understand why this little boy derived enjoyment going overboard about his hero to Godwina. But because she had an interest in psychology and about what makes people tick, his obsession with Conan interested her and brought up a number of psychological causes: *was his father mean to him so he used Conan as a substitute father? Was the student ignored by his father and this forced him to find another father figure? Did the little boy want to be strong like Conan?* Figuring this out and discovering what was really at the heart of this boy's excessive admiration made Godwina happy and kept her busy for months.

"Hero worship, 'from the Latin verb *Servo*' to preserve whole, is akin to the word *serare* meaning to safeguard, but etymologically it's thought to be from Hera guardian of marriage…," she informed me as the rest of the staff stood perplexed, but accustomed to hearing her academic trivia by now.

We all had our own ideas of how to spend our spare time.

To most people launching garbage out of the back of a pick-up isn't considered a high point in their month, but it was in mine. One of my favorite things to do was go to the local dump with Sr. Hyacinth. Because we lived so far out of town, we didn't have a regular trash day and had to wait for the city to schedule a pickup. When our ongoing yard work and ordinary rubbish had grown into an unusually large unsightly heap in the back of the retreat, Hyacinth would bring the truck up from the girl's home, enlist the help novices and we'd haul it away ourselves.

The dump was located outside of town and it was like no other dump I ever visited. It didn't have an attendant tallying up each load we dropped off. It was in a field the local people had decided was a good place to bring their refuse and somehow everyone knew where it was. It wasn't out-of-control dumping with broken washing machines, lumpy mattresses or refrigerators without doors because these items weren't generally used by most of the local Indian population. The dump was filled with reasonable loads of trash from everyday living. Most people burned what they didn't need and that kept throw-away items to a minimum.

There were no signs pointing the way, Hyacinth had been here a number of times and knew the way. I could tell we were getting close when I began seeing various stages of decomposition on the sides of the road; flat tires, springs that had lost their coil, pieces of indestructible plastic, corroded car batteries. A handful of carrion-eating birds always seemed to be picking at bacteria laden items near the main drop off point.

With the novices in their habits, we would pull ourselves over the opened gate of the pick-up and stamp about in leaves, clippings and rubbish from the retreat. Then it became a free-for-all with everything going every-which-way off the truck, their baggy black sleeves flapping, with gloved hands we'd fling the messy jumble; then drag our feet over the bed until everything was out. More than once my comb would find coffee grounds in my hair.

Even Sr. Hyacinth would struggle out of the truck, tighten an apron around her habit like it was a mantle of honor, move her crucifix around to her back safely out of the way, and reach over and throw whatever she could reach; always in black habit and veil, if there was the need throw trash, then she threw trash.

What made this dump special for me was an unusual rock formation nearby that was both grotesque and beautiful at the same time. It had rugged edges that rain had dissolved away that had taken years to sculpt into such a bizarre three-dimensional shape. The large free-standing rock abstract had a base of white sandstone that looked like a pedestal for a sculpture on which four separate heads rested on thick necks. I was puzzled how wind, rain and snow could whiten the base and necks but turn the heads a rusty auburn. The way the rocks were layered on top made them look like they were each wearing bad hair pieces.

If I *stared* intently at the heads, it was easy to see separate rough, craggy faces with wrinkled foreheads, protruding noses, accordion-like ripples in the necks. I picked out subtleties of eyes, cheek bones, chins, brows, clefts, and Adam's apples. Because the heads were joined at the base unable to move, I developed a feeling of helplessness for their position unable to detach from the physical, condemned to stay in the temporal world never to let their spirits fly, like they were in a continual state of purgation and stuck in the knowledge of their own misery.

If I *glanced* in the rock's direction, I imagined hearing a voice, scarcely audible, almost a murmur parched and raspy from being in the sun for decades, coming from the heads telling how hidden imperfections were holding them back, an outlook not unlike my own and a sure consequence of sin.

But if I let my eyes *sweep* over the large mass, four elderly Indians appeared to be sitting contemplatively like shamans, steadfast, and Buddha-like, acting as mediums between the visible world and the invisible world. This was when the trip to the dump turned into a pilgrimage for me, when the energy of the rock materialized as four spirit guides, wise Indians faithfully waiting for my return. I knew I had connected to the rock's deepest core by experiencing its quiet consciousness with my whole being, like it was a bridge between my imagination and reality.

All this picturesque beauty in the middle of nowhere was going to waste and it saddened me knowing its days were numbered. New Mexico's relentless heat and heavy downpours would act like cause and effect in a visible karma as the heads passed from one representation to another. Helpless, they accepted their fate as they had accepted earlier incarnations; four heads bound for eternity together like a mythological creature. The four proud Indian spirits resting on sandstone would eventually meet an ignominious end by crumbling away in the weather and pass beyond the world of existence to dust, their delicate balance would run down their faces to their necks and shoulders, wasting away to the base as if they had been desecrated by vandals.

Ignoring the reality I was actually looking at uneven piles of stone, jutting ledges and unbalanced rocks made me certain the scenery in New Mexico created illusions in contrasts and hues. There was no mistaking the intentional slowing of the mind, the deeper breathing and the restored flow of energy brought on by the beauty of New Mexico's landscape. Where most people would approach with caution fish bones, broken lamps, and bottomless buckets, the four wise Indians on the rock beckoned me. Standing back, I admired it every dumping day.

And then there was the rare occasion when a retreatant discovered one of the Sisters was a horse lover, Evangelista, and we accepted an invitation to go horseback riding. Jane was a divorced Anglo woman about 30 who lived by herself on the outskirts of a reservation, a brave way to live in anybody's thinking.

Sr. Evangelista drove us under a decorative metal arch with an outline of a pine tree leaning on its side and into Jane's *Lazy Pine* ranch at an elevation of 7,000 feet where we stopped at a corral lined with cowboys straddling old splintered wooden posts. They were an interesting lot in their jeans and leg chaps; mostly Anglo, a few Navajo, but all were real cowboys.

Jane galloped up to us and we all watched the action inside the paddock until a cowboy leading two horses interrupted us. Leaning over he handed Evangelista and me a leather strap attached to a horse but he stopped when he saw that Sr. Evangelista's legs were a *"might puny"* in the length department and her stirrups had to be shortened. He slid off his horse and landed as tall and straight as one of the fence posts and helped her into the saddle so he could make the necessary adjustments.

Evangelista gave the cowboy a shy thank you that sounded like an apology for needing extra attention, or for being short, I wasn't sure which. The cowboy headed off muttering something about *city slickers* and wondered what gave us away: my old garden boots or the baggy jeans Sr. Evangelista had scrunched up under her habit; a colored scarf had replaced her veil.

I've always enjoyed riding and relaxed when I felt the motion sickness tablet down in the crease in my jeans' pocket. Not thinking any more about how the bouncing would affect me, I went back to trying not to slouch.

I followed Evangelista who was following the slow gait of Jane's horse. And, in no time at all, the two were side by side ahead of me talking horse talk. Words floated back to me—dressage, reining, carrying the rider; equestrian lingo none of which interested me. As we clomped through the weeds urging our horses on, hearing the creaking sound saddles make moving with the horse's frame, I was right back looking through a wire fence at a race track when I was a child watching jockeys parading horses, some trotting, some whinnying, in a world of flowing manes and tails. As a child, I looked on with interest at the small whips tucked under their jockey's arms, at the long yellow teeth of the horses, at the rearing up of one unruly equine.

And there was something else; a selected few horses had a shimmering around their frames. Not all of them, I was to discover, just the ones that went on to win; I was too young to realize the implications involved in having a horse win, place or show but the memory of translucent edges on the *special* horses stayed with me. I hadn't thought of this memory in years but what better time to explore this interconnectedness while living in Navajo country with people who believe people, plants, animals and earth are all connected. Or had the memory surfaced *because* I was living among people who for thousands of years have taken for granted the earth is made up of this eternal interconnectedness?

The question remains with me to this day; if animals are purer than humans in regards to sin, could the other horses in the race *see* this translucence, and if they could, did they *throw the race* and '*let*' the *chosen* horse win seeing it was favored by God in this way? What did this say about free will?

With time to gain perspective, two possible reasons come to mind that are the closest I've come to understanding what I was *seeing*; the outline on the edges was part of an electromagnetic field or it was part of the universal field covering everything Einstein called *ether*.

It didn't surprise me I remembered this while in the land of enchantment, a land that uses its shapes to stretch the imagination until it is in the realm of the spirit. And even though I knew I shouldn't, I looked directly into the sun and for a time I was without sight, reckless and maimed, my purpose blinded, convincing me New Mexico is an enchantress that continues to charm the onlooker until they welcome whole-heartedly the deliberate bewitching under the orange red sun in the sky.

CHAPTER
13

In a town that didn't have much graffiti, it was only a matter of time before Gallup underwent a natural progression from faded advertisements and weathered storefronts to beautifying them with paintings of local history and Indian culture. The amount of unblemished wall-space alone called for outdoor displays of art but it would be years for the idea to develop into outdoor murals.

But back then, when Hyacinth said she was going to a place known as a *village of artists*, I had no idea what she was talking about.

With her background in art, Sr. Edith's ears perked up and she spoke first. Straightening her veil, she said thoughtfully, "With an introduction like that, I'd like to go, if you don't mind."

"You'll enjoy it." Hyacinth encouraged, building her destination up for the rest of the listening staff. "I'm going to a locale known as the *Middle Place of the World* also known as the Zuñi Reservation."

"What's that?" Evangelista said, suddenly attentive. "Did you say we were going to the middle of the world?"

"No, I'm going to a place known as the *Middle Place of the world*. It's only a short ride, about an hour away. I need to drop off paperwork to Fr. Paul at the Zuñi reservation. He's stationed there and we'll be able to visit the Mission too. No trip to the Southwest is complete without visiting a Mission and this is one of the best. Our Lady of Guadalupe mission church was built in the 1600's by the

Spanish but was abandoned in 1820 until restoration began in the 1960's. The walls of the Church have been painted with beautiful figures, *Kachinas* or spirits. Wait until you see. They are an attraction for people worldwide; Jackie Onassis visited once and even Mother Theresa came to view the paintings."

"Really, Mother Theresa was here?" Evangelista asked, who I was sure, was picturing the stooped figure of the old nun giving approving looks at the degree of simplicity of the chapel as she walked through.

On the other hand, I was imagining Jackie smartly dressed in dark eye glasses living a celebrity lifestyle, handing out autographs.

"Maybe I'll be able to buy another basket," Evangelista said hopefully.

I told them I wanted to go too but didn't tell her why; I didn't think it would sit well with them if I explained that as soon as I heard the phrase *village of artists* scenes of Haight Ashbury with its laid-back hippie culture came to mind. Puffing on a peace pipe would truly give a well-rounded experience of Indian culture.

I felt for the motion sickness pill in my jeans pocket for dizziness and vertigo. Unnoticed by the others, I slipped it in my mouth and felt confident I wouldn't have to excuse myself due to carsickness in the middle of a celebrity sighting; if the Mission attracted people of notoriety, I wanted to be ready.

We filed into the car. With Hyacinth at the wheel, instead of turning north towards Gallup, she made a hard left from of the retreat center. The only thing out this way that I knew was the Sunday school building. Hyacinth drove passed it, veil flying, and making good time.

After about thirty minutes, we slowed and pulled off the highway onto a dirt road. I may have missed it, because like the Navajo reservation, there was no sign indicating, **Zuñi Reservation Ahead** with an arrow pointing the way.

Once we were inside, I was surprised to see the houses weren't hogans but typical residences with flower beds alongside them. They weren't bunched together in an urban crowd that had been built to one design; they were built on large irregular plots of land big enough to grow small vegetable gardens situated every so often. There were no sidewalks and for that matter, the roads weren't paved either. We were only on the outskirts of the reservation so there could have been grey-stoned farmhouses to red-tiled domiciles the farther in we went.

Hyacinth parked the car in a field, and we walked to Father's office on a wide country lane. Seeing a middle-aged priest waving to us from the porch of a small office building, we hurried our pace. I followed the four Sisters in their black habits and veils up three steps to the porch where we each shook Father's outstretched hand.

Fr. Gary was wearing black slacks and white shirt and a cross on his collar. He had a quiet demeanor, the kind that comes from spending long hours on a remote mission alone where the days turn into weeks, then into months, and suddenly a decade has passed. He moved his black shoes in the slow unhurried gait of someone who wasn't under pressure, typical of missionaries working *out in the field* as compared to religious members who held fast-paced, stressful jobs. He was happy to have a visit from fellow missionaries who, no doubt, were dealing with many of the same issues he was; isolation, lack of community, solitude.

I was introduced but quickly excused myself, leaving the group of religious to their business and went looking for the Mission. It was midmorning and the sun was hot on my face as I walked through the quiet neighborhood along sporadically placed houses. It was easy to picture Franciscan monks in brown habits from the Mission strolling peacefully under the trees, prayer books in hand or fingering beads of a rosary as they prayed.

The Mission was in easy walking distance from Father's office. I could see a large wooden cross towering over the sun-soaked adobe building that more then anything else, typifies the Southwest. Solid off-white walls surrounding the perimeter made it impossible to look through and were high enough to prevent a look over. Logically I knew the walls had been a defense against intruders in years past but it was easy to imagine a garden of roses growing on the other side. I resisted the urge to hoist myself up on the wall to see if I could see any clusters of pink, white, yellow or red roses climbing gracefully on the sun-washed adobe. By the time I reached the Mission steps, I could almost smell their intoxicating fragrance wafting over the high wall.

I pulled at the wooden door and the darkness of the interior surprised me. Dipping my fingers in a small holy water basin, I made the sign of the cross and quickly took a seat on a pew to let my eyes adjust to the interior. I was grateful for this time alone to sit in the quiet church and let the ambiance of the southwestern architecture permeate my being like the holy water renewed my soul.

Sitting behind the progression of pews, I shook my head in wonder, there was so much to choose from, Hyacinth could have given a better indication of what the inside of the Mission looked like; a ceiling of large rounded beams full of knotholes gave the church a rugged outdoorsy look; to the left and right of the sanctuary, was a buffalo head, complete with horns sweeping back in an outward curve had been mounted on each wall; or she could have mentioned the two colorfully woven blankets hanging beneath the skulls reinforcing the unique blend of Zuñi heritage and Catholicism.

I settled back in the pew under wrought iron chandeliers taking it all in. In the front of the church behind the altar, a large window let in enough daylight to brighten the walls and together with two overhead panes, beams of daylight lightened the brown-red color of the tiles on the floor.

Looking back on a side wall, I was astonished to see life-size figures painted on both sides of the Mission facing each other across from the church making their presence known like obnoxious bodyguards. Most of the brightly colored figures were wearing unusual masks and it was easy to anthropomorphize and see spirits of humans seeping from the figures, fairy-like projections swirling about the church, regarding onlookers on the *other side* with suspicion.

A pictorial had been applied directly to the surface of the walls in bird of paradise oranges, atmospheric blues, and thundercloud foams. How unlike it was from other Missions that had oil paintings of departed saints encased in antique frames; these paintings were alive. Hyacinth had been right about the art; Our Lady of Guadalupe

Mission Church was a living portfolio of artwork transitioning from moccasins and feathers to shadows and clouds to dreams and visions.

I heard the sound of movement coming from a platform at the far end of the church, and as if someone had been eavesdropping on my thoughts and my private moments, suddenly I felt self-conscious. Turning, I saw a dark headed man on scaffolding high above dipping a small brush into paint. All this time I thought I had been alone and there had been someone else in the church.

It was my turn to be embarrassed having violated the painter's privacy by entering his Mission cum art studio uninvited. I continued to watch the lone artist painstakingly add small touches of paint to a figure of a bird on the wall. Observing him, it didn't take my shoulders long before I was tensing for him as I watched his repetitious actions of reaching up, extending and straining to paint a precise spot on the bird.

The sound of several sets of footsteps making their way to the door disturbed the peace of the Mission and Fr. Gary opened the door for the staff of St. Francis Retreat and flicked on a set of lights. One by one the accolades started, "Look at that," "Look over there!" and "I've never seen anything like this…"

A voice called down from rafters, "*Keshshi* (welcome), Fr. Gary," which made Evangelistic jump in surprise.

Father turned and looked up toward the voice.

"That's Alan," he introduced, waving an arm at the upper part of the church.

Alan rolled on his side to look at us, his dark hair shined as it caught the light of the chandeliers. He was wearing a long white T-shirt like a painter's smock over trousers.

"Alan is restoring the murals. He's rejuvenating the natural colors which will preserve the murals from further atmospheric damage."

"Tell them *why* murals are important Father."

The priest motioned those standing to be seated and began sharing what he knew about the kachinas on the walls.

"As I understand, Zuñis believe Kachinas live in a mythical Lake called the *Lake of the Dead* located near the Zuñi River. By preserving the tribal paintings, he is in essence, preserving the old ways.

"The figures are called Kachinas, or spirits, and they represent different events in Zuñi life. 'Look for yourselves,' he instructed, tilting his head to the finished wall behind us.

"Different tribes have different Kachinas: the *Kokopelli* Kachina is an ancient Anasazi symbol that provides abundance, fertility and rain. For the Navajo, the *Hemis* kachina brings corn to maturity while the *White Cloud* kachina reminds of the importance of rain, and the *Prayer Eagle* kachina is protector of all. You get the idea."

Shifting his weight, Father told us *White Buffalo Warrior* kachina brings hope and *White Bear* kachina brings wisdom, courage and spiritual strength. You get the ides." We sat very still on the pews grateful to be receiving this lesson of Zuñi culture and history. Father continued, "Zuñis are related to the other pueblo tribes scattered throughout the Southwest but the Zunian language is only spoken by them and bare no resemblance to surrounding tribes. Spaniards arrived in 1540 in search of the 'streets that were paved with gold' told by Francisco Coronado in his *Search of the Seven Cities of Gold* but Zuñis managed to remain unaffected by outer influences. I'd say generally the tribe has managed to remain intact because they didn't fight in wars or take sides in any conflicts; they managed to remain autonomous.

You happen to be sitting in the old mission Catholic Church that was built in 1539 and then rebuilt in 1968 when it fell into disrepair due to non-use. Our Lady of Guadalupe Mission is in the center of the old village and plans are to have over 20 murals of kachinas painted on the interior walls of the church.

My first impression of the Mission was the wall looked more like a fort than a church and recalled hearing the distant sound of a bugle in my imagination. The adobe walls around the Mission gave the impression the place was a well-fortified stronghold ready to defend from all direction even though the Mission itself is period perfect for southwestern architecture.

"Restoring the murals has become a lifetime project for you, isn't that right?"

"It's a labor of love though, Father," as he reached up and dabbed paint on part of a feather.

"Right you are," the cleric said as walked to the back of church. The rest of us stood and pushed into the center aisle following him, each of us genuflecting as we passed the tabernacle. This was a place where spirits of the ancients walked alongside you as living, breathing history and I wondered if Mother Teresa was able to pick up on their spiritual presence while she was here.

We followed Father to a dim wooden staircase. Hearing Sr. Hyacinth chuckling on the stairs above me I knew that it pays to travel with someone with pull; he must be giving us the grand tour ending with an overhead view of the backyard. My mind ran through the various species of roses; Cherokee roses, American prairie roses, Double Cabbage and dwarfed Lucinda's. I could hardly wait to see the budding climax of our tour!

I heard the sound of keys jangling at the top of the stairs and then a door opening and we were flooded with natural light. I stepped forward confidently and prepared myself to behold horticulture at its finest, fleshy pistils and swollen stamens loaded with pollen that had been cultivated in a garden of evergreen leaves. I readied myself to receive my first fragrant scent drifting up from a garden this size; maybe I would be able to take home a cutting or two.

At the top of the stairs we went through a single door and were in an open balcony that had a series of separated wooden posts for a front rail and were immediately hit by a wave of fresh air. With his hand on the waist high rail, Father stood overlooking the focal point of our climb, the enclosed pocket of land behind the Mission.

Eager to see what lay before me, I sidled up to the front of the balcony ready to feast my eyes on numerous varieties of roses my mind envisioned, but there were no roses at all—anything green had long since died but that was fitting because I was looking down on a graveyard! Cold hard head stones had replaced soft, pliable petals! I rubbed my eyes but another look at the dried weeds covering the head markers confirmed it, my flowery denouement had been replaced with dead bodies! So this was what the wall was keeping out of sight!

This was a disappointing turn of events and my thoughts went naturally to the holiday celebrated in November, All Saints Day, when we remember people who have died. Images of hybrids and blooms turned into skulls and skeletons, and to make matters worse, the yard was littered with trash. Papers were scattered about and unwanted items had been tossed over the fence, left to quietly decompose along with the deceased.

I think we were all astounded, standing with our mouths open, looking down at the grounds with confused faces while images of manicured lawns of Forest Lawn passed from our minds.

A subtle movement along the fence caused me to interrupt Father's accumulated facts.

What the heck is that? I said, pointing to the side enclosure. Out of nowhere an arm was reaching over the wall holding a crumpled paper bag. We watched in horror as the bag was slowly and deliberately lowered from the other side and let go, dropping to the ground with a dull thud.

My overall feeling was one of embarrassment; how could anyone treat their dearly beloveds this way?

Seeing the look of concern on our faces, Father quickly explained this was not a sign of disrespect at all; Zuñis believe that once a person is dead, their spirit is no longer here. "And in truth, it isn't here anymore, is it?"

All of us shook our heads. "Well, no," Hyacinth snickered. "Everyone knows the spirit leaves…"

The rest of us looked at the cemetery hoping we wouldn't hear screams of torment rising from the lower regions of the earth.

Sr. Edith, aware of the creative influence of such a momentous transformation said, "When the connection to the earth is over, the body doesn't need to continue to be respected; I can understand that."

"It's a matter of cessation beyond possibility of resuscitation…" Godwina taught, "however continuance is dependent on replacement of cells…"

Sr. Evangelista kept staring at the yard and said nothing.

After a while I said, "It was definitely a shock seeing graves at first and another shock seeing how the cemetery is used in such a disturbing fashion because Indians are the last people you would expect to see showing disrespect." But I knew if anyone should be embarrassed, it's was *us*. They were actually living what they believed, while we were hanging on, unsure, slow to react.

I regretted not having time to stroll up and down the markers like an anthropologist to see if anyone had left a final statement or if the graves had been decorated with a remembrance of moccasins or favorite pot, but remembering I couldn't read Zuñi, I went back to listening to Father explain the spiritual reasons behind this seemingly irreverent practice.

"Death is the heaviest burden laid on human existence, all flesh grows old like a garment... ." he was saying but I wasn't listening; I was busy ridding the scent of sweet-smelling *bourbons*, *gallicas* and hybrid *perpetuals* from my mind.

We weren't a particularly merry group descending the stairs but as Father pulled the balcony door closed tight behind us, I knew we were a more enlightened one. Back inside the church something had changed, there was a different feeling this time even though the same scent of incense still inundated the interior, the same two rows of empty brown pews were complementing the natural look of the adobe, and those were the same wrought-iron chandeliers flickering light from the ceiling. Similarly, the same expressive murals were still filling the Mission with their curious depictures of kachinas.

Foregoing all these pleasing elements that made up the whole of the Mission, it had taken a long time for me to understand it didn't matter that the yard wasn't a cadre full of beautiful roses or lovingly placed lily arrangements. It had taken a while but I was finally beginning to see the murals were not only displaying representations and figures; they were passing on a way of life handed down for thousands of years teaching the old ways in customs and tribal traditions. It had taken time for me to realize what I was really seeing on the walls was the spirit of the Zuñi people because it had taken all afternoon for me to think like an Indian.

CHAPTER
14

The flash of steel, the glint chrome and a shiny reflection from a long black car, Franklin and I looked on the new arrivals with growing interest; it wasn't often we had someone escorted into the yard. And as it pulled in front of the retreat office and stopped, noticed a car without Gallup's road mud splattered on its sides was carrying someone special.

A driver got out and in one movement opened the back door and stood waiting as a tall casually dressed man in a plaid shirt and tan slacks got out, turned back and offered his hand to a middle aged woman in the back seat who looked glad to be out of the cramped compartment. I couldn't be sure of course, but I bet there was a Madame in her name somewhere; she just had that air about her. She reached back in and pulled out a purse as shiny as the car.

A dignified figure of a man about 60 exited next wearing a smart black suit and the stiff white collar of a priest. He stood beside the other two visitors and was easily the tallest and thinnest of the three with a long neck just the right height for blowing out candles on an altar. The thin shouldered priest had neatly trimmed grey hair, the kind of short cut that wouldn't require much attention. As he stood by the car, a glint of gold from a cross flashed from his lapel.

The office door opened wide and out popped Sr. Hyacinth's head wearing a black veil anxious to greet the well-dressed gentleman.

"Bishop Struther; how nice of you to drop by!" Sr. Hyacinth said, holding out her hand in welcome. "Yah te hey," we heard her say walking toward him. And turning, she greeted the middle aged couple the same way.

Franklin and I kept our distance across the yard trying not to stare like tourists but St. Francis retreat never had a driver waiting in the yard before. I wiped my right hand on my sleeve in case I needed to shake hands.

Top ranking church officials drew attention and I wondered if Fr. Lighterman had noticed the important entourage too, prompting my eyes to scan the grounds for him. And there, wasting no time was Fr. Lighterman making a bee-line across the yard cutting his way to the group like a sprinter.

The driver, who I called *James*, just stood there although for a time I thought he'd move his body in a defensive stance in front of the Bishop like a bodyguard to protect him from the incoming cleric; no contact was made however and James continued to stand in readiness.

The Bishop! No wonder Fr. Lighterman came charging out of his room to meet the man who was essentially his boss. I quickly thought over the protocol involved in meeting such a high clerical member in case the group wandered over our way; I wasn't sure if kissing of rings would be involved and relaxed when I saw Hyacinth only shake his hand. I heard her usher everyone in the retreat building for coffee and cake. As soon as the door closed, James began to rub at a dirty spot on the windshield.

The *Bishop*, I thought again! I expected a person of this stature to be draped in flowing robes of purple velvet, leaning on a crosier and wearing a three pointed hat, not someone dressed like an ordinary priest. The word dapper came to mind with his silver hair and tall thin body that looked neat and trim. He used the white handkerchief sticking out of his pocket to gently dab his forehead, but I would never imagine him blowing his priestly nose in it. The only frame of reference I had to go by concerning clothing and shoes for religious comes from listening to chapter 55 in *The Rule of St. Benedict,* read daily in the monastery: *Monks should not complain of the color or texture of their clothing. It shall be whatever is available in the surrounding countryside or whatever is cheapest.*

In black slacks and white shirt, the Bishop as an active clergyman, wasn't far off the mark.

We didn't have a red carpet to roll out in welcome but at least we could have hosed off the porch if we knew he was coming.

It wasn't more than an hour when the kitchen door opened and the entire group walked back out in the yard again with everyone was smiling, including Hyacinth. James sprung into action opening the back door and stood poised for action.

I heard the Bishop grumble out a few words to the driver that made him walk to the back of the car, open the trunk and lift two suitcases to the porch. Next, James opened the back door for the Bishop who sat down ready to be driven home.

Bishop Struther waved goodbye to Sr. Hyacinth and Fr. Lighterman but gave a thumb's up sign to the deacon and his wife. Pressing on the accelerator, James moved the black car ahead with a lurch, leaving the couple standing next to their luggage on the porch and Hyacinth to make all the necessary adjustments. Fr. Lighterman seeing that the show was over and there would be no more excitement, went off to his room; the only thing to look forward to now being dinner.

Unable to grasp the obvious, I said in a low voice to Franklin, "Wait a minute, he forgot his two passengers."

Hyacinth quickly set me right calling over to me, "Anne, I want you to meet Deacon Walter and his wife June. They will be helping us this summer."

It occurred to me then that springing surprises on Sr. Hyacinth was the Bishop's modus operandi instead of a lack of preparedness. Getting the drop on people by taking them unawares avoided possible defensive stands and counter oppositions to why the undertaking shouldn't take place, like stationing Fr. Lighterman here as chaplain with little or no forewarning. This time the surprises were named Walter and June and like it or not they were here for the summer.

"A deacon," I asked bewildered. I had absolutely no experience working with deacons, Bishops either for that matter.

"Wasn't it nice of the Bishop to line up workers for us?

Hyacinth asked through clenched teeth.

Hearing the resignation in her voice taught me a valuable lesson. Bishops as overseers of pastors as well as laity, because they are appointed by the Pope are responsible for Church management and have supervision over all ecclesiastical institutions; in other words, the Bishop can do anything he wants.

With the couple standing there on the porch, Sister said, "They'll be a great help great help the Bishop assured me. After all, what would we do if something happened to Franklin? Then where would we be?" Hearing this, his usual serious face smiled.

"We can use all the help we can get," I said to Hyacinth hoping Deacon Walter would have some practical maintenance experience and he knew which side of the hammer to hold.

"Bishop Struther was most anxious to have them start working here," Hyacinth made clear. "And June is to work right alongside Walter," she said, knowing they where in earshot.

"We'll give you both a room in the new building next to the chapel opposite Fr. Lighterman," prompting them to reach down and pick up their suitcases. "Anne's in the Brother Sun hogan over there," pointing to it. Hyacinth handed each of them a set of keys and led them to their quarters. "From the front side, to get to your room, you have to go in through the chapel but from the back side you can use a hallway. After you get settled, I'll give you a tour of the whole center."

We were a full count sitting around the table at dinner; Fr. Lighterman at the head, Sr. Hyacinth on the opposite end, the staff of three Sisters, Evangelista, Godwina, Edith, and myself, now Walter and his wife June; we just had enough dining chairs. June wore a dress that had lightened pictures of fruit over it, fastened at the waist. She was fifty plus years old and was the epitome of the devoted housewife, loyal, supportive, championing her husband no matter what. She had brown shoulder length wavy hair and a large white bauble on a ring on one of her fingers matching her necklace; it got in her way each time she was asked to pass the butter.

Hyacinth stood and welcomed the deacon and his wife by telling the rest of us some of the duties deacons are allowed to perform such as distributing communion, conducting prayer services and reading the Gospel. "Deacons are clerics who rank below priests in the Catholic Church and as lay persons, they assist the minister. We should be very happy to have them."

"It will be like almost having another priest, won't it?" she said, running the thought by us to helping her become accustom to the idea herself.

"Their main responsibility is to identify with those in need," June spoke out as she fingered her white necklace.

"You've come to the right place," I said. "There are a lot of needy people around Gallup, especially the rural poor," picturing the impoverished dwellings back off the highways.

"So the Bishop tells us," Walter said. "June and I won't be going out on the reservation much during this trip. The Bishop wants us to devote our time working around the retreat. He has high hopes this place will become the spiritual center for the Catholics in Gallup, and be if not profitable then at least sustainable. Besides, I've been in Gallup before and have seen how enormous the reservation is. This is *June's* first time."

"I have a feeling the reservation is going to come to you," I interjected. "Did you notice the workman in the yard? That is Franklin and he does odd jobs for us. You can't get more of a Navajo than him. He helps with the pathways and does odd jobs."

June broke in, "Did you hear that Walter? Her eyes now wide with interest, "I told you we are going to meet our first real Indian! Maybe he can explain the meaning behind why the mudstone cliffs near the town of Kayenta called Baby Rocks we've heard about they say look like thousands of babies either laughing or crying, depending on which way you stretch your imagination."

"Now June, you don't want to scare the poor fellow," her husband cautioned.

I assured them, "Don't worry, he'll keep out of your way." Poor Franklin, I thought, doesn't know what he's in for.

"Oh, but I don't want him to. I'm just anxious to ask him some questions," June interjected.

Redirecting the subject, I asked Walter, "You were here before?"

"Not here at this Center but I've been through Gallup before. The Bishop and I go back quite a few years, you know," Walter said, explaining how he came to know the Bishop. "It's no secret; we were in the seminary together. One of us made it through, and one of us didn't," he said looking up and smiling at June. "We've been friends ever since. He was instrumental in my becoming a deacon. I feel I owe him."

I could tell June liked being in the spotlight and Walter seemed perfectly happy with this arrangement. The deacon was an unassuming person in a short-sleeved plaid shirt, not at all eager to add his thoughts to a conversation. He was much taller than Fr. Lighterman but the difference in their height Father made up in his bulging waistline and in how far he had to sit from the table just to eat. Walter had on a gold watch, the kind given to people after years of service with an insurance company; Father had a couple of toothpicks sticking out of his shirt pocket always at the ready.

"We're here to help, Walter assured. "If there's anything that needs doing, just let us know and we'll work at it till it's done.

"Like the Bishop told us, 'Deacons act like his eyes and ears' so it will be our duty to inform him of any need," showing us she intended on being on her best behavior. "Isn't that so, Walter?"

Hyacinth added, "That's very obliging of you both."

But I immediately felt by her telling us this, it was a way to let us know they were going to keep tabs on us and a feeling of resentment began to come over me, like we would have to watch what we said and did. Oh great, I thought, we'll have to act in a strained decorum all summer. I guess you'd have to expect goodie-goodie types to be friends with a Bishop. I prepared myself to work with real spoil-sports and resigned myself to be around a couple of wet-blankets. How'd they ever get to be so palsy with the Bishop anyway? Oh, right, the seminary.

"The Bishop told us for our first project he wants us to paint the hogans," Walter apprised us. "Right, Hyacinth? He was very clear about wanting us to start there."

June ended his sentence, "He wants our service to the retreat center to be our contribution to the community," finishing her husband's thought, something she quite often I noticed.

"You mean seal the hogans," I corrected, hoping they knew they difference.

"Yes, that's what I meant. And if we have time left over at the end of summer, the Bishop wanted us to seal the main buildings too. I noticed they do need a coat of red paint also."

"They take stain," I corrected once again, making sure they were aware of the distinction.

"There is a store room under the chapel where you'll find everything you need. Anne will show you where it is."

"I'll be glad to," I said, as pictures of dried and matted paint brushes stuck to various kinds of old cans of oil and acrylic paint, stain and sealer in the work room came to mind. If the summers' heat hadn't taken its toll, then disuse had

"There's one other thing," June spoke up. "Walter and I like to say the Office a couple of times a day and were wondering if it will be all right if we used the chapel."

"Certainly," Hyacinth answered, "as long as you schedule your times around retreatants, there shouldn't be any problem. Fr. Lighterman says Mass every morning at 8:00, and Srs. Edith, Evangelista, Godwina and myself, plus Anne, usually try to meet and recite it together, but it doesn't always work out that way. You're welcome to join us if you want."

Fr. Lighterman, sitting with a contented look on his face having finished a piece of Sr. Evangelista's famous blueberry pie for dessert, asked Deacon Walter if he would care to give thanks for the delicious dinner as his first act as deacon.

Walter stood and we all bowed our heads while he gave a heartfelt thank you for the food we had received, for our community that so graciously welcomed them, and asked for help during the coming months; officially kicking off the beginning their work stint, and one of the most bizarre summers I, and the retreat, ever had.

The next morning in the early light of the bright New Mexico sun, the sounds of someone rummaging around in the work room could be heard coming from underneath the chapel. The deacon and his wife were scrubbing paint pans, washing brushes, flattening out bristles, and checking paint rollers to see if they still rolled.

They then went to work on the hogans in earnest, scraping and sanding the logs preparing them for the new sealer. Franklin and I watched them lug ladders and tools from hogan to hogan getting the stacked logs ready to receive coats of golden, almost clear, sealer.

At noon everyone would stop what we were doing to break for lunch prepared by one of the novices. Walter and June would fill up on water, we could tell was being recycled as sweat on their brows, and then go back to work in the hot sun dragging cans, brushes and scrappers along with them. As it turned out, the deacon and his wife were very good workers!

A work routine emerged; hogan work in the mornings, lunch in the small retreat dining room at noon and then back to work again coating the timbers with golden tone sealer. By 4:00, they would shuffle off to their room to clean up and rest before we would all meet in the chapel to say the Office. Some days the Bishop would drop by unexpectedly and take husband and wife team on short outings into town, to see how they were doing and if there was anything they needed and I assume, to find out if Sr. Hyacinth was running the place to his satisfaction.

If I could, I liked to be in the chapel early to settle my mind and relax before the actual Office began. It was easy to do because there were no telephones ringing, no sirens whizzing by, and thank God it was before the advent of car alarms; all was peace over the hilly landscape all the way down to Main Street in Gallup. So quiet in fact, there should have tonsured monks meditating in the back row. These serene times were about to take on an odd if not laughable, quality.

Sitting quietly on a pew, imperceptibly the sound of muffled talking would begin to creep into my awareness. I couldn't place exactly where the drone was coming from at first but within minutes the monotony of verbiage grew in volume and intensity until I realized it was coming from Walter and June's room. It didn't sound like arguing, more like a loud discussion. Even though the chapel walls had been built with silence in mind, they weren't the thickest. Walter and June's room was next to the chapel making it impossible to ignore their robust conversation. I couldn't make out the words if I wanted to, but I could tell Walter's points were definitely louder and longer than June's and it was a sure bet he was finishing his own sentences. At some point, a hush would fall over their room as they noticed the late time, followed by a moment to gather themselves in a final effort of straightening clothes and mussed hair making each other look presentable. The hallway door would open a crack and slowly and the deacon and his wife would wander out like nothing out of the ordinary happened, ready to recite the hallowed ecclesiastic ceremony known as the Office.

The door in front would open a crack, a head would take a peek in, and I would have to duck out of the way as they made their way unsteadily to the pew closest to their room. I didn't allow myself to make eye contact with either of them and hid the fact their muffled conversation was somewhat audible in the chapel. They were personal friends of the Bishop and that made them untouchable, they could never do anything improper. I felt even *suspecting* them of wrongdoing would be overstepping my place at the center.

Deacon Walter had taken it upon himself to lead us in the recitation of the Office and rosary, which was fine by the rest of us. He was an articulate speaker, usually, as he led us in prayer pronouncing his words in eloquent fashion. By midsummer, I noticed the speech coming from the obviously more relaxed deacon, had gone into decline. He wasn't as careful with his enunciations and at times he skidded over articulations, stumbling over words like he had an extra thick tongue. Undaunted, he would stop and take great pains to rectify the slurs in his sentences, repeating the words until they met with his satisfaction. He didn't give the appearance of being tipsy because he was cognizant of his own mistakes; if you didn't think he *may* have been throwing back a few before prayer time, it would have been hard to tell. Except once when he noticed the vigil light had gone out in trying to bring it to my attention he the had trouble getting out the word *extinguished* and ended up pointing to the dark candle holder instead.

Over the next few days which developed into weeks, this loud talking was accompanied by a gradual slow melt down of the recitation of the Office and upcoming rosary; slow, slower, almost to the point of stopping. If Walter announced: *"The Third Glorious Mystery; Descent of the Holy Spirit"* to start the rosary, I would sigh and get ready for another long session. Generally the rosary takes a long time anyway, but it had become became a physical and mental strain of drawn out proportions because each decade was accompanied, at his discretion, by a longer and longer meditation on one of the fifteen mysteries. I usually left by about the second decade, and Sr. Hyacinth had long since gone; both of us preferring to finish at our own pace, before dinner.

June seemed to mellow out too. Her tippled state came with an air of patience and an unrivaled resignation which allowed her to put up with the longest pauses and division breaks without becoming impatient. She acted pink with politeness but not flushed red with fire water. One would never think she was intoxicated, dazed maybe, as if she had awakened from a long nap, but aware enough to swat off insects that had a fondness for her short-sleeved bloused arms. It was easy to picture her sipping sweet liqueur like a southern belle to counter the smell of turpentine in the privacy of their orange curtained boudoir as she lounged on the duvet. Now sitting peacefully next to her husband, she couldn't have looked more content, and was cultured enough to know there was no talking in church, for there and there alone, she quieted her jabbering, a fact which did not go unnoticed by the rest of us.

Summer played out this way, nursing hangovers or not, Walter and June continued would work during the week after the weekend retreat groups had vacated, and one by one the hogans were, scraped, patched, sanded and painted, I mean sealed. With the new statue of

Jesus, the new rock paths, the new finishes on the hogans, and a new staff to boot, St. Francis Retreat really looking spiffy!

As for their tippling, because we weren't *really* sure, no one said anything. Even if we noticed Walter slurring his words, no one, not Sr. Evangelista, Godwina, Edith or Fr. Lighterman or me said anything to them. Not even Sr. Hyacinth. I guess as long as they were sober enough to keep staining the hogans and not each other, it was a small price to pay so we didn't say anything. Without conferring, we were of one accord; all summer long, it was our little secret.

It was a day late in summer when the encroaching shadows were making their presence known the long way across the yard when Franklin noticed a soft whistling sound on the breeze. I stopped to listen and there it was, a low moan moving through the top of the pine trees on the back part of the yard.

I looked at the sky. "Sounds like any other wind to me," dismissing his comment. Franklin was a hard person to figure out, if the breeze was saying something to him, he wasn't telling me and I couldn't tell anything from his expression. "Let me know if it tells you anything interesting," I said, teasing him and put it from my mind as I went to lock up the hogans.

It always gave me an eerie feeling going through empty hogans after the retreatants left because I was never quite sure everyone was actually gone. I made it a practice to through each hogan shouting hello to alert anybody still inside; you only have to walk in on someone taking a nap one time and from then on, you enter buildings slamming doors and banging windows closed to make sure anybody inside knows I was coming through.

I went from hogan to hogan checking making sure all the quarters were secure, something we did after each group to make sure water wasn't running anywhere, windows were closed and all the doors locked. Still, the wind closing a closet door in another room was enough to make me jump. It was the contrast between having a large number of people in the vicinity to absolutely seeing *no* people around, that left me with an empty, lonely feeling. I think this is what Franklin was feeling too, only he felt it on the breeze.

By the time I had was finished taking stock of the hogans and stepped outside, the sunlight was having a hard time filtering through the shallow covering of clouds overhead. Franklin was still at it, raking back rocks on the paths kicked off by retreatants. "Shouldn't you call it a day?" I called to him as I made my way to him across the yard.

"Yes, the sun is no longer shining high in sky. I…"

We were interrupted by the sound of a woman's whiney voice.

"Yoo hoo! Yoo hoo! We heard from across the yard. We looked up and there was June barreling toward us. She had always been overly cordial to Franklin because he was a Navajo, intrigued as she was by his Indian past and parlance. Under direction of her husband not to do anything the Bishop might disprove of, she had restrained herself up until now not to interfere and or bother Franklin but with her vacation running out, it was now or never to find out Indian secrets. But instead of coming to the point, she began by making light conversation, telling him what a good job he was doing while she radiated approval, asking about his childhood and what it was like to grow up in a hogan, exhibiting a comradeship beyond their brief friendship. She asked about Sun Gods, Indian legends, medicine men, peace pipes and pottery, enjoying his answers in the unique idioms of his culture.

Visiting a reservation we discovered wasn't uppermost in June's mind; meeting an Indian was. All the questioning was leading up to something, something so important to her it couldn't be broached without all the preceding small talk in an effort to find out his opinions and what he might think of her idea.

Searching Franklin's face, after a time she felt it was safe enough to reveal her pressing plan. With her eyes wide with expectation, we found out what was really on her mind; she wanted to hold a Pow-Wow. She saw them as mysterious trance-like get-togethers where spirits appeared laughing and dancing. I told her not to expect anything like to happen certainly not at a Catholic retreat center, but I was convinced however, she was hoping to see a vision anyway.

I remembered Sr. Evangelista's experiences with a Pow-Wow, first and foremost was the drumming, all day; drums, drums, drums. "I don't think pounding on drums in the middle of the night will go over well with Sr. Hyacinth but if we held a quiet get-together without any drums, she might let us do it."

"Why don't we do it tonight?" June asked, her eyes widening with excitement. "We can build a camp fire and Franklin can tell us about the ways of the Navajo. What do you say? I'm sure Walter will want to come. It will be good for him to break out of our routine for a change."

I hoped the whole idea wasn't insulting to him so I asked, "What do you think of holding our own pow-pow, Franklin? Do you think we'll make contact with the spirit world" I was half kidding but there was a certain amount of seriousness in the question.

When he nodded yes, I told them before we went any further, I should clear anything we are do on retreat property with Hyacinth first and made my way to the retreat office.

"Ask the Sisters if they want to come," I heard June yell after me as I walked away.

"Good idea," I yelled back.

Always one for a good time, Hyacinth thought it sounded like fun as long as we didn't get out of hand but declined my invitation to join us, sitting in the dirt in her habit after dark didn't appeal to her. I asked her, "Other than sounding like a bad joke, how much trouble could two nuns, friends of a Bishop, an Indian and a volunteer make giving a Pow-Wow"? She saw my point.

Sr. Edith passed on the occasion too, but Srs. Evangelista and Godwina jumped at the chance.

"I'll bring some fry bread!" Evangelista volunteered. "It grows on you!

When it was dark, in the lowering light of a full moon behind the retreat house, without drums or dancing, we met on the west side of the hill. Walter and June, Srs. Evangelista with Godwina in their habits, joined Franklin and myself. When we thought the time was right, our shadowy figures could be seen slinking silently across the weeded hillside. There were no retreatants occupying the large meeting room and it was completely dark. We stopped to look at the moon reflecting in the separated panels of glass on the conference hall, and watched as a few gray clouds passed from one side of windows over the abrupt interruption of the brick chimney, to connect again in the windows on the other side. The night was cooling off, there was hardly a breeze in the air but still the sweet scent of wood smoke managed to float effortlessly around us. It was a good night for a campfire.

June and I traipsed around in the dark looking for dry twigs and anything that would burn. Franklin hunted for rocks and put together a circle around our pile of sticks. Evangelista crumpled an old piece of newspaper and stuck it deep in the pile. Lighting the paper with his lighter, it didn't take Walter any time at all to ignite the entire pile and the six of us sat on the ground watching it burn, each of us commenting on how much fun it was to camp, even if it is in our own back yard.

June asked everybody if we minded if she taped our makeshift pow-pow so she could keep it as a remembrance.

"It's fine with me," I said, and looked at the others who were shrugging their shoulders with indifference, even Franklin, so June placed her recorder to the side of the circle.

No one said anything at first. We just sat looking at the kindling dwindle in the small flame and watched as Walter reached over and dropped a larger stick on to keep it going. It was nice to relax and just look at the hot point deep in the flame. The effect was hypnotic and lulled as into a dream-like state, our pale shadows dancing in the light around us.

Walter, speaking for his wife too, told us how grateful they were to be taken in like they were members of the community during his training on his way to become a full-fledged deacon. "We couldn't have asked for a more perfect place, quiet and out of the way."

The two Sisters sitting on a blanket Evangelista spread out for them, told us they came from a retreat house in Oregon. "We went from rainy weather to this dry heat. We're here to see what it's like to be stationed on a mission," Evangelista said.

And Godwina explained, "Actually, the first Christian missionaries were the 12 Apostles. As the Church grew, its missionary work became systemized so that in medieval times it was in the hands of Dominican and Franciscan monks." Looking at Franklin, she added, smiling, "Among missionaries in America, *John Eliot* was known as the Apostle to Indians…"

As a volunteer I explained, like Walter, I was grateful to be taken in by the Franciscan community but didn't say a word about the fact I was basically here recuperating from an episode of M.S. At that moment I was just like everyone else, one of six shadowy figures huddled together sitting motionless under a galaxy of gleaming stars.

Franklin spoke up too, telling us he was happy he decided to turn up our road weeks ago. He told us the purpose of Navajo life is to maintain balance between the individual and nature and live in harmony with the Creator; he wouldn't have stayed if he didn't feel he wasn't walking in beauty, in harmony, and told us how his world was filled with thanks.

It was at this point, Franklin's personal comment was too much for the deacon. Walter pulled out a large, leather bound flask from his outer pocket and offered us all a swig and I knew the mysteries of the ever expanding universe were about to take on a new dimension.

Franklin was the only smart one in the group, bypassing the flask handing it to the next person, foregoing a taste.

Social peer pressure almost demanded I shouldn't refuse, so I didn't. I screwed off the top, took a swig, and let the unknown liquid slide down my throat. "Good Lord, what *was* that?" I squeaked, as the powerful liquid felt like it took the top layer of skin off my larynx.

"It's not your grandmother's mulberry squeezings, I assure you! *Tumbleweed Whiskey*, the best there is!" the deacon shot back with gusto. And with deep appreciation, he held the bottle up in front of him so he could eye the brown liquor more clearly in the light of the fire. "If anything will make you see visions, this will!"

In no time we were feeling pretty happy as the authentic rot gut hit our own insides with all the force of a tomahawk smashing our inhibitions to smithereens. Once our inner monitors had been loosened, stories flowed from us in record time. There never was a lull in the conversation; one of us was always ready with another one.

Sr. Evangelista was the only one who prepared handing us each a patty of frybread telling us it was served at Pow-Wows so if we wanted this to be more like a real Pow-Wow, we should each take one.

Holding up his disk of fry bread, Walter looked at it in the moonlight and tried to say "On this auspicious occasion…" but didn't quite get it out but that was all right, we knew what he meant.

I held mine up too, "You know, fry bread *does* taste better soaked in mulberries" and everyone agreed.

With the fire warm and relaxing, it was easy to reflect on my time as a volunteer here in the Southwest. Meeting Indians, finding straw effigies, and now sitting in the countryside in a mysterious Pow-Wow under a full moon. I felt lucky to be here and that my time at the retreat couldn't have been better and looking at the sky, I thanked my lucky stars. But my marveling couldn't compare with what was about to happen. Something that was so strange and inexplicable, to this day, I can't explain it, but I had never had Tumble Whiskey before.

With the flask almost empty, and her time at the retreat was nearly over, June found enough nerve to ask Franklin if Navajos still held rain dances.

Franklin, without giving her a wordy explanation, chose to sing in his own language sounding like *"heya, hoa, heya hoa,"* a rain song.

I sat in disbelief, not only because I was sitting beside a Navajo on a mountain who had started to entreat the rain gods, but because on this seemingly clear night the most improbable thing happened: it started to rain!

I don't know anything about meteorology. I can't predict precipitation by the swelling in my joints or tell by the red color of the sky if a delightful day is coming. I can't even forecast a front about to move in by the altitude of swallows (swallows fly low, rain we shall know). All I know is that while I was sitting in dirt on a side of a hill in the dark surrounded by New Mexico's wild country beside a Navajo Indian, it started to rain!!

Needless to say, we all went wild, congratulating Franklin, slapping him on the back and shouting our surprise. Words can't express how dumbfounded we were, each of us excitedly reliving the moment when we felt the first drops, going over the instant our eyes moved to the fire hearing the first hissings, knowing the surreal moment was one we would never forget.

The next day, thinking back on our Pow-Wow, I realized what a smart move it was for June to bring her tape recorder, because except for the phenomena of the rain, I had a hard time remembering *one single story* I'd heard. Coming prepared like she did, it made me wonder if this temporary loss of memory that in some circles would otherwise be known as a blackout, might have been a regular occurrence for her. So it was a good thing indeed she taped our Pow-Wow. The trouble was we were all too embarrassed to listen to it, even June. But what better way to cap off their volunteer months?

Walking through damp weeds to the location of our campfire, there was little evidence to jolt my memory either; the circle of rocks, little pieces of dried frybread, the charred remains of our burned out campfire, the lingering smell of smoke in my hair, and… one monstrous headache.

CHAPTER 15

It wasn't a subject I felt comfortable bringing up so I kept it to myself during our Pow-Wow; UFO's. Having been in New Mexico for nearly a year now, I can honestly say I never once saw anything strange zooming across the sky, but I wasn't looking for any either. I'd heard the rumors about Roswell and how it was supposed to be a crash site of a flying saucer and that was more than enough space adventure for me; I didn't want to search the heavens for anything more, not if I wanted to continue living in the hogan alone without being too unnerved thinking every noise could be a space creature.

I was sure the subject was on everyone's mind though. When you make yourself vulnerable by sitting out in the open like we were under galaxies of heavenly bodies, we were not only opening the door for extraterrestrial traffic, we were we were drawing them to us! I had enough trouble dealing with earthlings.

The retreat staff was allotted an unusual amount of time for star-gazing too. It was impossible not to notice the trillions of stars that had been tossed in the air like celestial confetti nor was it possible not to stand in awe of the galaxies hanging by magic in the sky like garlands as we walked, flashlight in hand, to the hogans escorting quests to their rooms or delivering messages; there was always time for a glance up to appreciate the heavenly bodies of our galaxy. At 7,500 feet, the retreat center didn't have to compete with the lights from a nearby city so when it got dark, it was *really* dark.

As a human speck under all this heavenly grandstanding the sheer disproportion made me think it was presumptuous to assume all the stars, moons, galaxies, planets, comets, constellations, meteors, the entire cosmos, had been created for one species, mine. Even so, the only way *I* wanted to make contact with anything flying overhead, was if it was like the time I was walking home from school, and an out-of-formation, low-flying goose turned its head to me and let out a surprisingly loud honk. I jumped at our chance encounter but it continued on unimpressed, flying off on the stream of its own consciousness.

Since the retreat center was out of the city away from familiar trappings of civilization, I didn't dare let myself think about beings from other worlds visiting us. I never let words enter my mind such as extraterrestrials, sightings, and I positively ixnayed the aductionbay word completely from my mind. But keeping it out of my consciousness wasn't easy having read Whitley Strieber's, *Communion: A True Story*. I still remember the first line "My wife and I own a log cabin in a secluded corner of upstate New York." *I* was staying in a log cabin at the moment too, which didn't make me feel any better. I kept telling myself New York was clear across the country, far removed from New Mexico. But considering how high we were and so vulnerable in it felt like we were almost goading them to approach us, offering ourselves as living, breathing specimens; theirs to do with as they wanted. There *was* security in knowing that here at the retreat center, saints and angels were protecting us; it was something anyway.

And because the retreat was at a high altitude, I was reminded of Merton perched in his lookout tower on fire watch deep in the forests of Kentucky, alone, scanning the night for lightning strikes and potential fires around his monastery, Gethsemani Abbey. This took courage but it also took a love of solitude. Not many people would welcome an opportunity to sit absolutely alone, hour after hour watching and waiting through the night. I wondered if Merton asked questions like *are we alone* or did he, like me, avoid asking leading questions like these, especially staying in a hermitage by himself. As a student of human behavior and spiritual psychology, transforming experiences for him were sure to be centered on God and not flying disks.

I suppose Merton, being a highly educated man, wouldn't have had time for such outlandish ideas like this. I on the other hand, had the time but chose to ignore controversial questions like these. As a relative newcomer to the Southwest, I had different priorities, I was sure the Navajo Nation had been rubbing off on my intuition the moment I stepped off the train using its natural beauty to continually assail me with its strength and beauty in the mountains surrounding me, in the rock formations and in the beauty of the deserts.

Elements trying to transform me were occurring all around me: gorges heavy with the scents of desert flowers worked to quiet my thoughts more effectively than soothing balms; shifting wind turned clumps of dirt into red plains evened my temperament as well; clouds chasing patches of light across the sky were replaced with beams of light helped to clarify my thoughts too. The very endurance of this multicolored land, eons old, filled me with peace, calmness and patience so it was logical to think all along, my consciousness was being transformed too.

I recognized other similarities too. Each time I saw a thick-limbed cactus on a bluff growing out of a group of boulders unaware of its precarious position it reminded me of the precarious predicament I was in on earth. How even though earth was moving through space at a rate of 45,000 miles per hour or 12½ miles per second, I was like the cactus growing on the steep bank paying no attention to its absurd predicament either. Just as it thrusts its limbs ever skyward developing into a large thriving cactus, I too keep living disregarding the fact I was hurtling through space at any given moment.

Looking thoughtfully at the sky, I regretted not bringing a pair of binoculars or better yet, a telescope with me to New Mexico so I could look at the planets from this high perspective. And if I happened to see an unidentifiable flying object, I would acknowledge our chance encounter, like the goose giving me a loud call of surprise, I would give a yell as a commentary on the wondrous absurdity of the others' existence.

CHAPTER
16

It was easy for me to imagine Gallup's persona standing on the side of the road as a rancher in dirty overalls chewing on a piece of straw waving to drivers as they sped by in their cars. People usually pass through Gallup on the way to somewhere else which is a shame because the town has a life and a charm all its own that, like the roads, is good and bad. The old buildings and worn façade show a time gone by that visitors *expect* to see in a frontier town, silver dollars, women riding sidesaddle and button down collars on men but the most appealing aspect of the town is lost in their acceleration; the slower pace.

The lazy pace had the power to transform me with every kind of challenging situation. My walking and balance had grown stronger over the months but it wasn't difficult to recall a time when I had trouble putting one foot in front of the other and why I am so taken with being handed a loaf of bread through a drive-through window without having to park my car and walk in, search up and down aisles for the item, stand in a long line and walk out; in Gallup I had found a true convenience store.

Gallup keeps up with the times but it does so at its own pace. Good and bad, the experiences I had here were very different from any in my past, from the BIA (Bureau of Indian Affairs) serving many different groups exerting its influence among the diversity of people, to the opportunity of seeing time-wizened faces and distinctive dress of the Native Americans coming in off reservations for supplies. By this time I was used to seeing entire families making the monthly trek into town together for supplies.

From Native American arts to exquisitely worked silver and turquoise, Gallup never ceased to surprise me. I recalled the warm summer night I accompanied Sr. Hyacinth on a routine errand, collecting one of the wards of the Group home. The unending taxiing involved in being a parental figure, brought home the fact you can't be two places at once and Hyacinth oftentimes was needed to collect one of the girls. Going anywhere with Sr. Hyacinth usually turned into an adventure and this time was no exception. The sense of the commonplace left about the time a wave of sickly scent rushed over me.

It was the end of summer and a number of girls from all over had been dropped off at this state-run institution which consisted of a large complex of buildings, where they waited until the responsible party came for them. Stopping at the city's health center is an important stop for those who had spent time on the reservation; chemical treatments, enzyme-based products, and silicon—based lotions hung heavy in the air. I remember the yellow bulbs in the windows of the buildings giving off eerie glows as I imagined the combing, shaving and washing employed behind the glass. Hyacinth and I had arrived after a session of delousing of those who had spent their vacation time on the reservation and the odor of the insecticide permeated the area. One person was bad enough, but multiplied by many individuals being treated, the full scope of the situation can be appreciated; I thought I would gag.

Because Hyacinth and I were carrying out this undertaking uncharacteristically at night, the peculiar scent coupled with the darkness made a deep impression on me. The yellow lights in the doorways, upstairs and down, made an indelible impression on me. From then on whenever I even saw the complex from the road, the medicinal smell of that night came back to me, swiftly filling my nose, memory and mind with the smell of shampoos and washes.

Gallup plays on other emotions as well. It was a helpless feeling knowing some families are unable to afford $350 for a wood stove in their hogans, a fact I thought of whenever I stood in the dining room looking down on the snow covering the whole reservation like layers of soft cotton. I still feel sadness when I imagine elderly occupants having to stoke a wood stove with paper, twigs, and pieces of wood they chopped up themselves. Those were the lucky ones, they *had* stoves. Or, reading a headline, "Elderly Indians Found Dead from Exposure" sleeping in their own homes. My thoughts turned to Leonard and his removable door.

One of the most entertaining afternoons I spent in Gallup was rummaging through items in a pawn shop. This wasn't a common occurrence; in fact, it was the only time I had enough courage to actually walk into a pawnbroker's shop. It started when Sr. Celeste mentioned that Sr. Hyacinth was going have a birthday soon and I set about finding a gift that would be more than just a birthday present, I wanted to show how grateful I was for taking me on as a volunteer, risking my health would hold up and I would continue to be an asset to the retreat. The idea developed out of need, and desperate times called for desperate measures; the scavenger hunt was on.

This brought up a problem. What do you give a nun? Clothes? Nuns wear the same thing everyday; habits. A fancy box of assorted chocolates? This was a gift that would keep on giving in the form of multiplying calories and that wasn't good for anyone, if Hyacinth kept it for herself and didn't let the girls pounce on it. Perfume? No, they usually smell of soap. I walked around for days thinking, but nothing was coming to me.

There was another problem. As a volunteer I wasn't receiving a paycheck and this was a problem. That's when the heading of an article jumped out at me while flipping through Gallup's *Visitor's Directory* in the television room: "LAY ASIDE YOUR MISGIVINGS ABOUT THE WORD PAWN."

I continued reading the directory *how the trading post that deals in pawn is really a unique forms of bank and art gallery rolled into one and how in American Indian culture, pawn means more than borrowing against valuable goods. You will commonly see signs advertising "cash pawn" which refers to the practice of converting artwork or possessions into income for daily necessities such as groceries, bills, mortgages and car payments. Pawns can also be items from antiquity, heirloom pieces of handmade jewelry or craft, passed from a family into the public marketplace. Because much pawned merchandise is of real day-to-day value in the seller's life (guns, saddles, buckskins, etc.), the percentage of pawn that goes unredeemed is very small, about five percent. Merchandise that remains for sale after expiration is referred to as "dead pawn" and items of dead pawn are among the most highly valued American Indian artifacts to be found on the open market."*

This is what gave me the idea I could pick something up out of the dead pawn pile; I wouldn't have to tell her I bought it a pawn shop. I didn't have much cash, but if I could find a cross on a silver chain or a hand painted icon, something worthy enough to give to a nun maybe the proprietor would dicker with me. I felt this was the answer to my money troubles, and how I came to be going through shelves of a pawn shop in downtown Gallup.

Choosing a parking space along the street was easy, I guess not many people were pawn shopping during the middle of the week in the middle of the afternoon. I looked up and down the street at the orange colored buildings with a number of pawn shops, most with security bars on the windows, and went into a shop with the sign reading Indian Rugs, Jewelry and Collectibles that didn't look too seedy. In smaller lettering, painted under it was, Pawn Loans Here so I chose this shop thinking the proprietor might be willing to help an out-of-towner needing some fast cash.

Opening the door sounded a tinkle of a bell and I watched closely as a shaggy dog lifted his head off his paw but seeing his only interest was in looking at who had disturbed him from his nap, he went back to sleep.

The room was jammed with useful paraphernalia. On the walls hung coats and skins, and furry coats that were made out of skins. I saw Indian blankets spread out to display their unique designs and plain army types folded and placed in a stack. There were kerosene lamps hanging from metal rings as I perused the crowded aisles working my way to the front of the store where I stood before a glass counter looking over the myriad of items laid out in an orderly manner. As soon as I realized the progression went from most expensive to the inexpensive, I felt myself leaning to the right as I looked over watches, key rings, and dozens of knives. There wasn't one teak wood rosary in the lot.

Seeing an artificial potted plant in the corner led me to yet another idea, one that would reflect where I came from. Yes, my mind was made up; I would give Hyacinth an orange tree! It would be a small plant at first and would take years before it produced its first orange filled with a pulpy interior and sweet juice, but at least this was one gift she'd have long after I was gone.

When the owner, who looked like he could have moonlighted as a bouncer for a dive somewhere, finally appeared through a curtain of sheets from the back, I was happy I wouldn't have to haggle over a price with the likes of him. Instead, I asked if he knew where they sold fruit trees in the area or where a local nursery was.

I think, like his dog, I may have awakened him from a nap too; he didn't look very pleased. He grumbled a few directions, took a peak out the window at my car and shaking his head walked back through the curtains, muttering what I thought was, *"Dang tourists…"*

I paid him no mind; I got what I wanted.

Following his directions, I was pleased with myself for having come up with the idea, and in the nick of time, too. I felt a gift to Hyacinth should reflect the special nature of my state and be a remembrance of me. The nursery was out of stock for my first choice but it didn't take me long to pick out a second variety.

I carried the five gallon plastic container holding the young fruit-tree to my car and hoped the ride up our bumpy driveway wouldn't shake off the few leaves from its scrawny limbs and throw it into shock.

That had been the easy part, sneaking it in the television room was harder. I fashioned a gold ribbon into a bow and carefully tied it to one of its tender young branches before Sr. Celeste arrived with the girls and the cake. It was hard keeping a straight face when I asked Hyacinth to meet me in the TV room where she stood with a puzzled look on her face, looking not on a sweet variety of a California seedless orange tree, but on another California import, a lemon tree and hoped she didn't think it was a critique of her managerial skills.

CHAPTER 17

I don't think putting on the dog was quite what we did when we heard Sr. Godwina's relatives were coming to visit, but we did make it a point to use the unstained tablecloth in the small dining room off the kitchen.

It was Thursday at 3:00 in the afternoon when Stan and Josephine drove in the retreat grounds in a long travel trailer pulling a small silver camper. I expected to see two giants step out outdoing their daughter's height, but the difference was negligible; they were all equally tall and thin. Godwina's parents were in their fifties and very fit. In fact, I was told 20 years ago her father put down his cigarette and never had another one since, quitting cold-turkey, exhibiting the kind of will-power, determination and personal resolve against addiction I could admire and liked him immediately.

As it turned out, the retreat staff didn't need to have a room ready or fuss with meal preparation because staying in the larger trailer, they were self contained, fully equipped and supplied with food. And like most visitors who come to Gallup, they too, were on the way to somewhere else. They were going to a hot-air balloon show, stopping long enough at the retreat to pick up their daughter, Sr. Godwina, because they weren't going to just any ballooning event, they were going to the biggest hot-air balloon demonstration in the world, the granddaddy of all balloon festivals, the Albuquerque International Balloon Festival.

It surprised me learning nuns in active Orders are allowed to go on regular family outings at times… with the superior's permission. However, my experience in the matter was limited to rules pertaining to Cistercians where everything is much stricter and visits have to be approved months in advance; obtaining official consent from the Holy See wouldn't surprise me. I never expected Godwina would be permitted to go and more surprised when I was invited to share in their adventurous vacation too.

Sr. Hyacinth gave her okay and good wishes to me to have a good time and I packed my backpack lightly for the overnight stay but it wasn't until I loaded my camera case full of film that I was ready.

It was autumn and the weather had already blasted the surrounding mountains around Gallup with snow that made mornings chilly but the roads were still without snow and the afternoons sunny, warm and dry.

Stan climbed into the driver's seat with Josephine in the passenger side, Godwina climbed in next and because I was craving the sun after the chilly morning, I took a seat on the right near a window to get the full brunt of the sun and have a clear view of the desert. From the back I looked over the interior and saw a bedroom with a tiny bath, a booth dinette with compartments over the doors and windows, a small kitchenette that had wood cabinets and a breakfast nook with two barstools. I noticed the trailer had electric tank warmers; everything you needed to make a vacation feel like you never left home.

It felt good to be able to go on a holiday and thanked Sr. Godwina again sitting across from me in the shady side facing north, for inviting me. She acknowledged me by informing us, "Hot air balloons are the oldest successful human-carrying tools in a class of their own known as balloon aircraft…" As she was talking, I inconspicuously cracked a motion sickness pill in half to guard against car sickness (something I would have done even before I had M.S.) and put one piece in my mouth and stuffed the one other in a pocket in my jeans. After making sure my sunglasses were in a pouch of my camera case,

I was ready and settled back to enjoy a relaxing ride as a passenger and felt the usual sense of beauty passing many species of cactus that were thriving, weeds that were withered and dry growth making up the prickly carpet of the desert.

We were about an hour into the journey before I remembered because of my illness I need to be cautious, especially in regards to heat. I wondered how this very important fact could slip my mind, but it did. Because I was healthy the first 20 years of life and then had a major health problem, I naturally remember how my body acted during the healthy good years. This is what having the relapsing-remitting form (the most common type of M.S.) does, it lulls you into a false sense of security; because you look and feel healthy for months and years sometimes after an episode, you think you are and cram in as much as possible before the next wave of symptoms hit. The phrase, burning daylight, has a very different meaning for me than a just clock tolling a later hour and is the very reason I accepted this volunteer position in New Mexico as soon as I was back on my feet, literally.

And why in my excitement about the festival, I completely forgot to consider things like vertigo, sensitivity to light, nausea or dizziness; the words 'heat intolerance' never entered my mind. I even overlooked the reason I had to give up my vocation in Arizona in the first place: heat. And why after I left, but still undiagnosed, I moved to a climate in California that turned out to be even hotter than Arizona. With my track record, one would think the subject of heat would be ever most in my mind.

The trip to Albuquerque is long made even longer by how slowly we had to drive towing the little camper. About the only diversion was seeing distorted pools of water always on the road just up ahead and being disappointed driving through the illusions of cool water with nary a splash. So I was glad when Josephine began bringing up interesting facts about hot-air balloons along the way to break up the drive.

"About 700 balloons will go up," she explained, and told us what started in the parking lot of a shopping center has turned into one of the most photographed activities in the world. "But back in 1972, the festival was about finding out who was the most skillful pilot and continues to this day evolving into special events of piloting and speed competitions. And of course, there is pride for balloon owners having unique shapes to delight spectators."

It was hard concentrating on Josephine's fun ballooning facts about special events and piloting skills now that the unsettling memory of my illness and hospital stay just a few short months before were back. The memory was too vivid to repress any longer and once the floodgates were opened they came back with a vengeance. These were the facts invading my mind and why, as I sat full in the sun, the word rosacea, a chronic skin condition characterized by a red discoloration on cheeks, nose and chin, came to mind. So even though I enjoyed having the sun beat down on me giving me chills, it dawned on me being in direct sunlight the entire trip probably wasn't the best thing for my health and scooched away from the window. "Rosacea? This is just great," picturing my face with a year-round rosy glow. Actually, looking like I just stepped off a beach somewhere wouldn't be the worst thing in the world, however it forced me once again to face an incontrovertible truth: I was no longer healthy.

A bead of perspiration trickled down the right side of my face to my lap.

Josephine, brimming with ballooning facts, told us earnestly, "We might even get to see races involving piloting, speed competitions or races testing landing accuracy."

I looked at the heat-soaked limbs on the cactus making them droop and my heart sank. What was the heat doing to me? Would my already my thinned myelin due to M.S. (material needed to conduct nerve impulses) make symptoms flair up and come out in squirrel health problems. Disheartened, I thought again, "Great, I need to stay out of the sun the rest of my life is just great," looking dubiously at the blistering pavement on the highway.

Only the most courageous creatures crawl from under stones to eat the moisture in plants in oppressive heat.

Stan was concentrating on driving the trailer dragging the smaller silver one with Josephine sitting next to him holding a large map across her lap navigating. Godwina and I were seated in back looking out our respective windows when I realized I had been sitting in the same position for a couple of hours without moving, confined to a restricted space, unable to walk around. What was this doing to my spasticity, specifically in my legs? More to the point, when Stan parks the trailer, will I be able to get out? "Great, one more thing to worry about."

The later hour caused the temperature to rise searing everything under it with heat like an outbreak of sustained violence.

Josephine's eager voice piped up one more, "There's a race to see which balloon travels the farthest too. Some balloons have even gone as far as Canada. And on some nights, large numbers of illuminated balloons go up," but her enthusiasm waned as she realized we were only staying only night out of nine of the scheduled event and would miss it.

Nine days? I gasped. It's a good thing we weren't staying for nine days; I had been warned while using the steroid prednisone to stay out of the sun, ultraviolet light could trigger a reaction that causes redness like with the disease lupus where a distinctive "butterfly rash" extends across the cheeks and bridge of the nose that may be flat or raised, or red to a mild blushing of pink on the skin that looks like a butterfly. "Oh great, if my unsteady walking didn't make people stare, a rash that looks like a butterfly on my face will." I put my hand on my face feeling around seeing if I could tell a difference in temperatures.

I glanced out the window at the bright sunlight keeping pace with our car as we rolled unswervingly on the straight length of highway and thought; medication has to run its course too. Not knowing how long drugs stay in a body, there was a good chance some of the steroid was still in my system, and imagining the worst, I sat in the back picturing my face with a scarlet butterfly adhered to it wishing fervently we were already at the festival so I could stop worrying about the sun reflecting off the hot sand of the desert.

By the time we finally reached our destination, it was dark. Stan turned off the highway and pulled our short convoy into Cutter's

Field, named after the first person to own a hot air balloon in New Mexico, another one of Josephine's fun facts. With D-day almost upon us and time running out, unable to contain herself, Josephine excitedly barraged us with the more facts. "And there are special events and competitions where the winner of the race... Then there's an aerial game where balloonists drop a marker to see who is closest to a target..."

Having listened to Josephine's rundown of activities the duration of the ride, barring my own uneasiness about what may or may not happen to my body, by then I was enthusiastically looking forward to seeing an orderly, systematic and methodic liftoff of hundreds of hot-air balloons in the air and thought, sincerely, "This *is* going to be great, just great!"

With Stan maneuvering the vehicles carefully around figures huddled near numerous open campfires and darkened tents, we passed dim lights identifying human lairs as he searched for a space long enough to park the vehicles. Our headlights bounced off one encampment to another lighting the way for the few pedestrians courageous enough to walk in the darkness and hearty souls bundled in sleeping bags willing to sleep outside.

He found a space long enough to fit the two vehicles and parked on the dirt among other trailers. The campers had already claimed their spots making us feel conspicuously like we were late arrivals in a theater but I was still looking forward to stepping outside the confines of the trailer away from each others' body heat and into fresh air.

I stood slowly, stretching and extending arms and legs, making sure the others got out before me, stalling as long as possible, hoping the others would be looking at the surroundings and not at me if I tumbled out the door; and suddenly the image of me flailing as helpless as a turtle on its back looking up at their concerned faces came to me. I put one foot on the ground and then the other and was grateful they didn't buckle throwing me to the ground. After taking stock of my body, to my great relief, there was nothing to worry about; everything seemed to be fine, I'd check my face for a butterfly clinging to it in the morning."

Although it was only 7:00, it was already dark. Stan secured the silver trailer putting big rocks in back of the tires and unlocked the door.

The fresh air felt good but cool so we didn't stand around talking especially when Stan reminded us balloonists need to get up before the crack of dawn when the temperature is low and hot air will lift a balloon. Knowing tomorrow was the BIG day and all of us tired from the ride, we turned in, preoccupied with what the morning would bring. I stepped into the trailer where luckily my head just cleared the roof and by taking two steps, I was able to touch the other side; this wasn't a trailer, it was a shell of a trailer; no water, no electricity, no cots: none of the comforts of home. There was privacy though, and no rocks to brush aside before rolling out a sleeping bag.

With Josephine's facts bouncing about in my head, I was looking forward to seeing the thrilling sight of hundreds of colorful balloons lifting one by one in the sky. I wrapped up like a cocoon: two sweaters, a coat, a knit ski cap and made sure my feet were warm by wearing socks that were good and tight, zipped myself in my sleeping bag and prepared for a restful night of slumber.

But nothing could have prepared me for the cold! Even after I pulled on the third pair of socks, a thick woolen pair Josephine loaned me, my feet still felt like they were solid blocks of ice. I rubbed my feet against each other like they were kindling trying to start a fire but this action took the last vestige of sleepiness from me and now I was more awake than ever.

Hour after hour passed and I was still wide awake. I lifted my head and listened to the quiet; no trailer doors opening, no talking, no dogs barking, no heaters turning off and on. It was a lonely feeling knowing everyone was asleep but me. I didn't know much about hypothermia at that point, when the body is exposed to abnormally low temperatures and blankets that usually help a person retain body heat are not sufficient to restore a core temperature. Meaning, even if I had more blankets, it was so cold, they wouldn't have stopped my shivering and shuddering anyway because my body temperature had fallen below a critical temperature level.

I felt puffy goose bumps on arms and I hoped the cold didn't cause poor muscle coordination to make walking impossible and thoughts unclear. Picturing the worst, in a last ditch effort to warm myself, I imagined I was in a balloon moving higher and higher out of the numbing cold and closer to the sun, then realized with a sinking feeling, I had hit the benchmark moment all sleepless people reach, the time when crickets, insects and all creatures cease making calls and the silence is followed by thin tendrils of cold air caressing your face like bony fingers which only means one thing; DAWN; I had been awake all night.

Shortly thereafter, as if a signal had been given by an unseen town crier proclaiming the hour, suddenly hundreds of people were wide awake shouting unintelligible directives to each other. It was incredible, one minute everything was quiet, and the next, it was bedlam. Having slept in my clothes and coat, I scrambled from the sleeping bag and first thing, checked my ankles and wiggled my toes seeing if the night of cold had affected my muscles and was happy to find everything working properly. Compared to the extreme relief I felt, the rest of the day was icing on a cake. I grabbed my camera and didn't stop taking pictures until we left. It made spending the night in a traveling igloo worth it.

The actual mass ascendancy proved anything but peaceful. Literally hundreds of people edged in the shimmering light from the lightening dawn appeared; balloonists, crew members, onlookers and the mad scramble was on!

I was standing in the hazy light with Sr. Godwina and her parents, all of us in a slight state of shock watching people scurrying every-which-way, putting things together, uncoiling rope, pounding metal stakes in the ground, readying baskets for flight, everyone highly competent knowing exactly what they were doing.

When I heard the first gush of hot air being propelled into an open section at the bottom of a red balloon it sounded familiar. I recognized the sound from when an air-force balloon went aground near the monastery I was in Arizona. It was fascinating now being able to see within a few feet what was making the sound; blasts of air passing through flames into the nylon balloons making them buoyant as they lay deflated, flat and useless, stretched across the field like discarded coats at a party.

Looking at the controlled hysteria with a mixture of amazement and jubilation, I was surprised onlookers were allowed to stand so close to the action. I watched as partially inflated balloons flopped and struggled like wounded animals bumping other balloons in a collision of color expanding next to their proud owners overseeing the operation. Lucky spectators were selected and offered rides in exchange for helping to keep the wicker gondolas earthbound by holding ropes. Many accepted spontaneous offers to go up, then ropes were cast off and the rest of us earthbound, admired their courage and watched their ascendancy on what was sure to be a ride of a lifetime!

It took time for the limp material to inflate fully. But when it did, it was magic. First one was a foot off the ground and then two, but once they all reached capacity, across the field gondolas were defying the pull of gravity by hanging incredulously on the blue of the sky alone and it was up, up and away as they soared higher and higher among the cheers of the crowd. Then suddenly the sky looked like a rainbow had exploded sending bits of color over it; grinning, I watched from below till my neck ached.

There were all kinds of balloons: multicolored striped ones, patriotic balloons praising America in red white and blue fabric, larger than life cartoon characters and colorful designs that all worked to help me forget the cold. Sometimes balloons rudely blanked out the morning sun leaving the field in cold shadows.

As the shapes played effortlessly in the sky and were floating above us, most activity on the field ceased and the only sound was the far off whooshing caused by the intermittent of blowers in gondolas blowing more hot air in for lift. The mood of the bystanders settled into a helpless state of unease as they worried about friends and family soaring hundreds of feet in the air without knotted ropes to climb down, guide-wires or large nets beneath them. Within minutes the field had gone from a jabbering multitude, to scattered thrill-seekers left imagining vicariously what it must be like hovering in baskets in mid air.

Stunned spectators wandered aimlessly over the field talking quietly among themselves, occasionally, turning their heads upward to track a particular color and feeling a flicker of panic when it was unaccounted, finding it again and relaxing realizing this was all part of the festival too. To take their minds off their wayward loved ones, many people occupied themselves during the long wait to touch-down by placing more wood on their fires, cleaning their camp sites and washing the windows on their trailer.

In the background, the clicking of cameras was everywhere.

As I watched the large colorful balloons drift over the desert, I thought it was a shame I couldn't rent one for a day to take on a flight of my own. I would fly it over the desert and land it at the retreat, putting it next to the bell in the yard in front of the kitchen to show Sr. Hyacinth who always liked a good laugh; I could see Sr. Edith, sketch pad in hand, capturing the moment in charcoal and Sr. Evangelista in pursuit holding a spatula full of frosting as she ran to get a closer look. I would show it to Franklin, the handyman, who might think the Great Spirit was sending him a personal message in the form of a big presence letting him know God is always near, and, that even though the balloon's path was in the air, I found it to be one of the all-time best routes I'd found in New Mexico. I'd be careful the balloon didn't frighten little Ruby, sure to be underfoot annoying Franklin, and ask her if she'd ever seen such a sight in all her born days. Before the temperature became too warm, I'd pick up Sr. Carol, the missionary, and ask her to point the way to the hogan of the reclusive Navajo we visited and drop it near his hogan to see if he put if he put his door back on yet; an unorthodox drop-in visit from a missionary might be the incentive he'd need to keep cold air out.

And if there was any daylight left, I'd veer it along the banks of the Colorado River to Lake Powell, until I discovered Fr. Lighterman's secret fishing hole, to his chagrin… if I wanted to risk hearing sermons on privacy issues, lectures on spying or possibly the evils of voyeurism in his next month of Sundays; it was a risk worth taking.

Because I hadn't seen a sign posted anywhere advertising rides, I gave up my dangerous idea of surprising my retreat associates and instead ended up sitting in the warm camper with Sr. Godwina and her parents eating pancakes, compliments of Josephine, while we excitedly exchanged stores about what we had seen during the thrilling aeronautic display describing in detail our favorite snapshot, discussing bragging rights over seconds. I told them the next time I would be sure to bring a fisheye lens so I could cover 180' at once.

The balloon festival was an eye-opener for me. From the window of the trailer I watched passengers *without* parachutes waving recklessly, rocking their baskets on purpose above horrified spectators, letting them know they were thoroughly enjoying the ride. That was the moment I was compelled to look at my own situation; working in the heat of Gallup's summers, enduring interminably long car rides, drinking alcohol occasionally, treating my body like it was a popsicle and going a full night without sleep, I realized, even with M.S. I could soar above it all too.

Like the balloons, living could be limitless.

CHAPTER
18

"Franklin's in the hospital!" Sr. Hyacinth yelled from the open window of the car.

"Come on, Anne," Godwina shouted from the passenger seat. "We're on our way to see him right now." I slid in with the worried group of nuns in the back seat next to Sr. Evangelista.

"Not somebody else down sick. What happened?" I asked.

"We don't know," Hyacinth answered. "His brother was tight-lipped about the whole thing. All he would say was Franklin had an accident and was in the county hospital, but I don't think his brother knows as much English as Franklin so he probably couldn't tell me more if he wanted."

Sr. Godwina bent her head toward the back seat so I could hear what she said, but her words were lost on the bumpy downhill hill of our driveway. Unable to make out a word she said, I shook my head and smiled at her; I didn't feel like talking anyway, no one did. We were a silent group wondering what happened to poor Franklin.

We turned right toward Gallup and joined the main highway. We were almost finished with the front part of the yard too, I thought regretfully, although with all things growing, there never really is a stopping point. Watching the weeds rushing by the car, I hoped poor Franklin hadn't pushed himself too hard. There was one thing I was glad about, that we hadn't pushed him into taking a drink from the flask at the Pow-Wow. I felt guilty anyway, remembering how my *perfectly sober* father with his own alcohol problem, was no match against the onslaught of non-stop beer commercials that acted like brainwashing; by half-time or the seventh inning stretch, he was out the door heading for a liquor store. For Franklin's shake, I hoped the thought and close proximity, within swigging distance, didn't have the same effect on him too. I hoped it didn't put the idea in his head, "Say, I really miss that *Tumbleweed Whisky*," and imagining it sliding down his throat until he could resist no longer and took a drink just to see if it really *was* as good as good as he remembered.

It seemed like we were taking forever to get into town. With little to focus on either side of the road there was nothing to distract me; no billboards, signs, or even hitchhikers, only sickly looking weeds that had been blasted by exhaust fumes leaning on one another lining the road.

At last we went from the fast motion of the highway onto a residential street passed sections of older one-story houses. Making several turns, we stopped in the visitor's section of the parking lot of a hospital.

Sr. Hyacinth, with her arm over the seat to face us in the back seat, warned, "I want to tell you, a county hospital is different from hospitals you're used to. This is an economically depressed area remember; you'll notice differences, I assure you, but on the whole the care is quite good. Sr. Celeste earned her nursing credential here and we bring the girls when they need care but it's up to each of them because some Navajos still use traditional medicine men, you know, who use herbs and entreaties for cures while other Navajos choose hospitals; it depends on what they want to do when they get sick. It's comforting knowing help is so close for her when I'm staying up at the retreat house."

I was nervous about going into the hospital, *any* hospital. It hadn't been that long since my own hospital stay when I was stricken with M.S., and I really didn't want to be reminded of the discomfort, unease and embarrassment of the whole ordeal. And now here I was about to enter the antiseptic, white-sheeted world of sick people again, walking straight into their germs; I already had one disease, I didn't want another. I didn't blame Edith for staying home.

I took one last long breath of clean outside air and followed the three Sisters through the heavy glass doors of the entrance determined not to breathe for the remainder of the visit. But glancing around the lobby, I saw it was like any other hospital, clean and orderly, and let myself exhale.

At the admitting desk Hyacinth inquired what room Franklin was in and was told #347. Like penguins, we followed her as she detoured through the gift shop and bought a green vase full of colorful flowers to give to poor Franklin. The four of us converged on the elevator and stood like freight going from floor to floor, listening to the squeaking and straining of the elevator's guide rails. They were so loud I worried if it had enough pull to make it past the next half floor; I didn't want to be stranded in this small cramped compartment filled with the lingering germs of other people. I stuck my hands in my pockets to remind me not to touch anything and held my breath for the remainder of the ride.

Unfortunately, I couldn't keep thoughts coming to me of my own hospital stay in central California. I remembered the emergency room doctor had treated a patient before me who had broken many knuckles holding on to the roll bar of a jeep when it rolled; I could feel my hands involuntarily tightening into fists to check how my own knuckles were working.

Snatches of my hospital visit played in my head like how the emergency room doctor told me he had completed his residency at this very hospital. Suddenly I felt a kinship which awakened a confidence in this place and its treatments. I knew poor Franklin was in good hands and stopped wondering when the elevator had its last safety inspection. On hearing the three dings announcing our floor, we scrambled out and I let myself exhale.

We pushed from the elevator and found ourselves in a long unventilated hall filled with the infirmed in various stages of poor health. These were the unlucky few who didn't have rooms and were stretched out on gurneys along the wall forced to conduct their visiting in family bunches in the open. As a visitor, I didn't expect to find spacious wards being cooled with murmuring fountains, but I wasn't prepared to see the overcrowding. What an imposition it was to have to wear a cheerful face for a passerby.

The three nuns in their habits invited stares and inquisitive looks plus a few "Hi, Sisters" as we wound our way around patients and their guests suspending their flow of Navajo conversation the closer we came, Hyacinth offering healing touches of support to those that held out their hands.

We walked around patients who were wheezing, snoring, or just plain groaning. There were patients being cooled with wet sponges and patients who were either dead or comatose; I tried not to look too closely. Thankfully, I didn't see poor Franklin squashed up against a wall in the long hall with the other unfortunates.

We finally found room #347 and walked through the open door of a small private room. We found Franklin in light green hospital garb lying on his back with his left foot in a cast.

"Franklin, what happened?" we each asked. Carefully, Hyacinth gave the flowers a quick plumping up and placed the vase of cheery flowers on a ledge of a high window so he could see them.

Casting his sad woebegone eyes at Hyacinth, he said sheepishly, "Ya te hey, Sister. I broke my ankle." Seeing her look of concern, he comforted quickly with, "Don't worry Sister, it is nothing. I feel fine," he said slurring his words, under the influence of pain medication.

"How did you break it?"

He looked at his ankle and then back at Hyacinth. "It was a bad road, Sister. I stepped out of my brother's truck and he thought I was all the way out, but I wasn't, only my right leg was and the truck kept going with me in it, half in and half out. I heard a loud crack and here I am in the hospital."

"That's okay Franklin, we get the picture," I cut in, still squeamish from my own hospital stay. It didn't take much to make me queasy and hearing about anything internal like a bone snapping like a twig was enough to give me sympathetic pains in my own foot with an overall feeling of weakness throughout my entire body.

Sr. Hyacinth broke the enfeebled mood of the room. "Had you been drinking?"

He didn't seem to be put out by the question at all and wasn't the least bit annoyed for he knew the question was coming; in my head I heard him answer, "***Of course***, *I was drinking Sister*! *Do you think I am this clumsy when I'm sober*? But what he actually said was a polite, "Sister, I can not tell you a lie. Yes, I was drinking."

At this point I chose to look out the door and down the hall as I pictured him with his head under his pillow trying to muffle the Hyacinth's inevitable tirade. And it came gently but swiftly, "See what drinking brings to you, accidents and misfortune. What do you have to say for yourself Franklin?"

Not wanting to pursue what he thought was a pointless conversation, he smiled dejectedly.

Trying to convince someone of the evils of drinking is an impossible uphill battle but Hyacinth thought she had to try to get him to realize that, like his ankle, alcohol would eventually break him too. Having made her case, she leaned back as though she had gone to a neutral corner, like she needed smelling salts to revive her, in this everlasting battle of wills.

He wasn't too put off by her light scolding, responding with, "I have nothing to say for myself, Sister. I promise not to drink anymore," his eyes moving to his foot again. He didn't want eye contact with her at the moment.

I thought of what my father used to say to finish the same sentence. "I promise I won't drink anymore… *or any less;* a tricky way of saying he planned to continue drinking. I never found any humor in it, and from the look on Hyacinth's face, she wasn't the least bit amused either. Aware that the worst of was over, he broke into a strange complacent grin making us aware his medication kicked in.

The conversation being too close for comfort, he abruptly changed the subject and looked to the novices and me, and asked if any of us had ever broken a bone.

"I broke a finger once when a horse threw me one time," Sr. Evangelista admitted, proudly holding out a crooked little finger as proof.

"I severely bruised my right forearm once in high school, but the ulna wasn't fractured so I didn't get to have a cast, only a splint," Sr. Godwina said, dejectedly. "I was hoping my classmates could sign the cast instead of my yearbook. Did you hear a crack Franklin? Then it was a fracture. Proximally, you see, it might have been the fifth metatarsal, depending on the position relative of the ankle to the anterior ligament."

Franklin looked to Hyacinth for help understanding her academic theory and practice of the scholarly words and said nothing; we all did.

Moving his eyes to me, he asked, "What about you? Did your ever break a bone?"

"No. The only arm I ever broke was the arm off a pair of sunglasses," I kidded him. "But seriously Franklin, do you know what one Catholic saint had to say on the matter. Have you ever heard of St. John of the Cross?" knowing he would have never heard of this obscure saint. "St. John of the Cross wrote that when God wants to purify a person's spirit leading to its purgation, or cleaning, sometimes the dislocation, or breaking, of bones happens. The imperfection of sin can't coexist with God Franklin. In other words, in breaking a bone, God is accommodating, or making room, in the sensual part sense of the spirit so He can come in."

"Is this true, Sister?"

Hyacinth perked up at the question and moved in closer. "That's right, *the corruptible body presses down the soul*," like St. John of the Cross said in his *Dark Night of the Soul.* You better **put off the old man** who likes to drink, Franklin! When the sensible part of the soul is weak, it can't take strong things of the spirit. Doesn't it make sense how an impure physical body will bring down the spiritual part of a man? That's why we go through a period called the dark night to make us spiritual, and oh, Franklin, it's really horrible," Hyacinth warned while shaking her arms for affect, relieved her message finally made an impact.

"That's right," Godwina expounded in her usual knowledgeable manner. "All habits, both good and bad have to be brought into subjection, control that is, until they are purged. Spirit against flesh; two contraries cannot coexist without warring against each other like it says in *Wisdom*. They have to be purified before God can occupy them…"

Growing impatient with the subject of miseries, sufferings and horrors of this dark night, Evangelista asked, "Haven't you heard of the dark night of the soul?

"I have never heard of this dark night," Franklin said. "Native Americans use sweat lodges for purification, a ceremony to purify the mind, body, spirit and heart. It's a place where we are renewed, like your retreat center. Using the Sweat Lodge will repair damage to the spirit, mind, and even the body. We fast before crawling inside and sit cross-legged near a sacred fire pit of heated stones. The sacred fire pit has great spiritual value. By my sweat, I am cleaned for the Great Spirit." A smile of relief spread gradually across his face and he said, "Besides, when I broke my ankle, it was in the light of day."

His drooping head and sleepy eyelids told us it was time to go. Smiling weakly, he told me again, "Sorry I can't work at the Center anymore but I broke my ankle. I'm extra sad I won't see Butterfly for awhile." And looking up at the flowers, he said, "Tell Butterfly I hurt my ankle and can't come to work anymore."

"Don't worry, about the Center Franklin, it will be there when you are better. I'll be sure to give Ruby your message."

He muttered a final "Yah te hey", as we shuffled out the door and back into the busy hall again amid stares of curious onlookers. Again we interrupted conversations of well-wishers and family members who turned to look at the Sisters in their habits and at me in my dirty-kneed jeans and bespattered tennis shoes in a procession of web-less feet, waddling our way, stopping and starting, around patients to the elevator.

We went back by the heavy breathing of sleeping patients, back around patients being sponged off and around patients who were either in drug induced comas or pretending to be asleep trying not to notice the activity of subdued commotion around them until it was time for them to go home.

Pressing through the heavy glass doors to the fresh outside air, I took long cleansing breaths before closing myself in the back seat of the car again. I had plenty to occupy my thoughts on the ride home: the family members in the hallway caring for their loved ones and how fortunate it was Franklin was able to get a private room. I thought about how white the cast was on his ankle to the bouquet of flowers on the ledge that brought color into his cheerless room. When the picture of the awkward way he fell while drunk came to mind, it ended my thinking of him as *poor Franklin*; he brought it on himself.

As we moved through the residential tracts and onto the highway, my mind was filled with thoughts of the Sweat Lodge. I imagined the glow of red hot stones in the darkness and could almost see spirit guides coming around me in prayer. I saw steam rise from the hot pit as water was poured over the stones making a large amount of humidity fill the lodge. I could smell the odor of hot vapors as they filled the enclosed space and could feel my eyes begin to water from the moist air.

By the time we reached the bumpy washboard grade of the retreat drive, I was sorry I didn't ask Franklin if non-Indians were allowed to participate in Sweat Lodges. I could see the benefits in attending one and my mind ran over the possibilities; I could wipe off the rivulets of impure perspiration containing white fatty material of lipids and lipoproteins of myelin as it ran down my arms, and I'd sop up toxic beads carrying the multiple sclerosis virus forming on my brow with a rag. It was worth a try.

CHAPTER 19

The bench had an empty feel to it, sitting by myself with only the statue of Jesus to keep me company. I doubted if I would ever see Franklin walking up the road again because by the time he was ready to come back to work, my volunteering days might be over; how long *does* it take one broken ankle to heal anyway? It was only a week since my hospital visit but long enough for an idea to germinate, to go on a walk with the sole purpose of helping Franklin heal his ankle through breathing and imagery. By keeping myself peaceful, my efforts were sure to help his ankle heal for the overall good of the retreat center.

Not many people had the drive to accompany me over hill and dale so I usually went by myself. There was one exception, Ruby; if she was helping at the retreat, she liked to tag along. Her fetal alcohol syndrome made her somewhat uncoordinated, yet she was light and lean and was able to match my steps by turning anger at her condition into sheer will, nothing could hold her back. "Ruby," I'd say, "It's dangerous to walk with your hands in your pockets, what if you fall?" She would look at me with laughing eyes and place her hands on her head. From then on whenever she wanted to go with me, she'd make a grand gesture of vigorously shaking her hands toward me to show they were free and clear; how could I turn down such a demonstrative display? It was funny.

Today was different; today I was walking to help Franklin by keeping myself in a prayerful state and I didn't want any distractions. This reclusive feeling wasn't just so I could look at the flora and fauna; today's walk was the serious kind, the purposeful kind that helps you center yourself, the kind of walking I used to do at the monastery. Letting Hyacinth know the general direction I planned to go, I headed for the hills behind the retreat to put distance between me and the antiseptic smell in the hospital, and tried not to think what Franklins' prolonged convalescence meant to the staff work-wise; we'd all have to pick up the slack.

It was late morning, about 11:00. I was taking long steps to match my deep breathing and could feel myself relax just by hearing to the rhythmic sound of my shoes as they crushed the hard ground. New Mexico has a similar terrain to Arizona with distant buttes and plateaus and rock formations but the longer I walked, the more I saw differences between the two states; the soil in New Mexico had a reddish hue, noticeable in the sides of cliffs. And although Arizona has spectacular rock formations too, it can't compare to the balancing rocks in New Mexico where boulders balanced other boulders which supported larger ones in balancing acts that could rival acrobats.

Keeping peaceful was a challenge. I ignored thoughts that were sure to agitate me, like acknowledging the winded pain in my side telling me I had walked too far, too fast and was in unfamiliar territory. As a precaution I stared dragging the toe in the dirt every so often to help me find my way back if need be. Breaking branches along the way helped to mark my trail too. All the while, I didn't forget the purpose of my walk was sending Franklin's ankle healing thoughts for the good of the Center. By acknowledging the strength in *my* ankles, I hoped by vicarious participation, it would help Franklin's broken ankle.

I could tell the up-and-down trajectory was ultimately leading me uphill and in no time, my heavy breathing turned into short snatches of air. The change had been subtle. I never noticed how the light desert scents of chaparral and sagebrush had been replaced with the biting scent of pine around me; I was now gulping the thin air of a higher elevation and having a hard time catching my breath.

This is what I was thinking about, distractedly hoping I wasn't lost when I when I stepped into a small clearing. Without realizing, I had crested the hill. Suddenly my walking came to an abrupt halt. In front of me was something so fantastic, so incredible I couldn't do anything but stare, unbelievably I had stumbled on the Continental Divide! Not ten feet in front of me was the deep natural boundary line of the hydrologic division separating the waters in the continental U.S. making them flow either to the Atlantic Ocean or the Pacific.

I stood back from the edge in startled surprise seeing the image of my inattentive body falling free-style from this steep height bouncing from rock to rock never to be found. Barely ever breathing, I stood very still and stared across a valley that was as deep and wide as the Grand Canyon to the other side miles away.

On the north side was a long mountain range that was made out of imposing block-like ledges, one on top of another that stretched the entire north and south length of the Divide. Clouds were nestled on both ends giving it a ground-less look of a dream and an ethereal look of a mirage. To offset this out-of-this world quality, I sat down in the dirt and put a palm flat beside me trying to make a connection with the earth like a ground.

I sat and watched an ever changing patchwork of colors pulling purple shadows across the sky almost eye level. It was inspiring and I was flooded with a feeling of insignificance that made me want to sit where I was and admire this long horizontal stratum on the parallel mountain miles away. This is how I came to be sitting cross-legged in the dirt on the side of a mountain, utterly taken by having something so unexpected appear before my eyes.

Looking at the extensive stretch of high ground on the other side, if there wasn't a hiking trail running the entire length, there should have been. I wondered if this was the *Going to the Sun Road* or *Logan's Pass* I'd heard about. As my mind raced to remember, I jumped up and began waving my arms hoping someone would see me on the other side but realizing I was too far away I sat down again, making a mental note to bring a mirror to throw a reflection on my next visit.

I picked up a dirt clod from the ground. Rolling the little clump between my palms loosening the dirt, a round stone emerged and I thought, "Eureka, I found my first geode!" The words of the group home girls came to me, *put it in a sock and smash it with a hammer and I would find a center filled with tiny crystals lining the sides.* Stuffing it in my pocket, I looked forward to breaking it open some day to see if they were right. The geode was a nice token of the day I accidentally stumbled upon the Continental Divide while on a walk. I thought of Ruby and how she would shake her hands in my face letting me know she wanted to go for a walk and decided I would give the crystals to her when I break it open.

I smiled thinking how Franklin called her Butterfly because she was so restless. When the image of Franklin's broken ankle wrapped in white plaster came to mind, I went back to sending him healing energy by imagining him whole again waiting on the bench in front of the retreat ready to go to work. I saw him shoveling rocks, pushing wheelbarrows, walking without a cast and seeing him doing all these things as a healthy limbed person. Plus he had the extra protection of the invisible force of God's healing energy I was sending him in the form of health angels swarming around his ankle. I planned to keep this up all the way back to the retreat.

Although there wasn't a *sheer* drop off on the verge of the little clearing, it fell away steeply and I kept my distance thinking of what *could* happen if a sudden episode of dizziness came over me or if the colorless shade of optic neuritis paled my vision while I was this close to the edge. Reassuring myself, I *could* crawl to safety, over the geodes, over the rocks, through the fence, all the way back to the retreat on my hands and knees if I *had* to.

Peering over the edge, I chose a suitable epithet to scream if this was my date with destiny, "*Precious is the death of the just!*" was a good one, and imagined myself yelling it on my way to my glory waiting for me at the bottom of the ravine. It was humbling experience sitting dangerously close to my own death. On one hand, part of me wanted to walk over the edge into the chasm and possess its beauty for eternity; on the other hand I didn't know how prepared I was for an untimely death. If previous indications were right, life was going to wear me away instead of forcing my hand but that was hardly a comfort.

Straightening up and stretching, I took one last long look at the panoramic view before tearing my eyes away, deciding there and then I wouldn't say anything about finding this colossal rip in the earth. Like I had found a channel to the great beyond, a divine opening, I wouldn't spoil my remote vantage point by bringing onlookers, sightseers, and curious look-i-loos to this profound place of peace and promised myself to keep this isolated sanctuary to myself, and then I was ready to face the lengthening trail home.

It was dusk by the time I crossed the retreat yard and opened the door to the inviting warm kitchen with the smells of dinner and the activity of the cooks stirring pots and tossing salad.

"Do we have news for you!" both Evangelista and Godwina exclaimed. The cooks wearing work aprons, continued, "Guess what Hyacinth did?" Godwina asked more calmly.

"What now?" I moaned, tired from the walk. As close as an employer thinks they are to their staff, the real camaraderie is always among the employees; putting up a solid front, if one employee acts inconvenienced, the others usually act like it bothers them too. I waited to hear what they thought about Hyacinth's latest undertaking.

"Hyacinth hired, or I guess the word is *approved*, two more volunteers! Not nuns either, they're students," Evangelista elaborated as she waved a spatula at me to help to help make her final point flicking bits of cauliflower at me with each word. "They're "students, *male* students!"

"What?" This overshadowed my finding the Continental Divide by a long shot. "When did she have time to locate more volunteers?"

"I guess they've been asking to come for a while, and now that Franklin is laid up, it's the perfect time. You'll meet them at dinner," Godwina explained, adding, Hyacinth thinks they're a Godsend."

"They might be." I said, trying to sound chipper about the new employs but my heart wasn't in it; all I wanted to do tonight was sit down and rest after the long walk. "So that's what Hyacinth's been up to all week", I said, panting.

It didn't take long for me to get used to the idea. I asked them, "After all, Walter and June were volunteers and they worked out okay, didn't they?" hiding my reservation.

Inviting strangers into your life is always risky, but this is exactly what Sr. Hyacinth did by securing the help of two male volunteers. Knowing she must have put them through a rigorous screening process didn't make me feel better because as much as I didn't want to admit, lonely, isolated places like retreat centers sometimes attracted individuals who weren't firmly grounded in reality; I didn't know if the word psycho was even *in* Hyacinth's vocabulary.

Hyacinth was more of a trusting soul than I. This may have been due in part to her robust physique; things better work out if they knew what's good for them! It made it hard not to acquiesce to her wishes. Even now, as her figure stood peacefully before me on the other side of the kitchen in habit and veil, crucifix dangling from her neck, for some reason the unprovoked image of her gently tapping a rolling pin against the palm of her hand comes to mind, although I had never once seen her lose her temper.

I knew I wasn't as trustful as Hyacinth. Where she was good at hoping things would work out for the best (I was living proof) I questioned the motives of the volunteers because even if references are checked, you never know what type of personality you're getting, balanced or unbalanced until it's too late. Were they running from something, if so, what? It could be anything from police record to a love that had gone bad. Or was ambition driving them? What did they hope to gain?

Our recent additions acquiring Srs. Evangelista and Godwina turned out to be good cooks. Maybe we'd have good luck again.

Washing my hands, I walked to the dining room and was surprised to see Father Lighterman already in his seat. I took my seat next to him.

"Have you heard the news?" I asked causally. "Two more volunteers out joining the staff."

"I heard," he grumbled. "If you ask me, it's nothing more than *onus-probandi*, a blind bargain."

I told him I felt the same until I realized the same could have been said about me too, or rather, the both of us.

"I guess you're right!" he said, with relief, straightening his silverware. Worrying about what the new volunteers would be like hadn't affected his appetite.

I was uncomfortable having to make conversation with a priest, as if he could discern my past sins just by looking at me and zeroing in on some past indiscretion. Hearing the food cart being pushed in, to distract him I said, "We don't have long to wait now."

Seeing his eyes widen as he looked over the choices, I sat back in my chair and thought about my prayerful day of walking on Franklin's behalf for the good of the Center. Without Franklin, the retreat didn't have the lifting ability of strong shoulders and the support of a strong back. Now, after one day of prayers, we had two. Call it a coincidence or just plain luck, but I felt the new volunteers were meant to be here.

It didn't take long to realize why the volunteers wanted to work at the Retreat Center in Gallup. It was located in a frontier town in the heart of Indian country. If they were going to volunteer for the church, it might as well be in a place that holds the promise of excitement and the possibility of real adventure. Like me, I wondered if they had been drawn to the cowboy and Indian mystique of the West.

One of the nicest things about working at St. Francis Retreat was it didn't feel like work. There was no one looking over my shoulder questioning my every little decision. The only harassing presence was the continual heavy awareness of silence of pressing on your ears like a flute that continually played only one note. Listening to the awesome sound *quiet* makes on its own was intimidating to some. One retreatant told me she ran the fan in the bathroom all night to make it sound more *normal* so I wondered how the new volunteers would adjust to it. An isolated place like this could turn out to be a problem for them.

The volunteers didn't know each other until meeting outside Hyacinth's office under the watchful picture of the Pope this afternoon. George was a student from San Diego and Thompson was from Wisconsin. It seemed like the only thing they had in common was the motive; they both wanted to volunteer two years of their lives for the Church.

Physically the volunteers were very different. George was over six feet and round-shouldered with a small paunch protruding from his belly. He was dark-headed and had a line of black freckles running across both cheeks that looked like they had been stenciled on with a permanent marker. It gave him a whimsical, impish look so even with his Goliath stature, it made him seem friendly and approachable.

Thompson was shorter, about five feet, five inches with a massive shock of red hair and a face that was plastered with red freckles. So many it was impossible to pick out a patch of plain pigment without splotches of red, I had to turn away when he caught me searching his face looking for one.

We were all surprised when Thompson uttered his first *Yah te hey* with an Irish accent! He, and his manner of pronunciation was going to take some getting used to and I wondered if this would be the first Irish brogue the Navajo girls ever heard. But as Hyacinth so eloquently put it, "If I can work through the mountain of paperwork getting his visa and traveling papers straightened away, they can bloody well try and understand his accent!" Hyacinth said kidding already picking up his slang.

With a classy accent like his, it was easy to picture him sipping tea with his pinkie in the air, a well-bred gentleman's gentleman, mannered and polite, just the type to work around self-effacing, taciturn Indians.

Hyacinth assigned them to two different small hogans; George to the *Sister Water* hogan and Thompson to *Brother Fire* hogan, with his red hair it was a natural fit. And like me, they understood when we had more retreatants than hogans they would have to graciously welcome retreatants into the extra bedrooms in their hogans during overflows. I told them, "Don't worry; it's only happened twice since I've been here."

Hyacinth explained they were expected to eat their meals with us in the small dining room. She walked them to the hall and showed them where the washer and dryer were, in case they had it in their minds volunteer work included maid service. This housekeeping chore didn't pose a problem for Thompson because he was older and had been out on his own several years, but even after George was shown how these appliances worked, in time it became apparent he seldom bothered to use them even though the machines weren't run by inserting quarters.

I was glad the two volunteers had joined our staff if only to show outsiders there were men here to stick up for us if need be. Fr. Lighterman was glad they were here too, to swing the balance more to the masculine side. Not that the women's movement was alive and well at the center because Hyacinth never flaunted her power or exerted her control. But after all, she was the director and what she said goes. If a difficulty arose, clergy *could* always go to the Bishop, but as far as I could tell, nothing like that ever happened.

Tomorrow was Sunday. It would be a good day for the new volunteers to meet the girls from the home before Mass. It was important since the teenagers oftentimes helped around the retreat, setting and clearing the tables for the groups and they were a big help; Sr. Celeste said it gave them a sense of responsibility so it was good for them as well.

It was Hyacinth's idea for everyone to go to Mass at one of the larger parishes in town. We did this occasionally when Fr. Lighterman wasn't available to say Mass at the retreat, if he had a meeting or if he had to council someone or I felt possibly when he heard the fish were biting.

Srs. Hyacinth, Evangelista and Edith just fit into the front seat of the truck, the white sedan was packed with the girls, and my car carried Godwina, with George and Thompson sitting in the back seat getting acquainted and we'd rendezvous at the bottom of St. Joseph's church steps.

Our convoy pulled in front of the church. The door of the sedan opened and the first thing Ruby did was run up the stone steps, then run down again. Youthful Ruby, keyed-up by the excitement of meeting the volunteers, found it hard to settle down even after Evangelista took her aside and pointed out how the mother bird in the trees overhead was telling her chicks to stop chirping because it was Mass time, did little to settle Ruby. Butterfly, true to her nickname, flitted from Sister to Sister ending up at the new volunteers asking who they were and why they were here. Sr. Celeste trying to fasten the ends of a hat under Ruby's chin gave up trying, murmuring "*Sacre bleu*," under her breath as she steered Ruby into church by the shoulders.

Noticing a woman's disapproving look as we passed, I directed a soft"Shhh," at Ruby which propelled her pell-mell up the steps again and into the church.

And Ruby *could* give both Sisters a run for their money! Sr. Hyacinth's thick waistline was no match for Ruby who was like a gazelle, quick and agile. Although Hyacinth's athleticism was evident in everyday tasks—controlling a vehicle, arranging furniture, carrying luggage etc. but she was no match for a squiggling child. Hyacinth's face was naturally ruddy but the few times Ruby truly exasperated her, Sister's happy florid face would go bright red; if Hyacinth was a tea-pot, she'd be whistling hard, bubbling over hot water and her lid would have blown off. It always ended the same though; a remorseful Ruby would slink up to Hyacinth and apologize, letting Sister know how sorry she was for making her collapse into a chair.

The rest of us straggled into a church already crowded with churchgoers. We couldn't all sit together because we were a large group; the retreat Sisters of Hyacinth, Edith, Godwina and Evangelista were ushered into a front pew, Sr. Celeste and her charges were directed to a seat behind them, with George blocking Ruby's escape route if she became fidgety or had the urge to break for freedom; his large presence was already paying off. Thompson and I ended up sitting in the back of the church.

Ruby was always ready for a game of catch-me-if-you-can, so I was relieved to see her finally sitting peacefully, even if it was under constraint between Celeste and George on her best behavior; now we could all share a peaceful and calm mass.

I knew most of the priests in town. Many had conducted or attended retreats and I was familiar with the priest now saying Mass. I knew he gave interesting retreats and for the sake of our new volunteers I was glad he was the one officiating today for the sake of the new volunteers as their introduction to Gallup. This Mass will show them what they could expect during their stay.

Looking past Sr. Hyacinth and company toward the altar, I saw Father swinging a long chain with an antique bronze incense dispenser on the end. He flung it first in one direction, then in the other, doing his utmost to have the purifying fumes from the incense reach as many areas as possible in preparation for Mass.

In his final pass, he pointedly swung the chain towards Hyacinth's group as if to purify her entire entourage in one broad sweep. I watched through a mist of incense and candle smoke, as the drifting haze settled on the colorfully robed priest, on the unnatural faces of the statues and on the shimmer of gold of the tabernacle making this religious tableau look like it had been rubbed from a lamp.

Everything was going along smoothly although I noticed the priest was reading parts of the Mass rather quickly, like he had an appointment to keep. His expert pace seem to pick up as he went along going faster and faster until he was speaking so quickly, I stopped trying to read along with him as he zoomed in a blur through doxologies, Gospel and communion prayers. He was reading the prayers *so* rapidly it must have offended Thompson's idea of the *proper* way to say Mass and when our new volunteer couldn't stand it any longer, he stood up and in front of Mary, Jesus, Joseph and God Himself yelled in a stentorian voice, **"What's your hurry? What's more important than Mass, nowt!"**

I am a shy person and don't like attention. I was glad we were sitting in back. Thompson's shocking outburst brought me out of the heavenly reverie at once making me want to crawl in the wooden hymnal holder on the pew in front of me until everyone had gone. Thompson's remarks were uncalled for, but what made it worse was his forceful tone. A stentorian voice is usually backed by something; anger, muscle, or even lunacy and I didn't like the idea of having to wait and see which one it was.

Most of the congregation was sitting to the front of the church, so maybe they hadn't heard Thompson's bold comment. I was relieved the priest showed no signs of being disturbed by the rude interruption and continued his lickity-split rendition of the Mass or if he had heard it, he was ignoring it.

The Sunday congregation was made up mostly Anglo parishioners, a number of Navajo, other tribes may have been present but during my limited stay, I found that Navajo, Zuñi, Hopi, Acoma, and Laguna Indians resemble one another making it difficult to distinguish one tribe from another. After Thompson's out-lash, I wasn't looking around to make eye contact. For second language Indians, it was probably hard enough understanding my accent, let alone an Irish one. What does the word *nowt* mean anyway? Some form of Gaelic? 'Good God', was Thompson going to yell out every time he didn't like something?!

Compared to Franklin's outburst, Ruby's scenes of impatience were minor; in fact, now I saw her as well-behaved in comparison, especially with her fetal-alcohol-syndrome background. I began to see that her behavior wasn't dreadful at all, it was almost exemplary for someone dealing with the amount of problems she had. She never ran from *me*, not since the day I entrusted her with *special* hiking tips; always keep your hands out of pockets to help break your fall, always walk backwards *away* from a bobcat while screaming as loud as you can which she, of course, had to practice, and never run downhill.

Priests may use any tempo they want to celebrate the Eucharist. It's not the momentum of delivery that is important, in fact, portions of the liturgy the priest recites are in a tone audible only to him. (These parts are known as the *Secret*.) Volume control and speed are not what mattered in the Mass.

Two pairs of lively black eyes regarded Thompson and me suspiciously from over the top of the pew in front of us sneaking quick peeks at the person with the strange accent who had the audacity to yell like that. It wasn't only the two little girls that were struggling to see us, curious adults turned to stare in our direction too, like Thompson and I were geeks in a sideshow and I was amazed how fast my body responded to what I thought was threatening; instantly my face felt hot from humiliation, my mouth went dry and my head started to pound with a debilitating headache. I wanted nothing more than to have this Mass over and with my body tensing with every head turn, there was a good likelihood I would awkwardly stumble down the church steps in my haste to leave.

Not wanting to be associated with the screamer and his insensitive remark, I lost Thompson in the mingling crowd as I walked from the stuffy air of the church. Moving down the stairs away from the churchgoers babbling good-byes, I could feel the cool, crisp outside turning the color of my red cheeks pink again.

What did Fr. Lighterman call it, a blind bargain? After taking Thompson out on his first jaunt, it felt more like *buyer beware* and hoped he wasn't going to act up like this every time we were in public.

Hurriedly moving down the steps, at the bottom it was with the combined sense of relief Mass was over but grateful when I thought of the favorable turn my thinking had undergone during Mass concerning Ruby. So when the priest expressly told us to "Go in peace," I realized this was one time I actually did.

CHAPTER
20

After the volunteers had worked on a couple of retreats and knew what to expect, they relaxed. George was the same reticent, bashful *type,* but humming now as he went through the hogans checking to see if occupants left anything behind. It was Thompson's tongue that loosened when he realized he was working in a casual atmosphere among a friendly, relaxed staff and not under pressure of a heavy workload with a slave-driver for a boss. And it showed, by the end of the first week, we all knew he was a person who loved to talk, yak, yak, yak! It was fascinating listening to his Irish accent but his talkativeness made it all the more surprising finding out he considered himself monk material; he was only volunteering at the retreat to prove he was novitiate-ready, humble, docile and obedient; definite requirements for any monk.

"I've applied to the Benedictines and Carthusians," he told us excitedly, "I'm waiting to hear which one accepts me."

Most Catholics know the strict reputations these two Orders have with one strictly enforced rule, no taking! Benedictines and Carthusians use minimal speech, if at all, similar to the Cistercian Order.

"Isn't that always the way?" Sr. Evangelista commented. "He loves to talk but wants to enter a community that doesn't allow it!"

I nodded. Making sure Thompson was out of earshot I said, if he can't even sit through a Mass that wasn't up to his liking, we know long-suffering isn't one of his strengths either.

She looked at me and smiled.

"If he does find a monastery to accept him, I told her, "he'll find out soon enough how hard it is keeping his opinions and helpful criticisms to himself."

Life developed into a daily routine for all of us working with the new volunteers. Just like Walter and June, George and Thompson turned out to be very good workers, they were capable and dependable and we learned we could count on them. And with two more workers, the extra help gave me a lot more free time. That's when I had the idea; since my health was holding up I would take classes at the university. Higher education was never more accessible than in the high desert country on the red rock mesa-land. That's what I need, professional development, I would take classes at the university!

Sr. Hyacinth was all for it, so I registered for education classes at New Mexico University. It will be good to continue with teacher training classes because after my volunteer years were up, I'd have to go out into the real world. I thought this a workable plan and registered at the modern looking campus with spacious green lawns and red brick buildings and began attending lectures. My classes had a good mix of students, Anglos and Indians and I recognized two religious Brothers, Jeremiah and Drake, from a religious community in town after they volunteered to help at the retreat on several occasions. Things were going along swimmingly—classes in the morning, work in the afternoon, studying in the evening.

I didn't have any problems with any of the material *during* classes; it was *after* class that a big problem presented itself and left me with the predicament I was now in. Returning from class one afternoon, I drove my car close to the office and parked. No one around and figured the Sisters probably went down to the group home and chances are Fr. Lighterman went fishing somewhere putting finishing touches on Sunday's sermon, and who knows where George and Thompson were. I didn't think any more about it, I was used to the solitude by now, that is I *thought* I was alone.

That's when I heard a branch snap. I turned my head to the sound and saw a large bull standing among the junipers! I had come as close as I could to being face to face with a wild bovine! Certainly it was within charging distance anyway. What a shock it was to look up and see this enormous animal, big as a buffalo, lumbering its way through the retreat yard!

I rolled up the windows and from the safety of the inside my car, inspected it more carefully. It didn't look much like a pet or a show-bull! This wild descendant of the once great herds of the American West had pieces of dried weeds and jagged leaves stuck to its stringy tail. This unkempt animal had all the telltale signs of being wild. The fact that it didn't look like a pet made my situation worse, would it charge, nostrils flaring, phlegm swinging and hooves stomping if I suddenly sprinted to the office door? Did I want to risk being gored by its two thick horns while fumbling for door the key? I knew as fast as I could scramble, the bull would be faster and I didn't want to take that chance. I was stranded.

I sat in my car watching as it leisurely scrounged the ground for something to eat. It had knotweed embedded in its scruffy skin which made me wonder how a mangy black hide like this, even if it was brushed, could produce soft leather for coats and purses from any part of its rough skin.

It knew I was there, turning its head to me every so often both keeping an eye on the other. After about a half an hour, to pass the time, I began to *will* it away by focusing my attention on a patch of green grass way over by the chapel, hoping it would pick up my brain waves and leave the brown patch on which it was presently nibbling and move to the other side of the lawn where the grass was green. Or better yet, go home. With my chin on the steering wheel, I sent out a series of thought waves aimed at the bull, picturing it wandering off in another direction. But for all my concentrated thinking, the only movement it produced was on my part, in the mounting pressure of a headache. The bull never even turned its head toward the green patch of lawn and I convinced myself I had weak brain waves and gave up.

As long as I was inside the car, I felt reasonably sure it wouldn't make any sudden lunges in my direction,

The afternoon shadows were growing longer as I waited in the confined space of my car. Like sitting on the edge on the Continental Divide, it was exciting being so close to danger as it moved on and off the gravel paths picking up undignified bits of pink gravel with its wet black nose. At times I would tempt fate by opening the door and stepping out of my car just to see what it would do. One time I even took a few steps to the porch but jumped when it gave a loud sneeze making me shrink back to the fortification of the car where I cowered in safety assured it wouldn't toss into the cactus garden like a rag doll.

Waiting for help to arrive gave me time to think. Maybe the animal keeping me from my studies was sent as a sign. Maybe it was telling me I shouldn't go back to school and that going back to school wasn't the right thing to do. If it was, wouldn't God have cleared the way instead of sending this living obstruction? For students like me who are undecided about a career path yet, this walking blockade moseying unperturbed in the yard made me wonder if it really was a sign, the equivalent of a ton of bricks. What more did I need?

Although the bull didn't have the four-compartmented stomachs of a cow in which its cud is forced back for re-chewing, it reminded me of my own situation. Wasn't I doing a similar thing by returning to school again? Hadn't I already paid my share of tuition, listened to enough lectures and crammed for enough exams, especially if retreat work turned out to be my calling after all?

That was the point I realized retreat work as a profession, was what I was meant to do. No other occupation meant as much to me or gave me as much satisfaction as helping people along their spiritual paths. From then on, whenever I convinced myself I needed more academia the image of the snorting and grunting mass of brazen brawn in the form of the black bull came to mind and became my bete noire in more ways than one. So what if I would never hold a title or have letters attached to my name indicating years of study?

Trapped in my car by myself, I realized retreat work was for me and I wouldn't have come to this conclusion if I hadn't been forced to spend time alone afraid of a bull lumbering through the yard watching it eat. Chomp, went the tops of grass and my misguided thinking that because retreat work didn't require an advanced academic degree, it wasn't a worthwhile profession. Chomp, went the berries on a manzanita and my notion that since retreat work wasn't a sought-after career, it wasn't valuable. Chomp, went the clump of dirt holding the weeds together taking with it my underestimation of the good retreats did.

This afternoon wasn't about watching a bull grazing on our lawn like it was pastureland. Gallup had used a four-footed animal roaming the countryside to show me what I wanted to do with my life. More than this, the imposed confinement made me aware that retreat work was not just a worthy profession it was a high calling as well. When I thought how God had directed this animal here just to give me time to realize all this, I smiled.

No sooner had I come to these conclusions, I heard the sound of a car crushing rocks on the road making its way to the retreat. Finally! The cavalry was here in the form of a Franciscan! It was Hyacinth! I stepped out by the side of my car and frantically pointed toward the bull hoping she could defend herself. I yelled to her in warning, "**Stay in the car! Stay in the car!**", waving my arms and pointing.

Sizing up the situation, I could see the puzzled look on her face, her eyebrows furrowing, her nose crinkling in puzzlement. She disregarded my frantic warnings. Evidently she thought I was a lily-livered city slicker, parked the car and got out with a groan. If I could hear her thoughts at that moment, they would be *I can't leave the retreat for one second…* . She took one step toward the bull, gave it a threatening flick of her wrist, and stood challengingly holding her ground in a menacing stare down.

The beast did not like this new turn of events, anything that brazen might have something to back it up with. Disturbed by its sudden lack of force with its position, and frightened by this bold interruption in its peaceful afternoon of nibbling, the animal turned and made its way between the hogans, escaping down the hill trying to get as far away from Hyacinth as it could.

The last I saw it was hightailing it off the retreat yard away from the big, bad sinister Sister, making tracks as fast as possible, retreating to the safe haven of the Reservation, looking over its shoulder with every step, its swishing tail tucked safely between its legs.

Feeling a flush of embarrassment, I watched red-faced from behind the impenetrable protective shield of glass and metal covering my car as Sister shooed the animal away without incident.

CHAPTER
21

The sun brought multicolored leaves to the retreat in the form of a canopy of living color. It also brought the dancing gods of Zuñi.

Ever since Hyacinth took the staff to see the Mission at Zuñi I wanted to return to see one of their dances. And I remembered what Franklin said, "First, you have to climb up a ladder so you can watch from the roof…" I stopped listening at that point and my sense of adventure took over and my mind made up, I'd go to Zuñi to watch one of their dances and find out for myself if I really did have to watch from a roof. It was just plain luck that this was one of the times during the year Zuñis held these events.

I had a traveling partner in Thompson. The question was, after his sudden outburst at Mass, whether I could I trust him to maintain his composure and keep quiet and not draw attention to us. Native Americans live by different standards than other people. They are quiet in word and manner and this mental calmness gives them untroubled and peaceful temperaments. Did I want to take unpredictable Thompson into a social setting filled with disciplined, soft-spoken individuals?

And not having Hyacinth with us in charge added extra worry to the trip, I was now responsible. I didn't think I could talk my way out of a problem like her, because as a nun, she had the whole Catholic

Church backing her. I asked myself again if I could trust Thompson not to yell or make a scene like he did during Mass in Gallup.

I decided it was worth the risk and I explained to Thomson in a serious tone how Reservations were under Tribal law and have culturally different expectations how people should act. As an example, I told him I left my camera at the retreat to hold off groups of well-meaning citizens prepared to make citizen's arrests because violators would be held accountable. When the fleeting image of him tied and stretched in the sun came to mind with the phrase *mob-mentality*, I knew his vocal outburst was worrying me. I told him the pueblo of Zuñi with a population of over 10,000 was a sovereign, self-governed nation with its own government, courts *and* police force; it took some time but I think he got the message when I made it *very* clear I didn't bring money for bail.

More than anything else, he listened when I told him that if he ever yelled again, it would be the last time I would take him anywhere again and I would find another willing traveling companion; big, strong George for instance, was probably a good tire changer and I wouldn't have to convert 32 pounds to metric either. I hoped Thompson's solemn word about behaving himself meant something.

Thompson was here on a visitor's visa and was anxious to see every piece of Americana he could. And since Native Americans have lived in many areas of New Mexico since after the time of Christ, what was more authentic than the genuine article, Indians? So after much deliberating on my part wondering if I could trust him to behave, we set out for Zuñi pueblo.

When we were leaving, Hyacinth yelled after us, "Remember, every dance *cuts a hole in the sky*; they're prayers, not performances!" Whether her remark was just her flair for the dramatic or not, now I was looking forward to experiencing an awakening of my spirit and wondered if we would experience anything like a *vision quest* and a message would come through for each of us. This was my mindset at ten o'clock in the morning when Thompson and I set off for the pueblo of Zuñi.

Regardless of the season, getting a late start like this, the blue-gray interior in my car was already too hot to touch and we rolled down all the windows in the Mustang driving down the bumpy driveway to the highway. Turning left, we were greeted with a pleasant breeze blowing over us the entire hours' drive through the high desert. We wondered out loud what the dances would be like but nothing we pictured came close to the exciting religious event we were to witness that day.

We traveled through the countryside looking at the beauty of low-lying mesas and cactus growing impossibly out of the hard dry sandstone desert floor.

Knowing we were going to what is considered a spiritual event even listening to Thompson's nervous conversation wasn't enough to keep me from being in a prayerful mood. I full of expectation, it wasn't everyday I was privileged to visit a traditional community to see a religious dance even if it turned out to be like the loud drum-centered Pow-Wow Sr. Evangelista attended.

I thought of June and how unfortunate it was she and Walter had gone home before I knew of these dances, she would have loved to explore the large Zuñi pueblo, and the Deacon could have actually seen the Zuñi River Fr. Lighterman mentioned in his sermons.

After about an hour I slowed trying to remember where Hyacinth had turned on our trip to the Mission. There wasn't a sign but I remembered the large clearing and pulled onto the empty lot and parked on the dirt. It was sunny and hot and quiet; nothing stirred except the cawing of a crow crossing overhead I took as a good omen. And like my first trip to Zuñi pueblo, it was refreshing not being bombarded by stores, hordes of tourists and noisy cars. There wasn't a soul around, all was quiet and peaceful.

We climbed from the car, stretching after the long ride and looked around at several houses, some with window boxes but none had vegetables growing on the roofs like on the Navajo reservation. The houses weren't the adobe-brick surfaces plastered in mud I expected, they looked the same as residences I was used to seeing on any residential block but without sidewalks, curbs or fire hydrants.

Walking on an empty road soon we were met by a smiling Zuñi woman wearing a calf length skirt, blouse and sandals offering directions speaking very good English with the distinguishing accent of her people. I informed her we were here to see the dances and she pointed to the end of the road telling us to turn right and follow the other people walking into the interior we would see walking too. We thanked her and before she left, she turned to Thompson and warned, "Remember, no applauding."

When she was out of ear shot, I told Thompson it must have been his loud, red hair that prompted her statement. Nevertheless, it worked to increase our curiosity and we continued on determined.

Making the turn, out of nowhere, came numbers of people walking on the same road coming in from different directions. The more inland we went, the more people came and joined in the steady, unhurried pace down the middle of the unpaved dirt road. It was peculiar how no one spoke, not even Thompson, as we all walked in a hushed and purposeful gait like a spontaneous procession or a walking meditation.

Walking along in silence, the lack of speech added solemnity and importance to the upcoming ceremony and it was easy to sense a feeling of camaraderie and a kinship of spirit. As Thompson and I followed the growing swarm, it felt like we were caught in a spiritual undertow dragging us deeper into a different state of consciousness. We walked faster and faster and I had a sense of urgency something important was going to happen.

Finally, we walked up to the front of a building and we could walk no more. Looking up, I gasped. One by one the bottleneck of people at the base were climbing a tall ladder to the roof meant I would have to too! In the back of my mind, I'd hoped my vision quest wouldn't have begun on a tall, homemade wooden ladder.

I gave Thompson a little push in front of me when he stopped to watch a woman on a rung halfway up disappear over the edge to the roof. I gulped. Having no knowledge about what goes on at these dances, for a fleeting moment my over-active imagination brought the image of a sacrificial pit with people voluntarily jumping to their deaths to secure prosperity for the tribe for the coming year; hearing no screams, I dismissed the notion.

A group of us stood milling around the base of the ladder waiting for a turn to climb as each person made their way up in an orderly manner until it was Thompson's turn, then my turn to scramble up the large precariously high ladder leaning against the side of a *kiva* (room used for religious practices) the entrance for viewing and the *only* way to see the dancers, was from the roof of the *kiva*. Mouthing the words, *don't look down on my lips* watching Thompson, I grabbed hold of a rough-hewed rung and started up after him.

Reaching the top of the adobe building and dismounting, we stood on a flat gravely surface. It was interesting looking out at the community of Zuñi from this high angle, over the buildings, over tall trees and intersecting roads; over the entire town. Thompson was taking it all too. We walked to the other side of a 200 foot roof with the rest of the onlookers to look at a spacious enclosed square courtyard with bare earth for the floor and secured partitions along the walls in preparation for the arrival of the dancers.

The entire time spectators were still coming off the ladder to the roof making their way to the other side in search of the best place to see. There were a couple of tourists among us who looked as dumbfounded as Thompson and I but everyone smiled and was friendly and polite. I was glad too, because the roof was full of black haired people; one very red-headed Irishman and one dishwater blonde Anglo in the crowd, we stood out like sore thumbs.

The dances are scheduled, but exact times were difficult to pin down. It was just by accident that we left the retreat when we did but it turned out to be the right time and it wasn't long when we were startled when someone yelled, "**Here they come**!" and like a wave, everybody rushed to where we could see the plaza and watched as men dragged two sides of a large wooden gate around opening the entrance for the dancers while I hoped Thompson would keep his mouth closed.

One by one the dancers trudged in, weary after having danced through the night along a nearby riverbed. There was no music but one by one trim and muscular men entered the patio gyrating to some inner beat that kept them dancing the entire way.

Thompson and I looked at each other in disbelief.

It took time for them to dance in but eventually about twenty bare-chested men their bodies smeared with mud and streaked with paint, wearing the ugliest face masks imaginable filled the patio. Their distorted countenances and disfigured facial parts were grinning horrible ghastly smiles as they gyrated and twisted in ungodly movements on the packed-down earth. They were outfitted in skins draped around their waists like loin cloths, and either wore sandals or they were dancing barefooted in the dirt. It was an unorthodox scene and I was grateful I was up above them on a rooftop with Thompson, out of harm's way watching such a bizarre scene.

There was no music, only an individual voice in Zuñi dialect would call out at times and Zuñi spectators would break out laughing. Sometimes a dancer would let out a loud undecipherable cry, all the while dancing to choreography of their own making. Thompson and watched and I wondered what it felt like to feel the sand in their toes.

I knew primitive dancing is usually religious in nature so I tried to figure out the meanings by scrutinizing their movements, like if the stamping of feet was a simulation of thunder and acted as an inducement to bring rain, or if the loud cries were a supplication for the Great Spirit to protect them, or if the duration of the dance had anything to do with bargaining for a long life. It was fascinating to think of the possibilities while watching the wild and primitive tableau in a place where the art of dance is still sacred.

Thompson and I watched, captivated, along with the others on the roof who were mostly Zuñi women I guessed were watching boyfriends, brothers and fathers. We all watched as the dancers leapt and hopped and stomped in the dirt of the square in no particular arrangement of dance routines I could determine. It was a fascinating display of steps and gestures handed down from generation to generation in an unprecedented show of Indian exhibitionism.

With the sun going down, Thompson nudged my arm and suggested we go. What he found repetitious was what I found captivating. Even without understanding what I was hearing and not understanding what I was seeing, I could have remained until the dance was over.

Before we were ready to climb down the ladder, I took one last sweeping look around, at the tumultuous dancers in the patio, at the smiling faces of the black-haired Zuñi women on the roof with us, at the eternal spirit hovering about a people and tried to hold onto the memory of this intimate sharing of an ancient prayer in a day I didn't want to end. Breaking my reverie, I followed Thompson down the ladder as inconspicuously of we could and the closer I came to the ground, the stronger the impression grew that, step by step, I was climbing out of my subconscious like I had been roused from sleep. Jumping off the last rung, I hit the ground startled, fully awake.

Turning to Thompson, I asked him, "It was worth the climb, wasn't it?"

"Smashing, I say, and how about those costumes? Most peculiar indeed, wouldn't you say, with the mud and all? Why do you suppose they muddied themselves like that?"

"I don't know. I was surprised to see mud instead of feathers and paint like I imagined; this was one dance I could never have imagined, not my wildest dreams. It was unreal seeing the dancers burst in kicking, spinning, twisting to the arena. What a surprise!

Nodding his agreement, we walked back along the empty road excitedly reliving the day. It wasn't long before we were approached again by an Indian woman wearing a rose colored skirt and sandals. She was about sixty and told us her name was Linda. I couldn't help noticing she was wearing a silver bracelet and silver studded earrings. When I commented on her lovely hair clips, she invited us into her home to see her collection which she sold. Thompson glanced at me with wide eyes just as I glanced at him, both of us thinking how fortunate we were to be able to go inside a Zuñi home.

Her house was furnished with the typical manner; a couch, coffee table, dining table and armchair. Except for a work table off to the side of the living room, it looked very much like the houses I had been brought up in, even the stack of dishes draining on the counter next to the sink.

While Thompson asked Linda questions, I picked out a couple barrettes with beautiful hand-beaded orange and black designs. Linda told us how Zuñi women worked in *cottage-based industry,* small scale industry by family members using their own equipment and is a main source of income for Zuñis, sculpting pieces of pottery as well as traditional arts and crafts items like baskets and Kachina dolls and were famous for their needlepoint and inlay jewelry.

We asked her to tell us about the mud-caked men and she explained how the dance of the Mudheads served as a warning against incestuous relationships. That's why they wear the hideous masks, to show what happens when relatives marry. The Mudheads or Koyemshi, were clowns.

I told her I wished I had known they were comical characters because the masks were so ugly and distorted, they gave me the impression they represented bad-tempered, disagreeable characters.

"It gets the point across." She explained that the dancers started in a nearby dry river bed and danced through the night, dancing the entire way to the Kiva and lasting until dawn.

She was happy to share, telling us there were other dances as well corresponding to the different seasons which included Sword Swallowers, Summer Rain-Dance, a Doll Dance called the Shalako, and Leaving the Gods dance.

She walked with us as far as the gate in front of her property. We thanked her for her time and she replied, *"Elahkwa,"* (thank you) back to us.

As she closed the gate, I told her every time I wore one of the barrettes I would think of her and the Mudheads and remember the extraordinary time I spent at pueblo of Zuñi, doubtful I'd ever top such an exciting time again.

It was dusk when we finally climbed in the car and readied ourselves for the hours' ride to Gallup. The highway was without traffic lights and cars were few and far between but it was a relief knowing we weren't the only ones driving in this unpopulated region miles from the nearest town. I was glad Thompson was with me as backup in case anything unexpected happened.

It wasn't long before I had to turn on my headlights. Black shadows crossed the road making it seem very different traveling this road at night than it was driving it in the daylight. Everything looked different as our lights threw out long black shadows over bushes turning fleshy-limbed cactus into human-like figures as we flew by the unfamiliar landscape narrowly escaping prickly outstretched hands.

I asked Thompson to help me watch the road for any number of animals that might to cross the road: deer, boar and even elk, not to mention black bears. When told him about seeing the mountain lion cub in back of the retreat, he set about watching for wildlife in earnest, eyes squinting, searching the road as far the light traveled. I told him the majority creatures roaming this area were bound to be tarantellas, snakes, scorpions and centipedes, little critters that thrive on dry ground instead of big game so he could relax; chances were slim of us running into a four-footed animal. But that you could never tell what lay ahead of you in this part of the country which made him move nearer to the windshield to see more clearly. As if on cue, he asked pointing, "What do you think *that* is?"

Being in the middle of nowhere, the thought of seeing anything odder than the Mudheads made my heart jump; I told him this was no time to start seeing things and that I had seen enough weirdness for one day.

"I'm not kidding. Look up ahead over on the left side; doesn't it look like there are colors floating in the air? Blue, then there's gold and red?"

From this distance I *could* see something peculiar. Up ahead above a slight depression on the hill, I could see colors, and they were suspended mid-air almost like a hologram; red, blue and white lights.

"Yes, but I don't remember passing a gas station or any store," he said, scratching his head.

With the design of lights fast approaching, a shape came into view and we were both pleasantly surprised. We looked at each other and smiled. Thompson couldn't have expressed it better for the both of us, "Why, why, it's a pub!" he stammered, not believing his eyes.

"Dry Gulch Saloon," he read, running his tongue along his lips in anticipation.

"Come on; let's go in for a wee one!" He didn't have to coax me, the last drink I had was at home, and after standing in the sun all day, I was thirsty. Besides, I was just as curious as he was to see what the inside of a real saloon looked like. So I pulled the car into the parking lot of the Dry Gulch Saloon, cut the engine and turned off the lights.

I wondered how safe my car would be displaying California license plates among a number of trucks that looked like they'd belonged to a bunch of good ol' boys, red-necks and rough types. So before we went in, I took Thompson aside and cautioned, "For heaven's sake, don't make anybody mad! You never know who we'll find inside." I told him that as far as I knew, there's always been a prohibition against the sale and possession of alcohol on reservations, but there wasn't a law prohibiting Indians from frequenting drinking establishments, so for heaven's sake, watch your step.

He was already walking to the door whenI heard the words "Don't worry," trailing behind him, "I don't fancy my head being bashed in either."

Dry Gulch didn't have the butterfly-wing doors we could push open like in Westerns but it did have every conceivable insect known to the Southwest stuck in its screen door. Attracted to the colors in the neon sign, the recently caught bugs were glistening green and blue in the light.

He opened the creaky wooden frame around the screen door and we walked into a large dim room filled with cigarette smoke.The saloon didn't have the long horns of a steer stretched decoratively over the fireplace adding to a western atmosphere, but it did have a long-haired black and white cat stretching sleepily at the other end of the bar.

Wemade our way through the sawdust on the floor and quickly sat down at the nearest round wooden table.

One by one heads turned to see who the strangers were coming in off the desert and I cringed inwardly. No one said anything. One man sitting at the bar in front gave us a slow up and down look, while the man on the next bar stool next to him, gulped and gave a hard swallow. Seeing the old-fashioned spittoon in the corner, I hoped our surprise entrance hadn't made him swallow his tobacco juice.

I quickly sized up the place. Rough knotty-pine walls were holding the stale air of the smoke filled room in and a fireplace made of stone contributed to the hazy atmosphere. The two men seated at the bar were Anglos, one wore a tan cowboy hat tilted forward, and the other's was hanging on the coat rack next to the door.

Although Thompson and I weren't looking to get in on a card game, I remembered the first rule for saloons was to *never sit with your back to the door*. Feeling this was sound advice I casually slid to another seat and was relieved to see there weren't any holsters packing six-shooters hanging on the coat rack too. Behind us, a few ranch hands were seated at round wooden tables nursing their beers, minding their own business. One gent sitting way in back was coughing, put me in mind of Doc Holliday. I didn't see any Indians though.

I was disappointed when I didn't hear a piano player belting out *She'll be Coming 'Round the Mountain*, but there was a juke-box in the back of the room playing a Willie Nelson song. I sat there self-consciously thinking how this was one time I wished someone would actually turn *up* the country music to take the attention away from us.

A gruff voice behind the bar took our order. We didn't get a, "What's your poison," but we did get, "What'll ya have partners?"

Thompson looked at me and I mouthed the word beer. Turning to the bar, he called out, "We'll have two pints please."

With his accent, now everybody knew he wasn't from around these parts.

The bartender, a burly man about sixty with a full beard, responded by asking, "Two pints of what?"

"Why, lager of course," Thompson said as pleasantly as he could showing him a mouthful of teeth in an ingratiating smile.

I added quickly, "We'll have two beers please," and we watched the taverner pull back on the spigot and filled two tilted glasses underneath with a golden liquid. Placing them in front of us, he said, "That'll be three bucks."

Always at the ready, Thompson handed him a five dollar bill and told him to keep the change. From then on, we had a very attentive bar-keep who exchanged our empty glasses with frothing full ones without our asking.

I tried to keep up with the drinking pace Thompson set but after a certain amount, beer just doesn't taste good to me anymore, so I stopped drinking. I kept him company while he continued in his rowdydow, which wasn't so much rowdy as it was continuous drinking. When he excused himself, I felt I had to take the opportunity to duck my head under the wooden table to see if he was pouring his beers into the sawdust because with all he consumed, he didn't show any signs of inebriation whatsoever, no hiccups, burps, slurring of speech or any unsteadiness about his person.

Crouching, I felt the floor with my hand, letting the small particles sift through my fingertips as I felt around in the sawdust; completely dry! There wasn't a hint of sogginess! I had to concede, I was no match for this Irishman.

By the time Thompson returned, I had wiped the sawdust off my knees and was sitting upright in my chair wearing my best poker face. But his inordinate drinking ability made me wonder if there was some truth to the idea certain groups of people can or can't hold their liquor; living proof was strolling sure-footed to his chair across from me and effortlessly draining about six inches of golden liquid down his throat that very moment.

The cat had long since vacated its spot on the counter in the late hour and we decided to do the same. We waited for the country-western song to finish before we got up and left, Thompson earning a respectful nod as he passed the barkeep, while I was expecting something aimed at me like, *"Good thing they're leaving, I was going to have to cut her off,"* came to mind after seeing me crawling around in his sawdust under the table. I avoided his judgmental look and walked quickly to the door.

Heading into the blackness outside, we swatted our way through powdery millers, hairy moths, shiny black flying beetles and everything else swarming the light at the entrance.

After we had taken a few steps, I motioned for Thompson to stop so we could listen to the quiet and we stood in the parking lot listening while I watched the side of his face changing hues with the colors of the neon light. If it hadn't occurred to him already, I pointed out how the strong scent of the sweet desert sage was one of the best reasons to live in the desert; I felt he should know.

"Right you are" he said, and we both took long sobering breaths of clean desert air.

I was relieved to see my car still in the lot and we climbed in. It was a challenge seeing through the un-splattered section of the windshield as I pulled farther and farther away from the lights of the saloon. With darkness ahead of us and darkness behind us, I turned on my lights and felt comforted Thompson was in the car beside me.

On one level I was listening to someone happily feeling their alcohol explaining the differences between pubs in Ireland and bars in the States. On another level I was thinking about all that had happened that day: climbing to the roof, watching the dancers, seeing the ghastly pig masks, and the friendliness of Linda. Feeling my pocket, I made sure I had her barrettes and felt grateful all over again for the hospitality she showed us, together with appreciation toward the Zuñi people allowing us to glimpse into their mysterious world.

Thompson continued describing his favorite pub meal with gusto, like he was choosing food items off a cart in front of him. But my thoughts were far from food, I was still trying to let it sink in we had visited a real saloon!

"You couldn't ask for anything better," he finished, licking his lips almost tasting the fried potatoes and onions he was describing.

"Exactly," I said, in firm agreement but imagining the Mudheads dancing through the night in the dark, perhaps now around flaming ends of torches...

CHAPTER 22

Hyacinth was an eager listener when she was approached by a Sister offering an invaluable commodity, spiritual help. I had never heard of the Blue Army before but I had been here long enough to know when an idea is the backed by the Bishop, there is little point in objecting.

Opening the slider in the staff dining room, she steered me downstairs. We stopped for a few moments on the wooden landing and a tentative smile formed on her face. "The Bishop is having an apartment built here as an adjunct to the retreat for a Sr. Norma who will be in charge of running the Blue Army, you may have heard of it. From what I understand," she explained. "The Blue Army is a group devoted to spreading the message of Fatima."

I told her I vaguely remembered the messages that were given in Fatima from my years in Catholic school but it was a long time ago. I'd have to go back to the encyclopedia shelf in the office to look up information on the Fatima messages so I would be informed regarding the apparitions when Norma arrived.

"Will Sr. Norma be joining our staff for meals?" I asked, trying to figure out her role at the center.

"No, the Bishop said the apartment will have its own kitchen so Norma will be self-contained and won't have anything to do with the retreat. She will have her own entrance so as not to interfere with the retreat or the retreatants. Work on the apartment starts Monday after our retreatants leave so when you see trucks barreling into the Center and men working in here, you'll know why."

In a town as small as Gallup, people know most everyone, and because Sisters move in the same circles, Hyacinth had heard about Sr. Norma. She knew Norma was from a different Order and had floated from one job to another but all in the general vicinity of Gallup.

I told Hyacinth it seemed there were many people like that in Gallup so Norma will fit right in. "You never know, this could turn out to be her final stop in her long quest to find where she belonged."

Hyacinth's own devotion to Mary made her rally in Norma's defense; she was grateful the new Sister would add a channel of prayer to the atmosphere at the Center. "I know the Blue Army is a very prayerful organization and I'm all for it being in Gallup too. It was at Fatima where apparitions appeared to three children foretelling how God would punish the world if reparation wasn't made for its offenses against Him. Repentance is a big part of their teaching. I remember there was some kind of solar miracle with the sun after too," filling me in.

"We'd better get used to having Bishop Struther dropping in checking on the apartment's progress and seeing how the Blue Army is progressing," Hyacinth said resignedly. "In fact, the Bishop is bringing her to see the location tomorrow."

"He doesn't waste any time, does he?"

"No, he doesn't, especially when he told me Norma needed a place to live."

I wouldn't want to have the Bishop as an immediate supervisor and felt Norma was braver than me.

I left for the office to read about the Blue Army so I wouldn't be completely uninformed. I selected the **F** encyclopedia for Fatima and one that had *Blue Army* listed and took them to my hogan where I spread them out on the kitchen table and read...

The Blue Army was founded in 1947 by Fr. Harold Colgan, a parish priest who had fallen ill and was hospitalized and when he prayed to Our Lady of Fátima and told her if she cured him, and she did, he devoted his life to spreading information about her and the Blue Army was born. At Fátima, the spiritual breakdown of our society was predicted to three shepherd children if her requests were not heeded she offered spiritual means for restoring moral order and establishing peace in the world through prayers and penance (turning back to God to receive God's forgiveness). Dramatic prophecies were given to the three children after they were shown a terrifying vision of hell part of which is known as Fátima Secret.

The Lady of Fátima promised that on October 13th she would reveal her identity to them and provide a miracle so all would believe. The Miracle of the Sun, where it zigzagged across the sky at high noon and advanced threateningly on the earth to an estimated 30,000-40,000 witnesses highlighted the importance of the central message of Fatima: return to God. According to accounts, the miracle of the sun lasted approximately ten minutes while the three children reported seeing Jesus, the Virgin Mary and St. Joseph.

Reading on, Blue Army members are required to pray the rosary daily, consecrate to God through Mary, wear a brown scapula, offer up sacrifices through daily duty, and accomplish the devotion of five first Fridays of the month including fifteen minutes of mediation on the mysteries of the rosary. A pledge is signed by the person desiring membership.

One thing was for sure, this wasn't an organization for spiritual weaklings!

It was hard enough for Sr. Hyacinth and Sr. Mary to entice people to come on retreat where we cater to retreatants without *any* demands to pray, how hard was it going to be for Sr. Norma to enroll new members with all the required praying? I wondered if this assignment was going to end up being one more job in a long line of endless job hunts.

I had to hand it to her though, right from the start, the newcomer at the Retreat knew she had a tough road ahead of her starting from scratch like she was. I wouldn't want to be in her shoes, especially having the Bishop watching her every move; maybe she was more desperate than I.

This was the first time I ever saw a Sister wearing a brown scapular. I wouldn't call Sr. Norma a go-getter; I couldn't imagine her rushing anywhere. She was about fifty with a patient way about her with wavy brown hair that matched the paper bag she carried in each day walking to her apartment. I couldn't picture her trading her veil for a scarf like Sr. Carol when she was involved in less than clean work, in fact, I couldn't imagine her doing any type of work that might snag the thick nylons gathering at her knees. She spoke slowly and softly and walked with her head half bowed giving the impression she was always praying, and maybe she was—*"Thank God I have a place to live."* A blue ribbon was pinned to her tan blouse signifying she was with the *Blue Army*.

The apartment was finished quickly. It was underneath the convent at the back of the retreat and I monitored its progress each day walking down the back steps after the workmen left. When it was finished it had turned into a beautiful little hermitage! The rooms were small but had everything she'd need to live comfortably, a tiny living room, a narrow bedroom, compact kitchen and a closet for a bath room; I know Merton would have thought this out-of-the-way cubby hole would have made the perfect hermitage. And aesthetically, the walls had been made out of the same redwood as the retreat dining room, inviting visitors to relax in their warmth.

On moving day, the workers made a space for Sr. Norma to pull in her older grey car, behind the retreat buildings and off to the side. A walkway emerged from the workmen having to carry materials the shortest way to this inconspicuous niche under the retreat. I was aware it didn't take Norma many trips back and forth before she was settled in.

That's when the Bishop made an appearance.

I watched Bishop Struther drive his long black car to the retreat office and his black slacks walk to the retreat office where the door was held open for him by Hyacinth. I followed them both to see Norm's newly finished domicile. He was a high ranking clergyman but not too busy check on his pet project at the moment, the headquarters of the *Blue Army* and the residence for Sr. Norma, keeping her new quarters in mind for future vowed residents in case she didn't work out, I'm sure.

Dressed all in black, he was very tall and thin and he carried himself in a dignified manner, the word dapper came to mind and I could easily picture a boutonnière of a white carnation in his light coat. Reserved but well-spoken when he did talk, I thought it splendid of a Bishop to personally take responsibility in providing Norma with a place to live and fulfill a worthwhile service.

Since her place was so small, he walked in, glanced around and promptly walked out again. With four good sized adults filling the small area, most of the time was spent saying *excuse me, excuse me your Excellency*, and soon all of us were climbing up the outside staircase like we had been attacked with severe claustrophobia, and went into the staff dining room where we could breathe.

Everybody at the retreat dropped what they were doing when the Bishop sat down to table; the cooks put down their spoons, Edith put down her chalk and straightened her veil, and if the girls from the home were helping, they sat quietly at the other end of the table aware this *high collar* was someone important; we all enjoyed being in the company this tall, poised clergyman.

Hyacinth served congratulatory coffee and pound cake, and the *Blue Army* was off and running.

The Bishop had another idea hatching under his silver hair. In his official capacity as Bishop and transmitter of the apostolate line, he took his appointment responsibly using prudence, sobriety, patience, firmness of character, and this influential minister of the Church told us he planned to have a *refugio* built on the next hill not far from the parish buildings.

"Let's not forget how Christ went into the desert to alone to pray in a place he could get away and *"wait silently for God* like Psalm 62 states. It will be a place where I can regroup from the busy chancery office. I plan to offer use of the hermitage to visiting family and visiting priests too."

"As long as the refugio doesn't take business away from the retreat," Hyacinth mildly objected, sidestepping the fact this was why

Bishop Struther had the retreat Center built in the first place, so people could get away from it all and reflect.

Between the Bishop's plan to fight temptation in the form of distractions, weariness and boredom in the confines of the refugio and Sr. Norma's plan of using an army that accepted new members if they promised to pray a long list of prayers, it was easy to guess which person would have the harder time.

The refugio went up as quickly as Sr. Norma's apartment and we watched its progress with interest. We watched with interest how the men dug a channel from the parish building to the refugio for a water line making it a fully functioning place for hermitage. A plain and simple cabin was erected before our eyes that could have passed as Davy Crocket's cabin over on a far hill with the front door facing in the direction of Zuñi, and not toward the retreat, for which we were all grateful.

Late one Friday afternoon after the workmen had gone, Hyacinth thought it wanted to see what the inside of a Bishops' hermitage looked like. All our retreatants had gone so Hyacinth and I walked over keeping our eyes on the road in case the bumper of the Bishop's black car should make an appearance. If locks were supposed to be put in, they weren't in yet. I let Sr. Hyacinth knock on the rough timber of the door a couple times while staying behind her and let her push the door open and followed her inside; I didn't want to be the one to run into the Bishop while he was reading, napping, gargling or something.

The Bishop didn't keep us abreast of his schedule so we had no idea when he planned on moving in and it gave me the willies being inside *anybody's* homestead uninvited but especially in an out-of-the-way place of a Bishop no less. Because it was undergoing final touches of construction, knowing he *could* be driving up the road any moment made me nervous and stayed behind Hyacinth.

We gave the refugio a quick walk through to get an idea of the room layout. There was a small living room, a bedroom, bath and cooking area. We weren't looking for anything in particular, but because I am the product of an alcoholic father, I couldn't help keeping my eyes open for beer cans, shot glasses, anything incriminating but the first thing we happened upon was a table fixed up as a place to worship giving an ecclesiastical look to the room.

"This is probably where he'll celebrate liturgy," Hyacinth said, noticing the white alb hanging nearby. A makeshift altar consisted of a crucifix on a white lace doily, a picture of Mary and a partially melted candle; and something else, a purity, an indescribable virtuousness which made me wish my conscience was clearer than it was or at least that I wasn't here snooping.

Beyond that, there was a table with another crucifix and a small reading lamp next to an arm chair; a kitchen outfitted with four electric burners, a sink and a student's half size refrigerator gave the refugio the feeling it was everything you could want in a hermitage. That was all, no television no Vatican hot-line, no ground phone; proof he intended on keeping distractions to a minimum while he laid low in his small hermitage, a cell in every sense of the word.

I didn't know what I was hoping to find; a ring, a crooked ended staff of a crosier or the jeweled headdress of a miter, maybe a long garment of a cassock, or a skull cap. But there was nothing, finding an escutcheon with a coat of arms lying around was asking too much. Pulling the door closed, we left the premises as we found it, almost empty.

As the weeks passed, it turned out like Bishop Struther said, *don't worry, Sr. Norma will keep a low profile and will not be in the way.* The only time I saw her was when she walked to her car, usually carrying an armload of papers. We never heard a peep from downstairs from the Sister or from any of the Blue Army or its members.

The Bishop was high in the spectrum of notables in Gallup's religious community whereas poor Sr. Norma had been pigeonholed for a ministry just starting in this diocese and she wasn't so well-received. As the weeks passed and word got out there was a chance the Bishop may be at this location, unavoidably messages needed to be delivered to him and to Sr. Norma downstairs as well. Being a true refugio with no telephone, I enjoyed traipsing across the hills to the new hermitage to drop off a message or walking down the staircase for a brief visit with Norma too, although messages for her were few.

Walking to the two dwellings over time, I noticed Sr. Norma's space was as clean and neat as when she started, except for a woven prayer mat on the floor and a red flower in a vase adding a splash of color to the living room. Her apartment engendered an atmosphere of order and peace and impressed me as being a reflection of a well cared-for inner being.

I was surprised to see the inside of the refugio in much the same condition: there were no messy piles of newspapers, no dirty glasses left about the living room, no shoes and socks dropped where they had be taken off; like Sr. Norma's home office, the bare condition of the refugio told me it was free of anything that could distract him from God too. The only difference I detected from my first visit was a holy water fount had been attached to a wall near the door in the living room.

Even though the two religious were on opposite ends of Gallup's religious hierarchy, seeing the scarcity in each place made me feel the presence of God was an important aspect to each of them, and it followed interiorly their spiritual space inside had been cleared for prayer as well. Being a courier over the months did more than just give me exercise clomping up and down stairs and walking back and forth in the hard dirt, it showed me they were two religious who really understood the practice of poverty and took the passage Fr. Lighterman used in his morning sermon from James to heart:

Come now, you rich, weep and howl for the miseries that are coming upon you. Your riches have rotted and your garments are moth-eaten. Your gold and silver have rusted, and their rust will be evidence against you and will eat your flesh like fire. You have laid up treasure for the last days. Behold, the wages of the laborers who mowed your fields, which you have kept back by fraud, cry out; and the cries of the harvesters have reached the ears of the Lord of hosts. You have lived on the earth in luxury and in pleasure; you have fattened your hearts in a day of slaughter. You have condemned, you have killed the righteous man; he does not resist you. Jas 5:1-6.

I would walk back to my hogan promising myself to go through all the personal treasures I'd picked up on walks. It was a practice that started after learning a former volunteer found an old gun while taking a walk. There was evidence I had thinned my collection of useless items I'd found; I finally sent that old rusty key to my cousin Craig as a memento of my stay, and had taken the arrowhead to an antique shop only to learn it was just a dirty old piece of angled wood, so there was evidence I had made *some* progress. I stopped short when I came to the geode I'd found looking at the Continental Divide, it was difficult tossing out something that instantly brought memories of awe and astonishment even though I knew the tighter I clung to it, the less room I had to let God in my life.

Holding the geode in my fingers toward the window I admired its perfectly round design, rolling it gently between my palms, I had yet to part with something that gave me such tactile pleasure. This beautiful little stone reminded me of all the quiet times I spent gazing at the Divide allowing its depths to transform my intuition into contemplation the longer I stared. How could I part with anything that reminded me of something so powerful?

Thinking better of it, time and time again I would carefully place it back on the windowsill overlooking Gallup. The geode had come to represent my mystical stay in Indian land and was one personal keepsake I wouldn't let go.

CHAPTER
23

When I first came to St. Francis Retreat, it was customary for Sr. Hyacinth to ask the visiting facilitator, priest, a nun or lay person giving the retreat, to join us in our personal dining room for meals. It was the hospitable thing to do since the more retreats they gave, the more we saw them and became our friends.

Fr. Clark was one of these people. He ran a retreat center similar to St. Francis in a diocese in eastern Arizona and was a person of particular interest to Thompson and I after hearing his center was located in Apache country. From then on, even though he was talking about mundane experiences that happen at any retreat center, adventure showed from his eyes and his words were charged with danger. An invitation was extended to Thompson and me (the idea of moving again didn't interest George at all) to visit *Canyon Retreat*, arrangements were made over dinner. Hyacinth felt it would be good for us to see as much as we of the Southwest and we both couldn't resist the idea of venturing into the forbidding realm of the Apache.

The thought of being cooped up in a car for hours with someone who liked to talk was a difficult choice. I knew my speech and voice muscles would be sorely tested and I hesitated; did I want to risk having Thompson hear my speech deteriorate along the way? Neuromuscular weakness, a common problem for people with M.S., had affected my speech in the past but thinking of a worst case scenario, I reassured myself the only thing that might happen was I would slur my words and chances are he wouldn't even notice.

Why is it I am always in the company of people who want to talk right away instead of those who want to think and feel before they speak? But my wanderlust outweighed my choice of passengers and I decided to risk the embarrassment; I wouldn't have gone by myself.

"I know about Captain Jeffords," his words rushed out even before we reached the freeway onramp.

"Good, then you can tell me," I replied, resigning myself to making the best of a long drive next to a person who liked to talk; Thompson's tongue was up and running. When I admitted I had never heard about this Jeffords fellow, his words increased with the velocity of my car like it was a race. My heart beat faster as I approached the onramp heading east on a course for Apache country through the desert of unspoiled land that was not much more than long stretches of deserted highway. That's when hearing Thompson's voice was a comfort.

"Captain Jeffords was a red-headed…"

"No wonder you remember him, another red head."

"Quite, I suppose that's part of why the Captain's name stayed with me. His bravery with Apache Indians made a big impression on me when I was a lad. Jeffords worked for an outfit that ran a mail service and he persuaded Cochise to stop killing his riders. Cochise was so taken by the way Jeffords entered his camp *alone*, they became friends.

"How do you know so much about this?"

"Whenever a Hollywood cinema came to town, especially a Western, I made it a point to learn all I could from it, hoping to see it for myself one day."

We were both full of expectation looking forward to seeing Fr. Clark's mission operation in Apache country, if only for a weekend as pieces of action-packed scenes of bloody cowboy and Indian fights faded in and out of my mind as easily as I moved in and out of traffic. Images of battles that were impossible to expunge from my memory of scalping and torture that were made more real with the required school reading of James Fenimore Cooper's *The Last of the Mohicans*.

I was aware how much the exploits of Apaches have been sensationalized by the film industry, attributed with a reputation beyond all credulity and wondered if these graphic images had been shown in shown in the theatres in Ireland too. Was Thompson aware these images were meant to shock and thrill audiences? This wasn't the best time to be asking him, I thought, when we were driving into a culture even other tribes viewed with trepidation. And, I was entering with someone who had a hard time keeping his mouth shut. Apache methods of warfare were unsurpassed and even the name Apache struck fear into the hearts of all as they raided settlements and seized everything they could. I'd heard a warrior could run 50 miles without stopping and could even outrun a troop of mounted soldiers.

As far as I knew, I had never met an Apache before. All my preconceived ideas had been formed by television and movies with the only lasting trait I remembered about their entire tribe were that they were good trackers able to trail through shallow waters, over double-backs, up catwalks and across tree branches, even along ropeways, yet they themselves were trackless, giving them an air of immateriality.

Entering Arizona, the landscape began to change the farther east we traveled. The familiar forms of cactus, tumbleweeds and scrub bushes were now wild tendrils of long wiry weeds sticking out between the rocks like arms of the dead buried before their time reaching out for help. As if to accommodate the unearthly quality of our uneasy speculations, we were now driving between steep-sided slabs of black rock towering dangerously high on both sides of the highway. I couldn't shake the feeling the corridor was a real Valhalla filled with the souls of slain warriors; I could almost hear wails of agony coming from the spirits of famous Apaches, Cochise and Geronimo, as we passed.

I wasn't sure if our conversation was unnerving the both of us or was it the severe look the country had taken on, but we both recognized a shift in our moods. For the rest of the trip we spoke of a creepy feeling of apprehension following us and it was easy to imagine Apaches climbing on the rocky ledges as lookouts ready to warn the rest of the tribe that intruders were fast approaching. In the effort to restore the original calm of our trip, I told Thompson I thought most Native Americans believed spiritual power was everywhere, but this did little to reassure him. Me neither. If anything, it increased our paranoia.

Time passed slowly on the road having to listen to someone who had a strong opinion on everything and I was weary from the strain of having to keep making conversation. His noisy outbursts of words were like he was firing a Smith & Wesson and I felt myself ducking for cover each time he got off another round. I realized some people talk when they're nervous and Thompson was one of them. Miles down the road when the landscape changed into one that was less threatening, Thompson's conversing slowed, and I involuntarily felt myself ease off the gas.

We reached Fr. Clark's exit at dusk with the last of the light weakly blanketing the area. As the darkened landscape passed our windows we drove a couple miles along level countryside scattered with medium size pine trees and searched for his street name in the twilight. Seeing the lights of the retreat in the distance had the immediate effect of fading images of bushwhackers creeping behind every shrub, it dimmed bloody hand-to-hand fights, and vanquished the elusive Geronimo. It felt like we reached a fort when we finally saw the Retreat sign and pulled in a driveway taking comfort in finding civilization much like the pioneers did, glad to have escaped with their scalps.

Canyon Retreat was a series of buildings along a paved country road that ran along a long a narrow valley and I was glad to see the glow of a welcoming porch light chasing our road specters back into the shadows. I turned off the engine and we sat for a moment listening to the quiet disturbed only by the engine coming to a rest. I would have liked to have let my body come to a rest as well but it wasn't long before a door opened on the building to the side of us and Father Clark walked in the illumination, his brown hair gleaming yellow under the light.

We climbed from the car into the cool evening air, stretching our limbs while I gave the car and myself a quick once over. I was pleased to see the tires were still up, and other than the usual tension in my shoulders from being in the same position for hours, I could feel the soreness that comes from sitting many hours in a bucket seat. As long as things on the car were working and on my body was working too, I could handle a little soreness.

Fr. Clark was wearing the casual clothing of an off-duty priest: white shirt, black slacks and black sweater. His combed brown hair moved with his vigorous handshake in greeting, happy we had made it without any trouble. He told us he had made the all day journey many times so to him it was a trivial matter; I was sure he didn't have imaginary warriors from the past following him, the spirits of Cochise and Geronimo were probably his old friends by now.

We stashed our overnight bags in his office and went into a comfortable entry room where we reintroduced ourselves and exchanged pleasantries.

"Wasn't the scenery spectacular?" he asked proudly, as we sat a dining table.

"Yes, really beautiful," I agreed, and gave him a tense smile.

"Quite nice," Thompson added, not mentioning how we both found the towering rocks threatening and driving next to them for so long, we could sense a presence, like we were being watched the entire time.

I had worked on retreats long enough now to be able to tell the day of the week by what was served at dinner. The rule had been relaxed for Catholics to abstain from meat but there are still holdouts that keep the rule so the typical Friday retreat dinner usually is fish-sticks, baked potatoes and peas to be on the safe side. We were happy to eat whatever Father had warming for us in the oven since fast-foods weren't lining the highway and we hadn't eaten since breakfast.

Fr. Clark talked about all the benefits of volunteering in Apache country. Like St. Francis, as a non-profit organization there isn't any compensation other than room and board for services rendered. He told us there were many forms of volunteering, from serving food in soup kitchens and homeless shelters to helping in disasters so a volunteer should be certain where they want to be stationed for a couple of years before applying.

It might be what Thompson was looking for trying to see as much of America as he could, but I preferred to work in desert surroundings to enable me to follow in the footsteps of the Desert Fathers in the emptiness of the desert. I was settled in my work at St. Francis was happy I had picked an open and interesting director to work under and knew volunteering in Apache country wasn't an option for me but noticed Thompson giving it serious thought. He was in a different country and *should* try to see as much as he could.

As volunteers, we were subject to the vagaries of superiors, directors, managers and administrators and if you were tolerant and could put up with it, it was a good life. I was all for Thompson keeping Fr. Clark as a backup in Apache country.

We couldn't stop yawning, so Father grabbed our bags and walked us to our respective bedrooms, said good night, turned off the light in the hall and the next thing I knew, it was morning.

The next day my muscles were weary but rested. I had no numbness on my face from spending hours in the sun and my vision was steady; I knew it was going to be a good day. Thompson and I planned to start the day by attending Fr. Clark's morning Mass. So after a quick cup of coffee by ourselves, Father was up and out already, we headed down the paved road and entered a small Catholic church joining the few parishioners willing to get up on a Saturday: a few older women, one couple, two older Anglo men and a couple of Indians.

This was in the time when most businesses closed on weekends and *all* stores closed on Sunday. After Mass, Thompson and I strolled up one side of the street and down the other admiring window displays of Indian art and crafts. The town was quiet and peaceful and I could see why Fr. Clark was taken with it, it was smaller then Gallup and there was not much to see here either. We sat on a bench under a poplar tree and filled out a postcard to Sr. Hyacinth, Having a wonderful time, we both decided to stay and volunteer here. Thomson & Anne. P.S. Just kidding!

After attending Mass, the next big event for today was to meet Father at the only diner in town for lunch. At 12:00 we met at *High Feathers* diner where the priest was waiting for us outside in shined shoes and white collar, his good Mass clothes. He led us into a small diner that had a counter in front and six small square tables with laminated plastic gold flecked white tablecloths. I was taken with how *50's* it looked even way out in nowheresville.

We ordered three hamburgers and three chocolate malteds from a middle-aged Indian waiter who was also the cook. There were just a few other customers around us, all Indians with long straight black hair and high cheekbones who could have been anywhere from 15-25 years old. I thought this must be the local hangout except for one fact, adolescents are usually loud and boisterous; these weren't. There was no horsing around or loud music blaring top forty hits. They weren't whispering; they were speaking softly.

It seemed like the more food Thompson consumed, the more animated he became. He was really wound up after eating all the sugar in his dessert but this is what he had come for; this was his big chance, to present a convincing argument why Fr. Clark would do well to take him on as a volunteer in the future.

Finishing our lunch with Thompson's running pitch in the background, his enthusiastic conversation had grown in decibels; so much so, I had to wait for his persuading line of talk to lower before I could cut in to ask Father an obvious question, "Why is everyone in the diner so quiet?"

"Really?" Thompson asked, looking around. "I hadn't noticed."

Father Clark made a motion for us to put our heads together and explained, "It is the way of the Apache. Even though they are known for being storytellers and it's an integral part of their culture," he said in a low tone, "they feel speaking loudly is rude and a sign of bad manners and although that's true in most cultures, it's especially true for Apaches. Loud talking as an unenforced standard of conduct *is* uncultured and impolite but it's something frowned upon and considered unwise here."

Hearing this caused Thompson to be physically taken aback. Excited and now nervous, he let out a loud, "What? You can't be serious!" Laying his right palm flat on the table, he pivoted around looking at the patrons as if for the first time. Seeing they were all Indians, he said, "I say; is that so?" voicing his doubts in a somewhat lower tone. His exuberant personality decreased in timbre but I couldn't tell if it was out of politeness or if he was embarrassed.

Leaning over to speak, I told Father, "Now I know why Indians have always interested me, stillness is a part of their make-up." And raising my glass, said softly, "Here's to Indians; true contemplatives."

"Ah, you are right," he agreed, touching his glass to mine.

Although loud speaking is rude and unmannered anyway, what is considered mannerly in one geographical location may be unpopular in another.

The diner's food was favorable but learning we should have consciously worked at keeping our voices down made me feel like we were gate-crashers and I breathed a sigh of relief when we left the confines of the diner and our words were lost in the open air. Although speaking loudly *is* rude behavior and Thompson was just speaking at his normal excited level, in this part of the country where speaking pianissimo is the norm, we should have made it a point to speak softly. I was embarrassed by what Apaches deemed discourteous behavior on our part, but walked away with a privileged feeling of learning an obscure bit of information about their behavior, one I would never read as a footnote in a book about the Southwest.

As the three of us walked on a sidewalk to the retreat center, I realized how up and down the state of New Mexico, from the family of patient rug weavers I once watched outside of Gallup, to all the isolated Indians living in remote areas on reservations, to the quiet customers in the diner in Apache country, I was convinced the spiritual energy so easily felt in New Mexico was due to the peaceful lives of these individuals; their humble presence bestows blessings over the land under the guise of scenic Southwestern beauty.

As the three of us walked back to the retreat center, the entire time we were pressed into hearing the Irishman's campaign as to why Father should take him on as a volunteer in the future. Hearing this, I flashed back on all the religious promotional material I'd read over the years, volunteer programs included. No matter what Order, I would invariably receive a brochure containing a picture of a bright-eyed woman about 22 usually wearing glasses, a big smile on her face because she'd made the right decision. Her make-up free face was scrubbed so clean you could see where the washcloth had wiped the epidermis off her cheeks leaving only innocence and purity shining through. She would be standing in a room bound to have a statue of a female saint, usually the demure St. Theresa of Lisieux, the little flower.

Religious organizations send brochures to prospective male members of religious Orders too and I wondered if Thompson had received any such material. Even if he had, I doubted if the brochure would feature an opinionated youth, standing at a podium thumping his fist, expounding on one thing or another in a room bound to have a statue of a model saint off to the side, possibly St. John Bosco, educator and teacher of youth whose teaching methods were based on love rather than punishment.

As we walked, I noticed Fr. Clark was letting remarks from Thompson go unanswered like the priest was deciding then and then about whether Thompson had the special qualities needed to be a volunteer here. Weighing the pros and cons for this territory, the question was whether Father thought Thompson's lingual dexterity would be an asset or a liability; I felt his decision could go either way.

It all seemed to come down to words for Thompson; first, calling out at Mass in Gallup, but redeemed himself when he watched the Mudheads at Zuñi and was quiet and subdued. Now the loudness of his regular speaking voice was in question, and at a retreat center where a soft voice is welcomed, I wondered what Father would decide.

We walked to the retreat office and huddled next to the door waiting for Father to unlock it. Tugging thoughtfully at his collar, he turned to Thompson and said with a serious face, "You know, Thompson, controlling people with words is another way of getting your own way, isn't it?"

The enormity of his statement hit Thompson like Chief Seattle's spear hit him in the gut. But instead of giving a long-winded rebuttal, Thompson stood very still thinking and replied, "You know Father, you're right. All my life it has been for me to get others to do what I want. Now I see I was using words to distance myself from others. Words were really controlling me."

With that revelation, Father unlocked the door and we walked in, Thompson looking around the lobby like he was seeing the furnishings for the first time.

On our trip to Apache country Thompson came away with a contact person and back-up plan if he needed one in the future; Fr. Clark tentatively signed a hard working volunteer when the time was right; and I saw the great beauty of an area that turned out to be one of the most mystical and transforming regions this side of the Pecos River. It had to have been; thank God, Thompson didn't say much all the way home.

CHAPTER 24

George was testy when we returned from our tour of Apache country. The idea of working for another retreat didn't interest him until Thompson described how much fun our trip was in terms he could relate to: adventurous, daring and even dangerous. Then he acted like a spoiled younger sibling who hadn't been asked to go along with the older relative. Recalling George saying he didn't want to go through all the trouble of moving again, I assumed he didn't want to tag along to check out another retreat and I never knew he wanted to go.

Hyacinth, truly wanting all the volunteers to see as much of Indian country as we could while we were here, and to stop George from moping about, had an idea. It was the Sister's practice to let the girls at the group home connect with their Navajo heritage whenever possible, Hyacinth, together with Sr. Celeste, decided *everyone* could use an outing, one that would be educational yet interesting to everyone: Sisters, girls, and volunteers. A location was decided. We were going to Canyon de Chelley National Monument to see the 26 miles of sheer sandstone cliffs, prehistoric cliff dwellings and pictographs on a unique sightseeing trip. Checking the retreat schedule, plans were made to go on a sightseeing excursion the following week that included us all.

Taking a group of active, energetic teens to a place that had high drop offs wouldn't have been my first choice of locations but she knew the girls would act responsibly and safely particularly at a place that had descendents of Ancient Pueblo inhabitants still living there. Hyacinth, who had been there before, told us what she remembered about Canyon de Chelley (pronounced de shay), how it literally means *inside the rock*) and how artifacts of indigenous tribes who lived in the area have been found and preserved. "The park," she continued, "was established in 1931 on Navajo Tribal Trust Land within the boundaries of the Navajo Nation. The girls won't be visiting a playground, they know they will be visiting distant Anasazi and Navajo relatives and will be proud to pay a respectful visit and be on their best behavior, I'm sure."

To George's delight, Hyacinth planned on taking us to see Canyon de Chelley's 83,000 acres from a rim. She told us we would see Ancient ruins, 26 miles of canyon walls, and ruins of prehistoric cliff dwellings, 1000 foot walls and pictographs at a distance. We were all excited!

"To access the floor of the Canyon, you must be accompanied by a park ranger or Navajo guide. It's worth having a guide explain about the five periods of Indian culture represented on the walls of the canyon: Archaic, Basketmaker, Anasazi, Hopi and Navajo. We'll see about finding one when we get there."

Both our vehicles stopped alongside each other at the visitor's center but only Hyacinth got out. Because it was after summer, we were lucky there weren't many tourists mushrooming out into the street, flagging down taxis, searching for the cheapest hotels, looking for parking spaces; in essence, mobbing the historic and cultural environment. We couldn't have asked for a milder day too. It was a day for pruning roses, stringing morning glories or growing peonies. And it was quiet, very quiet; at 1:00 in the afternoon all I could hear was Thompson's voice entertaining the girls in the other car.

"We might see Spider Rock," I heard Ruby telling the rest of the girls excitedly while waiting for Hyacinth to return. "It's so high, you can see all over. We might even see Spider Woman too," Ruby almost screamed, happy she was just about ready to be let loose at the top of the Canyon. "She taught the Navajo how to weave. "

"Actually," Sr. Celeste explained, "Navajos believe the taller of the two spires, called *Spider Rock*, is home of *Spider Woman* and she showed the Navajo how to weave."

"We'll see ruins of Anasazi known as the 'Ancient People' too," Celeste continued. "This lookout will take us back thousands of years of Indian culture, as far as 350 A.D.," excitement creeping into her voice.

We were all excited, even George seemed to be pulling out of his funk.

"No guides," Hyacinth said, leaning into their car window. "We'll have to depend on our eyes and ears to pick up information and use our imagination to fill in the rest."

Getting in the truck, she drove it down the road and parked at a good vantage point where we could see as much of the canyon as possible. Sr. Celeste driving the sedan, followed.

Everyone seemed in a hurry to get to the edge of the canyon. There weren't many protective restraints or guard rails at the edge to keep people from tumbling over the side and Hyacinth yelled, "Make sure you hold on to Ruby!"

"Don't worry," Celeste called back, "Evangelista and I have hold of her."

I had spent many afternoons looking over the Continental Divide meditating on its grandeur. But when we walked to the edge of this canyon, it was nothing like that; this was closer and made it more personal. We all lined up on the edge of the enormous canyon, and for a moment the world disappeared as we looked bug-eyed at the tremendous opening of red stone. As if we had sunstroke, we stared speechless, dazed by what we were seeing and listening to the ancient silence of different epochs of Indian culture drifting up from its depths on cool draughts. And looking across the canyon, we saw sheer sandstone cliffs and the remnants of the Anasazi ruins perched high on the canyon wall, faded pink in the sun, and nestled in front of a large natural crevice that looked like it had been split open with a knife.

On a lower level, structural foundations of walls that could have been old work rooms or abandoned houses were all that was left of the buildings that had been formed by piecing rocks together on the canyon floor. The leftover shells of a once thriving community lost through the ages made me feel the shells of the Indians who once inhabited the ruins, timeless beings were still carrying on with their lives to this day.

Looking at the very bottom of the Canyon, like an oasis, full-grown Cottonwood trees and flowers were growing instead of cactus and tumbleweed. A river was straggling through between the towering trees and it was easy to visualize goats, horses and thirsty people bending down for a drink along the verdant banks at the bottom of the Canyon. It was just as easy to picture Anasazi Indians sitting peacefully under these same trees working on their pottery, shaping pots and vases, sitting next to a bush full of flowers, offshoots of that very bush perhaps.

Hyacinth was right, it was best to use imagination to *feel* what it was like to live in such an isolated place, to imagine what it would be like to live in one of the cubbyhole-like openings on the cliff, or how it would feel to be one of the inhabitants farming the little patches of land at the bottom.

Our group stood on top of the Canyon admiring the long dark streaks deposits of redstone left on the canyon walls and didn't miss having a guide telling us the strips were formed of oxide or manganese. Not even Sr. Godwina missed hearing about the mineral origins, crystal structure and physical properties of the minerals or their utilization and/or their geographical distribution. It was that visually stunning; the rocks were red, the dirt was red, and it was the time of day when even the sky was red.

I stood in awe of this breathtaking scene regretting I didn't bring my camera but I would never have been able to capture on film the most valuable aspect left by this ancient civilization for future generations to enjoy, the complete and utter silence. It was wonderful imagining people waking up in the quiet and going to sleep in it too, compared to the noisy pace of city life I would have to go back to eventually.

At one point, everybody, Hyacinth included, wanted to see where the walking trail in front of us led. While the others went happily on their way, I stayed behind to soak up the quiet and knew this was how the Canyon was meant to be experienced, at an uninterrupted pace by simply letting the peacefulness filling the gorge, fill my inner being as well. I watched as an eagle with a wingspan of six feet or more soared silently in the intensified quiet, coasting round and round on the quiet energy in the Canyon.

My thinking was suddenly interrupted.

"That was the last straw!" I heard Hyacinth yelling in exasperation as she came into view over the hill. Holding Ruby by the arm, she said, "I've had it with Ruby! She keeps darting away from us to the very edge and scaring me half to death!"

"I won't do it any more, I promise," Ruby begged. "Let me go with you!" Her small beady eyes on beside her broad nose were squinting with resolve. I could imagine Ruby pretending to throw herself into the canyon in dramatic fashion to get Hyacinth's goat and pictured Hyacinth's reddish hair now white from fright under her veil.

"She can stay here with me if you like," I said. We can sit in the back of the truck. It will be fun."

Ruby agreed and climbed in the truck bed.

Hyacinth walked away slowly looking back at times making sure Ruby was staying put.

Ten minutes went by when George's head appeared over the hill, he was wondering what we were doing sitting so quietly in the truck. Smiling, Ruby happily told him we were *sensing the place* with our whole being, repeating what I had said. And as we sat still taking it all in, her look of concentration told me she was doing her best grasping what I meant.

George climbed in the truck bed with Ruby and me.

I asked them, "Don't you hear it?"

"Hear what?" George asked, straining to listen by cocking an ear to one side.

"The best sound in the world." I said.

"What is it? I don't hear anything," Ruby asked, hanging over the side of the truck.

"That's what I mean. Listen how quiet it is."

"I can fix that," George scoffed and jumped up and out of the truck bed again.

Ruby looked at me and I looked at her, both of us wondering what he had in mind.

He walked to the edge, took a deep breath and began a series of what he thought were Indian cries.

On my sightseeing trip to Canyon de Chelley, I think I'll remember the first time I looked over and saw how deep the Canyon was. I might even remember the dark striations lining one of the walls like long strips of mahogany brown colored wallpaper. I'm confident the Anasazi ruins made a deep impression on me and will stay with me for a long time.

But I *know* I will always remember standing on the edge of the deep canyon looking far below and hearing George's loud Indian cry reverberating off its walls with, "Oh, oh, oh, oh, oh, oh, oh, oh, oh, oh, oh," as he thumped his mouth repeatedly with his fingers. His monotone voice is forever etched in my mind and will always be connected to my utter amazement at seeing a habitué walk out from underneath a canopy of lush, green Cottonwoods at the very bottom of the canyon to a clearing to make his presence known, look up, and with a scything sweep of his right arm, give us a prolonged wave!

CHAPTER
25

I don't know if other retreat centers have had a problem of volunteers not wanting to leave, but we did at St. Francis. When a person is getting three square meals a day and basically their own house (hogan) to live in, along with the camaraderie of well-adjusted, wholesome and happy people, George and Thompson didn't want to leave after their volunteer time was up.

We were into winter now and there was really nothing else Hyacinth could do but to let the matter ride; tossing them out in the cold isn't an option for a nun, it wasn't for Hyacinth anyway. Other than Hyacinth asking every so often what their future plans were, she didn't ask them about their future plans and we assumed they were looking for new work avenues to pursue.

I don't know who brought up the subject first, but his renewed interest in the Pow-Wow gave me an idea; I would seize the opportunity to remind him how Walter and June, the instigators of the idea in the first place, had gone back to their former lives after their volunteer months were over: *hint*, *hint*.

I didn't question why he was so interested holding another Pow-Wow. Surely he wasn't interested in learning more about the song Franklin sung, what the words meant and if they were really capable of bringing a the change in the weather. I know he wasn't interested in how *much* rain fell, like that would nullify the mystifying quality in any way; under an inch, it had been a fluke, over an inch, Franklin indeed had powers. He didn't seem interested in getting his hands on the tape June recorded; he was out of luck anyway because they took it with them. And as one of the main voices on the tape, *I* was even too embarrassed to listen to it, let alone have anyone else listen to it.

What could Thompson be after? There was something about that evening that fascinated Thompson; out of everything that happened that night, the camaraderie, thc fire, the dark adventurous night, what was the one thing Thomson was after? It didn't take long for the name *Tumbleweed Whiskey* to come to mind.

To hurry their moving-on process up, I agreed to hold a Pow-Wow with Thompson thinking after one a drink, I'd have the courage to ask him when he and George would be moving on. I could see Hyacinth thanking me for taking the initiative and taking care of this awkward task. My intentions were good.

Of course Thompson jumped at the chance. So I tried to locate a bottle of the exact brand of whiskey Deacon Walter had. How many brands of Tumbleweed Whiskey could there be? I stopped a local liquor store. There were at least two. I didn't want to spend an over long time selecting one in case I would be recognized, *"Say, don't you work at that retreat place up there on the hill?"* Looking at me and then at my purchase, the clerk might put two and two together, "What no *retreats this weekend?"* It wouldn't be good word of mouth.

I pointed to the right label and the salesclerk slipped it in a bag and hurried from the store like I had just robbed it.

Usually Sisters go to bed early. But before Hyacinth called it a day, I asked her if it was okay if I asked Thompson in so we could talk in dining room. The way was now clear for us to use the fireplace as are focal point instead of a bonfire.

I won't go into all the unpleasant details. In a matter of minutes, the volatile liquid completely wiped out my plan to ask Thompson where he was going after volunteering here.

He didn't show up for work the next day, *sidelined by a touch of flue,* at least that was the excuse he used, and asked George relay his illness to Hyacinth.

Everything worked out though. The Bishop transferred both Thompson and George to a parish in town that needed a couple of strong volunteers. They loaded the last of their things from their hogan on the retreat truck, climbed in and Hyacinth drove them to the chancery office in town to meet with the Bishop and the three of them worked out the details of their new volunteer positions.

Sr. Evangelists and I stripped their beds and went straightaway to the fireplace in the conference room where we lit the grimy outline of George, imprinted like a brand on his sheets, on fire, never having mastered the complexities of the washing machine.

I wondered if the speed in which they finally *did* leave had more to do with Thompson's Irish upbringing and his disgraceful loss of face when I saw he was no match for a 100% proof bottle of liquor, not many people are. It was either that or how it aggravated his colitis. Too close to call really.

CHAPTER
26

There was a good chance I was becoming spoiled and there was nothing I could do about it, it came with the territory positioned as I was behind three square meals a day, in-between serving generous portions of tasty meals to retreatants, I had the dubious honor of accepting the fact that my gravy boat, had indeed, come in.

As a person trying to live as a Trappistine in theory, the retreat lifestyle did present something of a problem. Though I didn't receive a weekly pay check, it was a life where good measure may not have been running over, it had at least been pressed down and shaken together; just about the antithesis of the half-starved underfed monks I'd heard about during the refectory readings at the monastery I wanted to emulate; having more than I needed was not my ideal way to live. I did try not to overdo, but taking three pancakes instead of five is not my idea of fasting. I was nowhere near the faultless perfection of monastic practices I had in my mind's eye.

This was brought home to me one day on the way to a Food Bank in Albuquerque with Hyacinth and the novices from the retreat. The self-effacing episode still makes wince. I was in a monastery of Trappistine nuns who were *real* hard core ascetics—a group of austere, self-mortifying, penitential, self-denying nuns who taught me I was in no position to judge the spirituality of others. I remember the telling incident like it was yesterday and not three years ago.... .

Tapping her teaspoon against a water glass, Reverend Mother Eleanor, the monastery's superior, announced that a couple of the abbey's benefactors asked if they could prepare a special side dish for us. Due to their generous donations in the past, and not wanting to do anything to jeopardize future contributions, I'm sure, the husband and wife cooking team were allowed to prepare a gourmet dish for all of us to enjoy. They went to work in the guest house kitchen where they were staying.

When 12:00 dinner time neared, we were seated around the refectory table anxious to experience the mouth-watering dish. We watched as the side door opened and the two visiting cooks entered carrying a large pot filled with some sort of gastronomical delight and placed it on the stove. They fiddled (in silence) over the pot with salt shakers stirring in last minute seasonings like proud grandparents grinning from ear to ear. When it at last met their approval, they took their seats at the guest table and waited to watch our expressions as we sampled their culinary masterpiece.

After Rev. Mother said grace, out of politeness she motioned them to serve themselves first. I watched with anticipation as they dipped a large ladle into the pot filling their soup bowls in one try. They were beaming when they took their seats across the room, close to our chaplain, Mac's, seat, and were ready to monitor our expressions closely as we ate. They genuinely wanted to share their favorite dish with Sisters who'd think they'd died and gone to heaven when they tasted their flavorful food.

Smiling broadly, Rev. Mother smacked her fingers against her lips making a sign of 'bon appetite. As the newest novice, it was my turn next to serve myself behind our guests. Walking all the way around the long wooden refectory table I tried to distinguish a savory aroma that would give me an indication of what the pot contained, but I wasn't able to detect a thing. Hungrily I closed in on the pot. Picking up a pot holder, I lifted the lid and to my amazement (and revulsion), I saw a bubbling pot was full of onions! Big ones and little ones, some the size of pearls and some as big as golf balls stewing in their own juice; *Onion soup!* How could it be they think food fit for the Middle

Ages was also fit for us too? Assuming it was a delicacy somewhere in the world, I thought, here goes nothing, and plunged the ladle into the mix, trying my best to keep an 'it looks delicious' look on my face for their benefit. I lifted the ladle full of little round onions in various shapes, pea size, marble size, ping-pong ball size; concentric edible bulbs floating amid fleshy transparent coverings. The rest of the community served themselves after me.

I have always been a lover of onions, the stronger the better; onions in tuna with mayonnaise, onions alone on a wedge of cheese, onions diced into just about everything, so as I was carrying my bowl back to my place I looked forward to my first mouthful and thought I'd really enjoy this unusual fare. The first spoonful *was* good and I smiled widely, and looking across the room, I gave the cooks a *thumb up* in appreciation.

The first spoonful *was* good. It was after about the fifth I started having trouble and it wasn't long before I realized I had already reached my onion limit. At some point into an onion meal, the very thought of the large amount still to be eaten is enough to turn the stomach. I looked at the other novices, who I noticed were taking their time bring their spoons to their mouths as well, in fact, we all were. Not wanting to be wasteful, we tried to eat as much as we could, but after a quick and inconspicuous hand sign from the Novice Mistress of 'stay' which had a variety of meanings: remain, wait, endure, rest, to name a few; in this case it meant '*leave* what you can't possibly eat'.

I suppose it was the right thing to do, but in the back of my mind were nagging doubts, should I have forced myself to eat the remaining onions in my bowl? What would have been the spiritual way to act? But making yourself sick wasn't spiritual either. This was what I was reflecting on as I sat staring into the lumps of bad tasting globosity remaining in my soup bowl. I waited for the visiting cooks to leave so as not to insult them when I made my way to the table in the back of the room to fill up on peanut butter and bread. This confirmed it then, I was in no position to judge spiritual behaviors.

This is what I flashing back on and I could almost feel the slimy skin of an onion clinging to the roof of my mouth when Sr. Godwina walked to our waiting car, her sandals slapping their way across the pink rocks on the paths at the retreat.

It was typical of Hyacinth springing this surprise trip on us at the last moment; it was always adventurous going with Hyacinth *wherever* she went. That's what made Hyacinth, Hyacinth, she had a strong will that wouldn't back down but could back *you* down; her red-colored cheeks had something to do with her temperament, giving the impression she was holding her temper and could blow at any moment, it was better not to chance it. For the most part, as I observed in her dealings with people over the months, she was usually right anyway.

I was looking forward to visiting Albuquerque, the neon sign capital of the world. As soon as Godwina was settled in the passenger seat, I felt the car lurch and we moved down the decline on the driveway and we were on our way. Godwina mirrored Hyacinth and Evangelista in black veil and habit as she sat next to Hyacinth in the front seat.Because of their *Sister* status, I climbed in back and sat next to Evangelista in case they wanted to discuss community plans, finances, or directions and prepared myself for the three hour plus car ride to Albuquerque.

Hyacinth made good time on the road. It didn't take long before we were out of the outskirts of Gallup and on the open road with the desert stretching endlessly flat and low on both sides of the highway and I settled back to enjoy the scenery. I could hear the Sisters conversing in an informal chat, but it wasn't until Sr. Hyacinth momentarily turned her head so I could hear her, and shouted, "You hear that Anne? We're going to a food bank."

I pulled myself up closer to the front.

Yelling so I could hear her against the wind, she said,

"A food bank distributes to those living in poverty. It's an organization that distributes food items. I spoke with a Sr. Elaine last night, she told me now would be a good time to come and collect so we'll pick up staples to hand out at Christmas." Hyacinth continued,

"Elaine does not belong to our Order, but they provide help…" her words were lost in the noise of a passing truck.

"We'll bring back emergency foodfor people who wander in to the retreat who are hungry. Some food banks serve only a few families each month, but some provide food to hundreds of families. The one we're going to distributes canned goods and hygiene items like shampoo."

Godwina picking up where Hyacinth ended… "Food banks are underground operations. People don't like to advertise the fact that they don't have money for food and avoid being seen. They try not to look directly at people."

"I'll remember that," I said, making a mental note not to not stare.

"But if people are going hungry, why aren't there more of them?

Speaking in short bursts, Godwina filled me in. "They attract the wrong element, down and out types; homeless, disabled, sick. They provide food to the hungry. In some respect they…" halfway turning her head to face me trying to talk over the wind whistling from the window.

"Oh you'd be surprised. They're out there, you just don't where. It's Sr. Elaine's job to distribute what people donate. You know, bread, flour, rice, staples. You'll see."

"You mean it's all donated?"

"Most of it; the government supplies some, like peanut butter and cheese occasionally, but mostly it comes from donations."

I went back to looking at the open land as it passed; we all did.

The first thing I noticed about Albuquerque was how flat it was, almost as flat as Tucson. If it wasn't for scenic Sandia Peak pressing its way into view it would be hard to tell the difference. With an elevation of more than 10,000 feet distinctively coming into view, it would be hard to tell the difference between the two cities. Hyacinth told us about an serial tramway that gives an amazing view of about half of New Mexico from the top. And because we were so close, she was taking us there first, not for a ride, but because she wanted us to see the spectacular view.

"Don't forget the Sangre de Cristo mountain range to the east of the city," Hyacinth added, pointing her hand in an easterly slant. "It's known for its beautiful red color," prompting me to look harder out the car window. "And the Rio Grande on the west side of the city is known for its slow meandering beauty, and although most of it is underground, it waters the whole central valley. In spring and summer, on each side of the road, you can see a beautiful fertile sight of fields and orchards."

Quite a difference from the plain hard desert floor I was seeing now to picturing it with lush green cover.

"Settlers were still able to run irrigation ditches and sow fields," Hyacinth said, adding that the Villa of Albuquerque was named after the viceroy, Fernandez de la Cuerva, Duke of Albuquerque in 1704. But it was Catholic missionaries that first settled in the area in the 1600s," giving us facts about the early missionaries.

The second thing that caught my eye as we drove over the clean streets were the numerous bunches of red objects hanging on doorways and windows. Hyacinth explained they were chili peppers called *ristras* and they were what gave spice to New Mexico's food. I told her I knew this for a fact after accepting a taste of one from one of the group home girls soon after I arrived and added, "*Never* again!"

Strands of the fruit had been arranged with great care and attention, were hanging under eaves and gateways like red icicles drying in the sun. The end result was works of art consisting of sometimes 500 firmly fastened fruits on a strand. They were formed in irregular shapes— teardrop shapes, cylindrical, and circular, hanging at different lengths pulled together neatly in foot-long lengths to two yards. Chilies the size of cherry tomatoes on top were followed by fatter radish size and longer cigar size chilies at the bottom producing most unusual displays.

And there was something else besides the way fruit was hung out to dry that was very odd, rooftops were lined with lunch sized brown paper bags strategically placed about a residence or business a few yards apart. I was told they were filled with enough sand to stabilize a votive candle and were called *luminarias.* Hyacinth explained how

Luminarias were related to *las posadas,* the ritual in which the search by Mary and Joseph for an inn is reenacted during Christmastime to illuminate their path.At night during the Christmas season, the candles were lit giving a decorative and festive atmosphere. "You might see them tonight, Hyacinth said smiling. "And in fact, Gallup carries on this tradition, but on a much smaller scale."

Albuquerque was not the adobe lined streets I was expecting. The buildings of New Mexico's central metropolis were a mixture of history of buildings from the past and today's culture; cappuccinos sold out of adobe shops, modern offices next to old courtyards with balconies above restaurants advertising biscuits and gravy, and country fried steaks. I did see a slower pace with a boy crossing a street wearing cowboy boots who could have been rolling a hoop with a stick, and older Indian women in traditional long skirts and blouses sitting peacefully against modern buildings that had panels designed to absorb heat. And squinting against the sun at the few pedestrians, I knew this was one town my cowboy hat would fit right in.

Passing the center of town,Hyacinth warned, "That's what happens to people when they cross the desert mid-day in the summer," pointing to the two cattle skulls hanging on the front of a Rattlesnake Museum & Gift Shop.

"We'll remember that," Evangelista said rolling her eyes.

"Ycs," Godwina enlightened, "I read Albuquerque, as the geographical center of the state, frequently reaches triple digit temperatures. Summer daytime highs range from the upper 80s to the upper 90's, but drop into the low 60s to low 70s overnight. The heat is quite tolerable because of low humidity, except during the late summer when the humidity surges in a monsoonal pattern."

"That skull we passed in the desert painted on a sun-bleached white side of a wall on an empty building with drips of sweat coming off it was enough of a warning for me: ***700 hundred miles of desert— WATER BAGS and ICE** next right.*"

It was well after lunch but instead of continuing to drive on city streets, surprising us all, Hyacinth turned on an entrance leading up a mountain.

"Where are you taking us? Evangelista whined, expressing the tired sentiment of us all.

In no time we climbed to a considerable height and pulled into a parking lot of a hilltop restaurant. We followed Hyacinth through an eatery to a window seat where we could see, putting it in her own words, half the state of New Mexico. The view was spectacular but in a moment we knew the *real* reason why she brought us here.

While admiring the view, all of a sudden something zipped out from over us! So this is what Hyacinth wanted us to see, **Hang Gliders**!

"Wow!" exclaimed Evangelista.

"Would you look at that thermal updraft! A launchable craft like that is likely to soar for hundreds of miles! Watch how it gains thousands of feet of altitude…" Godwina summarized for us.

"Are they **crazy**?" was my comment as I watched another one take off following it with my eyes over a patchwork of terrain going from mountainous woodland, coasting on the air in a gradual descent all they way down to the bottom of the mountain.

Letting out muscles stretch and relax after our car ride, we ordered drinks and watched for a half an hour sipping our drinks, in preparation for the next leg of our day while watching one glider after another fly out from over us every few minutes.

"Okay, let's go, Hyacinth suddenly said. I'm hungry and I know a tasty place we can eat. It doesn't have hang gliders but it has its own ambience, good food!"

We all stood; we were all hungry and anxious to eat.

By-passing the fast food places, Hyacinth stopped at a modest restaurant serving authentic southwestern food that I was sure was prepared with *ristras*. But as long as they were cut up, diced or mashed in, they added gusto, a southwestern twang to the food, and not the fire I remembered. The food was delicious.

The Food Bank wasn't a warehouse at all. It didn't even have a sign out in front. It was located inside a regular family home that looked like it had been built in the fifties. It had a side entrance hidden by two large overgrown bushes on both sides that obscured visitors from the view of the rest of the neighborhood. An arch opened on a low entryway where visitors waited surrounded by yellowed flowered wall-paper above worn dingy linoleum giving the impression it was a high trafficked area.

Sr. Elaine greeted us with friendly smile. She was all business letting us know what was available for us to take and what had been marked in advance for certain groups. Moving to one side and pushing doors ajar so we could see the cardboard **DO NOT TAKE** signs holding items, she commented how the local market dropped off large amounts of groceries during the Christmas season and told us the food-bank received nearly double the amount of donations in December, so we could take what we needed, telling us the spirit of human kindness is stronger during the holidays.

Sr. Elaine had a seraphic smile, a preferred quality for someone to have who deals with the down and possibly out types. There was a calmness about her which exuded an attitude of *there's enough for everyone.* Aware there were people waiting for what could be the first meal they had that day, her kind smile helped to mitigate a patron's dire circumstances.

Sr. Elaine continued explaining that while some Sisters regularly pick up food to distribute weekly, other Sisters came only when there was an urgent need. "Much of the food that is dropped off is surplus, so there is no telling what the day will bring, canned goods, jars of mayonnaise, even stuffed animals. It's kind of exciting to see; God knows what's needed and it's uncanny to see the very thing that is needed, dropped off the same week."

We followed her from room to room seeing some rooms literally piled to the roof with stuffed burlap sacks and boxes that were overflowing with food. It was a sprawling ranch style house with many small rooms and the food had been separated accordingly; canned goods, bags of flour, oatmeal, peanut butter, sugar and so forth.

In one of these rooms I saw an Anglo woman off by herself choosing items in an unhurriedly manner. I only had a glimpse of her as I was following tall Sr. Godwina and a stout Sr. Hyacinth; Evangelista and I followed. The woman had shoulder length brown straggly hair, snarled and knotted on the side.

Making sure the woman was out of earshot, I asked Elaine about her. "Oh that's Maggie. She's been coming around here regular like. She's fallen on hard times but she'll get back on her feet again. She has that kind of spirit. Food-banks are made for people like her. It's true what they say, most people are one check away from being homeless, and that's true in Maggie's case."

"What would she do if nothing was dropped off that week?" I was having a hard time imagining what hunger felt like with a plate of frijoles, chips and salsa lying heavy as lard in my stomach from our late lunch.

We heard the faint sound of paper rippling out in the hallway as Maggie carried her bags toward us. Elaine switched the topic telling us about the food-bank's charitable distribution of food. "We won't let anybody go away hungry," she said. "We can always find something, even if it's from our own larder."We pretended we were busy for Maggie's benefit, acting as if we hadn't been talking about her. Sr. Evangelista and I opened a few shopping bags and busily began to fill them with a variety of cans of vegetables.

Maggie walked into the room with her loaded shopping bags. Without staring, I glanced her way. She wasn't much older than me, and close up I saw her hair was knotted and there were light smudges of dirt on her face and arms. Turning toward her, her clothes looked wrinkled and had the drab look of needing a wash. Understandable, why would she put quarters into slots in a washing machine, when she could buy a loaf of bread?

She flashed us a faint smile as she readjusted her grip on the bags. Turning to Elaine, she said, "Thank you Sister" and she left carrying her food.

We muttered polite good-byes after her, but her fleeing figure was already gone.

It was late afternoon when we finally drove back through the town of Albuquerque passing the old buildings that made up this unassuming town of yesteryear. My last remembrance of it was of a tethered horse standing on the end of town silhouetted by the late afternoon sun before we picked up speed and went roaring onto the freeway.

On my first trip to Albuquerque I saw first-hand how food-banks work. I saw how they touched the lives of many needy people allowing them to at least get through the month. I learned some restaurants and supermarkets, instead of discarding food for whatever reason, cooperated with food-banks by passing along food. I came away with the strong sentiment to be more generous and to make it a point to consider the poor.

During the drive home, the lone figure of Maggie moving from room to room gathering food, half hidden by the stacks of food was disturbing. Was it because she was so close to my own age I found unsettling or was I bothered by the fact I knew she had to go without food at times? I couldn't figure out why seeing her bothered me so.

Hours into the trip as we were closing in on Gallup, up ahead in the spreading darkness my eyes picked out an unusual sight. I could see hundreds of glittering luminarias dancing with light brightening the dark streets of Gallup outlining walkways, edging curbs, bordering rooftops in an up-and-down procession of illumination.

As I watched these twinkling lights of Gallup sparkle brighter and brighter, it was as if my intuition had brightened too. In turning the reasons over in my mind, I finally realized what was eating away at me concerning Maggie and it had little to do with another person's underprivileged situation and everything to do with my own behavior because somehow I knew that whether they had been pickled, soggy or crunchy, Maggie would have eaten all the onions.

CHAPTER
27

Up until now we had only dustings of snow, not nearly enough to fill the banks on the sides of the road to the retreat that would force us to cancel retreats because the road would be impossible to climb without traction devices on the tires. The snowfall around Gallup was enough to the turn the broad landscape of the reservation into one great gigantic white sheet with fireplace pipes in hogans sticking up here and there like dandelions on a lawn and was fun while it lasted.

It was with great joy I found to find my feet guiding me unheeded to the end of the dining room and stopping, so that I could admire the pristine scene. At one time or another everyone on the staff wound their way around the tables to this beetling overhang to look on the reservation and enjoy the miles and miles of clean, untrodden land.

This afternoon Sr. Hyacinth had taken Srs. Godwina and Evangelista down to the girl's residential home in town so they could spend time in community praying the Office together as Franciscans and attend an afternoon Mass in their cozy, snug chapel leaving Sr. Edith and me by ourselves at the retreat.

During times like this, when there were no groups here and nothing was going on at the retreat, I was permitted to use the community room in the convent part of the retreat. The room had a fireplace and I enjoyed the novelty of trying to start fires which gave me a new respect for Leonard and all Indians who had to use woodstoves in their hogans if they wanted heat. The community room also had a television; but, because we were situated so far out of town in the country and the reception was poor, it only picked up a couple stations. The room felt comfortable and homey and I would make popcorn, put my feet up and watch whatever was on TV.

Tonight the reception was worse than ever. We were lucky though; the passing storm had waited until the last of the retreatants had made it safely down the steep driveway before making the road hazardous. Sr. Edith and I could see the angled trajectory of snowflakes as they hurtled past the windows and I remarked how it looked like the snow had picked up considerable momentum when the phone rang. Excusing herself, Edith stood straightening the belt around her scapula and went to the office at the end of the hallway.

Moments later she was back announcing, "That was Hyacinth. She said she and the novices decided to stay the night at the girl's home and not risk driving back to the retreat tonight in the snow."

"I don't blame her," I said, yawning. "The highway is probably a long sheet of ice by now. No doubt she wanted to wait till tomorrow to come home, they would have to use chains and I can't see Hyacinth lying in snow on her back trying to put chains on the tires." I called it a night and made my way to the door.

"You'll be okay staying here by yourself then Edith?"

"No problem. I like having the place to myself for a change," Edith said confidently, tucking her white blouse inside a black skirt, something I'd seen her do a hundred times. She was always prim and proper in her appearance, her well-groomed appearance ended at the neck though with a lopsided veil. She pulled an old prayer book out of a side pocket in her habit, sat down and began turning its pages.

Telling her, "Be sure and lock the doors before you turn in," I left her sitting comfortable and relaxed, prepared to read. I got up and walked to the front door and picked up a flashlight. Buttoning up my coat and pulling a ski cap over my head, I opened the door to a wind that was pelting chilling daggers around me, covering me in snow. I pushed at the door making sure it was closed. I could sleep soundly now, knowing Sr. Edith was safe and secure in the warmth of the convent.

Stepping off the porch I blindly made my way across the yard using the faltering light of the flashlight stepping over the rock borders lining the paths. The storm had caught me by surprise and I was only wearing tennis shoes instead of boots and the snow collecting on the shoe tongues was soaking my socks. It was only a short distance but was made longer by my intense concentration trying to remember where the paths were. Shining the failing flashlight, I picked a direction around where I thought the plot of cactus should be giving it a wide turn. I knew I was close and left the walkways, cutting my way across the remainder of the yard to the front door of my hogan.

Finding the door, it felt good being in the shelter of my windless hogan. I turned on the electric heat but knew it would take a long time before it made any measurable difference in the temperature of the room, the majority of heat rising to the white bubble on the sky hole. I changed quickly into my pajamas, turned off the light and climbed under the covers, listening to the muffled sound of the wind buffeting snow against the sides of the window by my bed. When the world is covered in snow it sounds deadened, mute, like it too had gone to sleep. I lay still, listening to the quiet and easily drifted into a deep sleep.

It seemed I had been asleep for hours when I heard…

Bang! Bang! Bang! I came suddenly and violently awake. *What in the world,* I thought, waking up. I glanced at the clock; 2:00 AM! Getting to my feet, I tried to remain calm but the first thing I thought of, of course, was the unbalanced person who left the straw dummy on the road had returned and was looking for more trouble! *What am I going to do?* I quavered showing no fight at all at this time in the morning.

Bang! Bang! Bang! I heard again.

Anyone who has ever been awakened in such a shocking manner will recall the pounding heart, the blood-chilling apprehension and absolute fear bordering on hysteria as you rouse yourself to action. Gathering myself, I took hold of the club I kept at my bedside, staggered over the cold linoleum in bare feet to the front door and asked the visitor to identify himself before opening the door; I wasn't anxious to take a peak at the cold, bleak world outside not with the memory of the hideous straw figure in my mind and knowing the crazed angry person was still on the loose.

"Don't be scared! It's only me," I heard a small voice answering."

"Who is it?" I asked sleepily, my shaky voice questioned once more, unable to put two and two together at this early hour.

"It's only me, Edith!"

"Edith? What in the world are you doing out in the snow at this time of night?" Pushing the door open, I caught a glimpse of the moon through the snow behind her. She wouldn't let me pull her inside the warm hogan, saying she didn't want to risk collapsing in the entryway.

"You feel that bad?"

She turned a pale face toward me. Her color was grey and looked drained.

"Yes, I don't feel well at all. It's my stomach, the upper part, if that makes any sense."

Abdomen? I didn't know if anything that could affect just that part of the diaphragm but I wasn't going to argue. She really did not look well.

"I'm in a lot of pain."

"Can I do anything to help?" The picture of me trying to negotiate the steep icy driveway flashed in my mind.

"No, I already called Sr. Celeste. She's a nurse and she's coming to take me to the emergency room. I just wanted to let you know what happened to me when you couldn't find me tomorrow," she said, holding her stomach, doubled over in pain at the doorway.

"I hope Celeste can make it up the hill," I thought anxiously. I wouldn't want to attempt coming up the drive and shifted uncomfortably seeing flakes of snow in the porch light.

"I didn't know what else to do. I thought of asking you to drive me to the hospital but since Celeste has lived here for awhile, she knows the area and called her."

"Sr. Edith, you did the right thing; I don't even know where the hospital is."

Behind her lights of a car moved dimly through the flakes snow. "There she is now," I said, pointing beyond the statue of Jesus. We watched from the doorway as the white sedan made its way around the top of the hill through folds of snow glistening in the headlights, stopping at the office door.

"She's a good driver. You have nothing to worry about," I said as calmly as I could, trying to convince myself while preventing the image of the car skidding and plunging off the side of the road into the ravine below. I wondered if Celeste had *any* experience driving in snow over patches of ice or if the muffled words *Sacre Bleu* would be the last words I'd hear from her as the car came to a rest in a snow drift at the bottom of the gully.

Edith carefully stepped on the snow, her boots crunching on the walkway as she made her way across the yard to the office in the light of her flashlight.

"Everything will be all right," I yelled after her" following her with my eyes. I saw Sr. Celeste get out of the car and take Edith's arm, helping her into the passenger seat. They drove away illuminating the snow covered statue of Jesus on the way out, making it glisten and glean as they passed around it at the top of the drive.

Back in my bedroom, I debated whether I should dress quickly and run to the top of the hill to see if they made down the drive okay. It was 2:30 and freezing cold; I thought the better of it.

I fell asleep trying to recall stomach ailments, Edith looked so poorly it must have been something serious; ulcers? No, she was a easy-going, care-free person who took things in stride. And the strongest thing she put to her lips was caffeine in her flavored tea. I lay back hoping it wasn't anything serious. Could it be food poisoning and ran through every illness I could think of. By the time I discounted lupus that I finally fell asleep.

The next morning I awoke with a start and dressed quickly layering myself with clothes. As I put on my snow boots and tightened the red laces, I hoped Sr. Edith had made it through the night. I trudged my way to the retreat house and added kindling to last nights' embers that caught quickly before adding a thick log so the fire would heat the room. The moment the log caught the flame, I left to check the phone messages. Nothing was blinking; no messages. I was left wondering what happened and if Edith made it through the night.

All day I couldn't get Edith out of my mind. I hoped it wasn't anything serious. What could be causing her so much pain and knew it must have been extremely painful for her to wake me up in the middle of the night like that. I felt so helpless. It came to me the best way I could help her was to keep myself peaceful and send healing thoughts her way. At least this made me feel I was doing something to help her. And it wouldn't hurt to tell Fr. Lighterman, who had slept through the emergency last night. Between the two of us maybe we could change the unhealthy energy around Edith by bombarding her with healing energy. If this could happen anywhere, New Mexico would be the place where it was easy to feel the interconnectedness of everything through its beauty. It was the ideal place to treat someone spiritually and make me feel I was doing something to help.

All morning I checked the message machine. It wasn't until I stopped for lunch and went to the office to check the phone messages again. It was from Celeste. "Anne, this is Celeste. Edith is all right. It was, well, I'll let her tell you. They want to keep her here a few more hours for observation though' she should be home by dinner."

I breathed a sign of relief. Whether or not our earnest attempts to help her had any effect on her or not, it was better than doing nothing even if I was the one who had deepened.

As I was stoking the fireplace in the community room taking the chill off to the room for Edith's homecoming, I heard the front door open and a loud voice yell, "Hello, anybody home?" It was Hyacinth. Behind her Celeste was holding an overnight case for a rosy-faced Edith, looking bright eyed, and composed, but with her veil askew I knew she was back to the same old Edith. She went straight to the fireplace to warm her hands while Evangelina and Godwina pushed their way to the fire as well; it was good having everyone home.

"Sr. Edith, you're back!" I exclaimed, delighted to see her looking so well. "Fr. Lighterman and I were praying for you. I must say, you look *so much* better. How do you feel? What was wrong with you?" I *knew* her condition must have been serious.

In good spirits, cheery even, like she was about to relate a fable with a solid moral at the end, it was disappointing hearing, "Oh, it was nothing, nothing at all."

I was *really* deflated hearing, "The doctor gave me something and it was **belch, belch, belch, belch belch!**

As the group pressed out of the room I heard her refrain again trailing all the down the hall, "I tell you it was **belch, belch, belch, belch belch!"**

I always thought religious people were like androids, automatons programmed to work and pray, asexual beings with no bodily functions whatsoever to slow them spiritually. They were too special being picked by God as they were for boorish, low class, uncultivated behaviors. They were enlightened individuals, cognoscentis on pedestals far from earthly behaviors like these. So it was quite a come down for me, almost shocking to hear Edith's diagnosis because it was so uncharacteristic for her to go against her genteel nature. I didn't think Edith even knew *how* to do anything uncouth let alone belch and *brag* about it!

CHAPTER
28

It had always been a winter fantasy of mine to hike into the mountains over snow covered trails, untracked and unexplored, in a winter wonderland of pine searching for the perfect Christmas tree. Sitting in a cold truck waiting to be rescued, wasn't part of the vision.

I thought back to this morning. I was in the retreat kitchen looking through the window at the snow in the yard when a mud splattered station wagon pulled into the yard and parked next to the statue of Jesus. It was a dramatic entrance when the car doors opened and one by one six Brothers stepped from the car wearing long dark blue cassocks with matching soft brimless blue caps; each with a chain and crucifix around his neck.

They walked to the kitchen, dragging their habits in the melted snow, everyone but forward thinking Bro. Drake who kept his hem unspoiled, clean and dry. In an instant he had gathered handfuls of his blue material and stuffed the excess in his belt that was holding up his slacks underneath and was standing to the side pulling at a loose thread from his shoulder.

The Brothers were a religious community who lived in a residential section of Gallup and taught and tutored at elementary schools in town and on the Reservation, too, along with being involved in as many different charitable works the Bishop found. They often worked at the Retreat when we had extra large groups and helped in a variety of ways: traffic control and parking, moving tables; sometimes offering to cook and would even stay late to help with the dishes. Usually, they would show up on Friday, and Sundays to help with the biggest meals, zooming about the pots and pans with panache in their long garments.

Brothers Jeremiah and Drake attended the University like I did and I would see them in passing. Tall Jeremiah ran a 12-Step program at a local high school and was quite talkative and outgoing, differing from Bro. Drake who was shorter, introspective and reserved. The Sisters and I looked forward to having them show up for KP because of their good-natures and jovial demeanors, joking and kidding around with everyone; they made time pass quickly.

It was during our Advent retreat when Pam, one of our regular retreatants, suggested we cut down a fresh tree for the dining room as a gift to St. Francis Retreat convincing me the retreatants will enjoy the Christmassy environment while they're here, and it will be a nice surprise for Sr. Hyacinth too.

I didn't need much persuasion and Bro. Drake was all for a little adventure too.

It with was thrilling expectancy that Pam, a long time resident of the area, drove us an hour to the nearest mountain to a thick alpine forest for our search to find the perfect Christmas tree. She stopped at verdant cone-bearing conifers crowding upward on a lawn of sticky pine needles that were spongy to walk on. Everything about the day was like I expected; a heavy fragrance of pine around us, a hillside thick with evergreens, trees in various stages of growth showing a variety of the shade of green as we wandered breathless from tree to tree at a cool alpine elevation; yes, this was the real way to choose a Christmas tree. The only thing that would make our tree finding expedition better was if we happened on an elk, a bighorn sheep or a mountain goat nibbling on a Piñon tree.

Enjoying the search, we settled on a very large fir, just the right size for the large dining room; big. It had a thick trunk supporting many well-shaped branches proportioned in the ideal Christmas tree shape.

We carefully cut it down taking turns sawing and let it flop into the bed of the truck careful not to bend its weighty limbs backwards. We drove homeward with the strong scent of pine in the cab and sap sticking to our hands but didn't complain; there was satisfaction in bringing the tree in the age-old way while a light dusting of snow fluttered from the sky. What could be more perfect?

Our inspired trailblazing ended abruptly though, when Pam driving her truck, could feel the traction give way on the ice-packed tires. We lurched, we spun, we jolted, and to our astonishment we started sliding sideways down in a snow packed ditch off the road.

Pam driving her Mazda truck, traveling over icy back-roads had lost control the moment the tires lost traction; no matter how deep the tread, when it becomes packed with glistening ice there is nothing to hold onto a surface. And if the truck happens to be on a steep embankment, gravity takes over and pulls it in a freestyle slide off the road. We ended up at the bottom of a ditch with the passenger window squashed against the snowy mountain as we came gently to rest.

There had been no warning; one minute we were driving on a remote backwoods road, and the next, we were holding onto the interior of the truck to steady ourselves, hoping the truck would come to rest gently against the side on the hill. We knew the traction had given way when we heard the tires spinning without a lurch or a jolt and a hopeless feeling hit us when we realized there was nothing we could do but ride it out, sideways, all the way down to the bottom of the ditch.

Relief at our deliverance from harm superseded all else as we looked at the pure white ice smashed against the window next to me. This was all part of the looking for a Christmas tree adventure, I told myself, never mind if the three of us were trapped in the cab like turkeys in a meat locker.

When we finally stopped, our shoulders jammed together, we sat very still, stunned. I know we were all thinking the same thing, keep quiet or else our voices could cause something else to give way like an avalanche. Pam broke the tense silence by recalling the catchy jingle for her model of truck; "Mazda, we are DRIVEN!" If the ice didn't move from our jarring howls of laughter, we figured it was safe to change positions and started extricating our entangled limbs.

Holding onto the steering wheel for support, we pulled ourselves out one at a time and scrambled up to the icy road where we stood in the snow looking down at the truck in the ditch. Crashed against the side of a mountain, this can't be good for M.S. Shivering, we decided to walk to keep warm and groped our way along the road in the freezing cold until we ran across an entrance way of some kind and picked up our pace as it veered to the left into the backwoods.

It gave us a good feeling seeing a trailer in the middle of nowhere and an even better feeling to see smoke coming from a pipe in the roof. I closed my eyes an envisioned a grizzled hermit with a wild beard opening the door after we knocked but was relieved when two women, identifying themselves as missionary Sisters in street clothes who were enjoying a quiet afternoon, opened the door. Looking us up and down, in seconds they decided they couldn't help us and the door was closed suddenly to keep the heat in.

Pam's well-intentioned tree hunting expedition had taken an unexpected turn. We decided to walk back to the road to be near the truck so we could flag down help. Brother Drake uncharacteristically threw himself into this wholeheartedly, stepping in front of any slow moving vehicle that came along, waving his arms as a figure not to be denied. Standing along the road waiting, our teeth chattering in the cold, I was glad we had Brother with us.

Finally a farmer in overalls wearing an old straw hat driving a tractor came moseying down the road. Seeing Brother Drake, dirty and disheveled hailing him to stop, the old-timer kindly offered help. He climbed stiffly off the tractor, took an unenthusiastic look down in the trench at the motionless predicament of the truck, grabbed a heavy chain and hitched it to the Mazda's bumper; the strong engine of the farm tractor strained and groaned but hauled our truck back up to the road, none the worse for its self-moving glide.

We thanked him profusely while he climbed back into the seat on his tractor, giving us a wave with his hat goodbye. Wishing him a chorus of "Merry Christmases," we went on our way expressing our profound gratitude to him over and over as we drove away.

Back at the Retreat, I don't know who was happier: Sr. Hyacinth seeing us driving in with a tree for us, Hyacinth stepping inside the dining room to warm ourselves near the roaring fire. Sr. Hyacinth was glad to see we had picked out such a large tree and taught us the country way to stabilize it instead of using a metal holder with screws to wind into the bark. She had us hoist the tree into a plastic gallon container which we filled with large heavy rocks. We secured it by piling on more rocks. I was surprised when it actually worked.

The rest of the Brothers had long since gone so Pam offered to give Brother Drake a lift. We thanked her for an adventure of a lifetime they got back into her truck and she delivered him at the Brothers doorstep in town.

That evening ended by stringing lights and popcorn, hanging bulbs, and laying strips of glittering tinsel on the branches. With the fire crackling sap from the firewood, we sat on the couch with our feet stretched to the fire sipping homemade eggnog, admiring the decorated tree.

The next day I read in the local newspaper 23 people had been ticketed over the weekend for illegally cutting down trees without permits. I wondered, with all the commotion we made, how was it possible they could have missed us.

Retreatants enjoyed the tree well into January, but permit or no permit, my Paul Bunyan days were over.

CHAPTER
29

I felt the same excitement seeing Hyacinth driving the white truck driving into the retreat now as when I first arrived; *what is she up to now?* Pulling the pickup to a stop, she got out and I walked to the truck where we both looked at the bulky piece of lumber lying under a tarp. It was not just any lumber, I recognized it as butcher block, thick and beautiful with a tough and durable surface; I should last so long.

I hopped into the bed of the truck to inspect it, exclaiming how beautiful it was close up.

"I thought so too" the Sister said, I couldn't just let them throw it out. What a stroke of luck!"

"Someone just gave it to you? Where did it come from?" I asked pleased Hyacinth had used her scavenging insight to bring it to me.

"It was leftover from the addition to the market. A workman recognized me from the retreat and he gave it to me. I was thinking it could be turned into a bench to put outside the church for retreatants. Do you think you could do it?"

I have always been a lover of wood and told her I'd try.

Hyacinth drove it to the back of the retreat near Sr. Edith's apartment, opened the truck gate and we laboriously lowered it to the ground.

I spent several days sawing off a smaller piece then cutting the piece in two again so I could bolt them on for legs. This was no easy task. Butcher block is a thick, hard wood and was very difficult to hand cut. With every pull on the saw though, I thought how good the natural wood was going to look after I oiled it with linseed oil, picturing the streaks in the bare wood turning darker as the oil soaked in; painting it would be criminal.

Who knew there was something so beautiful beneath the rough exterior of bark: wood, beautiful wood. Used for shaping figures, carving ornaments from teakwood kachinas and fetishes to duck decoys and grotesque masks to totem poles. I don't know what kind of endorphins the body emits when stroking a beautiful piece butcher block, but smooth finishes of deep rich grain demand to be touched. Building a bench out of it wasn't work, it was a privilege.

In the middle of this woodworking there came an announcement to deflate my expanded mood. And even though I knew it was coming, it was still a shock when Sr. Hyacinth announced she would be moving to the girls' home in town permanently to help Sr. Celeste take care of the girls; this had been her plan all along. Sr. Edith would become the new director of the retreat. That's the thing about volunteering, you have to take whatever's presented and some people are unable to sit back and smile as their circumstances change. And because her decision came near the time when my two volunteer years were up, I decided it was time for me to move on too.

The finished product turned out better than anticipated, especially under a coat of linseed oil. We moved it by the door of the retreat chapel and it gave me great pleasure to see retreatants sitting on it, enjoying the quiet while preparing for Mass. It was my gift to the retreat and was something I knew would remain long after I was gone and there was satisfaction in that.

I didn't know it at the time, but the novices who had been here over a year already, had decided Gallup wasn't the place for them either. Sr. Godwina decided to leave religious life altogether and Sr. Evangelista asked to be transferred back to her motherhouse. If I didn't know better, it seemed Gallup was the last stop for novices struggling with their vocations, like they had been thrown out of the pan and into the fire. But because their meals were promptly on the table, there was no indication things weren't going well for them both. It hadn't been that long since I left my community and I felt sorry for Sr. Godwina knowing the violent overthrowing of your life it causes and how hard it is going back into the real world. Sr. Evangelista would have it easier; she was going back to her former community and to friends. My ears pricked up hearing about the other retreat center near their motherhouse and kept it in the back of my mind now that I would be looking for work again.

In the days following, scenes came back to me reminding me what I would be losing; the happy gathering of retreatants chattering during meals amid an inviting aroma of coffee, the welcome and accepting camaraderie of smiling Franciscans, the wizened faces of Native Americans, *Yah-te-hey* the first thing on their lips, and luminarias that made Christmas a special time of year in the Southwest.

Most importantly, I was reminded I had *remained healthy the entire two years* volunteering here and the real journey wasn't in gallivanting over the landscape, the real adventure for me had been in the almost insurmountable journey back to good health using the experiences in the Southwest like object lessons. But as exciting as it all was, I found more satisfaction in realizing I could trust my body again and I wasn't going to give out on a moment's notice. Appreciating this miracle, it wouldn't have surprised me to learn the deep aesthetic pleasure I felt lauding nature here had had a ripple effect that went all the way down to my DNA. It's wonderful what being happy will do. I was living proof.

In the meantime, I had discovered Gallup was the hub where all trails begin leading to the fascinating lives of Indians in their hogans, to the mystical feelings found in the endless regeneration of land formations, and to an unalterable peace so deep it could be mistaken for a place. I still see Gallup as a slow moving rancher standing on the side of the road but after spending two exhilarating years here, I realize its persona is actually motioning visitors in to explore the natural beauty surrounding the city and to look in on the curious happenings going on in and around the locality.

Tightening the orange and black barrette on the back of my head, I thought of Linda, the Zuñi Indian, and the time Thompson and I spent watching the Mud heads dance. There were so many adventurous memories I was taking with me from Indian land, I filled with pride knowing I was a privileged person leaving with memories of friends, Franciscans and the intoxicating beauty of the southwest, but most of all, I was leaving with something worth more than gold to me; a vocation lasting decades.

Years later I had the opportunity of visiting the place that meant so much to me, to see it all again. Gallup was no longer a hodgepodge of stores; it was now clean, modern and fashionable.

And like the town, the retreat had changed too because nothing and no one remains forever unchanged . . .

I admit missing the Retreat Center as much as the people, maybe more so; the beautiful conference room, the retreat center grounds, the endless view of the Navajo reservation. Driving up the bumpy driveway to the Retreat, I passed the place where the statue of Jesus should have been but to my surprise it was gone and after all the worry I put into attaching its fingers and coloring its eyes, it was like losing a friend. As a gift to Hyacinth from her brother, I wondered if she had had a say as to its new location, this was where being a nun and not possessing things really hit home; the bench where I met Franklin every morning had been removed too, like our three forms never existed.

On my nostalgic return, I stopped the car and got out and stared. I couldn't believe the yard had returned to its former natural state, overgrown and wild with weeds! It wouldn't sink in how all our hard work had vanished, along with the people I grew to love as we worked together. The only thing left of the bustling retreat center was in my memory.

If the practice of feng shui is based on the belief humans are affected by their surroundings and should live in balance with nature, from the total disorder of the yard I assumed anybody living here would have disagreeable, ill-tempered, unenlightened personalities and were incompatible with the universe.

It saddened me to see weeds using the barrel cactus like spools of thread, tightly wrapped and choking the life out of the plants and I felt a sympathetic shortness of breath feeling their struggle. The pink rocks Franklin and I spent hours arranging were scattered about the grounds like pieces of my heart, mashed into the ground by uncaring strangers. Considering the effort Franklin and I put into organizing the grounds and laying down rock paths, it was almost too much to bear. It was viscerally hard seeing the yard back to its former overgrown state but without an attentive staff to drag a hose to the shriveled cactus garden once in a while or keep the weeds from climbing over the bell or sweep dirt off the benches, I couldn't keep the question from surfacing over and over in my mind: how could this beautiful place not be loved and cared for anymore and it hurt.

In my heart I knew somehow, someway, the center would bounce back again when another community was ready to take on the challenge. I could forgive the extended interruption of retreats; I could even forgive the doing away with the statue; but I didn't think I could *ever* forgive the person responsible for covering the butcher block bench with pink stain!

This is all water under the bridge now. R.I.P. Fr. Walchars, who made the comment on a postcard how retreat work might be the right occupation for me, I owe my retreat career. As someone who devoted his life conveying the concept of inner stillness in talks and books on prayer, meditation and mystical theology, *The Splendor and the Silence, The Unfinished Mystery* and others, it's too late to tell him I was listening but hoped he saw how I felt stillness every time I looked on the beauty of low-lying clouds covering the reservation like a big white sea, or when I located the brightest star through the skyhole every night, stillness was there. Watching from heaven, Father would be pleased I had found physical calm in the endless beauty of the Southwest: mysterious, solemn, sacred, stillness.

I was sad learning Franklin the workman had died, R.I.P., and when no one came forth with details of his death, I had the feeling alcohol was involved. To celebrate his rebirth into spirit, I cracked open the geode I'd kept safely for years I found at the Continental Divide.

I knew it was the right time to break it open and reassured myself that even though the crystals dispersed into nothing like Franklin, he would come together in my heart each time I thought of him.

I remembered how I had put the little round geode on the ground in front of me and giving it a good whack with a hammer, I saw it was true, glass-like crystals burst from the rock like I hoped Franklin's spirit burst from body. I scooped up a few crystals and blew them in the air off my hand to acknowledge his entrance into the Great Beyond watching them disappear into nothingness.

Standing among the weeds, I thought how nothing would rival the night I sat at a table with an abbess who refused to turn on a light to spoil the mystical mood, but hearing Franklin sing a rain song during a make-shift Pow-Wow producing rain, came close. A mystic in his own right, to this day I try to make out what is communicated in the singing of birds. And knowing how he enjoyed parades, I wondered if there were banners and baton twirlers to greet this Navajo veteran in Heaven.

Every time I see the little Navajo basket, I think of Sr. Evangelista the cook, R.I.P., and how after spending the day at a Pow-Wow she was sure her hearing was impaired by the pounding of drums. Patient and kind, she *made* time to take Ruby on many walks and Ruby learned to look up to her as a friend. I think of the cook/baker whenever I cut into a blueberry pie, her specialty.

The retreat's priest, Fr. Lighterman, R.I.P., had had a heart attack in the parking lot of a convenience store and I like to think he was running in to buy bait. As the Retreat's resident priest, he made life easier for the staff and for the retreatants knowing we could count on him to say Mass daily. As a Jesuit, and as smart as he was, he endeavored to keep his strong opinions out of his sermons; I am happy to report I only had to walk out one time.

Bishop Struther has gone to his great reward also which makes me wonder if a Mass said for a dead priest is the same for a Bishop; as humble as he was, I know he would have wanted it that way. Power and position did not keep him from listening to his subjects whose welfare he promoted like his own children; his intentions were always in the right place. Whoever was in charge of making him look presentable at his funeral, I hoped they'd tucked a piece of a white handkerchief showing in his breast pocket the way he liked it as he took his place on the end of a long line of Gallup's ecclesiastic hierarchy.

I learned Sr. Edith, the artist, had a quiet passing with members of her community by her side. I see the scene as a watercolor in soft pastels, rays of light shining down from heaven, her hands emanating light as her essence returns to its source. I remember her sitting on the porch sketching Franklin and me as we worked, her way of getting to know us, and we her. My memory of her changed little when it was decided she should take over as director of St. Francis now that a staff was in place; it was the right time for Hyacinth to live to work full-time at the girls' home, the plan all along. My mental picture of Edith shifted into capable corals and practical plaids as her creativity turned businesslike. Maybe it was the shock of responsibility that did it or the straightforward way she conducted business, but her black veil finally righted itself. As a sensitive artist, I hoped Edith didn't pick up on my feeling I was abandoning her. Volunteering is a good way of life but without an income, it doesn't last indefinitely and I had to go back to the real world eventually. I hoped Sr. Edith knew my decision to leave was based on the fact my volunteer time was up, and not because she had taken over as director.

Someone I thought would outlive us all, I was surprised learning Sr. Carol the missionary has gone from this life, too, probably kicking and screaming the entire way. She was a help to many families on the reservation who would have otherwise gone without, a heavenly Autobahn a suitable reward. I remember her fiery personality and by her example, keep a medicine wheel hanging from the rear view mirror to ward off evil spirits in the form of belligerent motorcycle cops.

I expected her to be gone and she was, Sr. Norma, who threw herself headfirst into making the Blue Army take hold in Gallup, ended up with few soldiers and not enough to make her stay on, so she rolled up her mat and moved on; a kindred spirit if ever there was one, seeing how I was about to do the same.

I was happy learning Sr. Hyacinth and Celeste are still going strong, true pioneers in the retreat trade, elite members of a dying breed of hearty souls to be sure!

In the day-to-day life of a Retreat Center, Sisters visit periodically to see if they would like living in the Southwest, so taking a few days to judge if they liked the workload, the desolate surroundings and most importantly, the rest of the staff. One such Sister visited and aftcr a couple of months decided if wasn't for her and left. But like they say in the monastery, it's better to know sooner than later it isn't the right place. Everyone who visited helped in their way and the retreat was better for each of them.

Clays, desert dust and biological particles may have been a factor when I learned little Ruby, the alcohol syndrome child, living on her own, ended up on the bad road many Indians take walking to and from town in winter. The day road conditions were terrible, making walking impossible; a normal person would have realized this. I asked myself whatever possessed her to venture out seeing large crystal clusters falling as snowflakes from the sky. Did the electrostatic attraction in the flakes pull her toward the crystal center of the winter storm, or did rosette shapes move her to chase them?

Normal people know that when ice crystals accumulate it is very cold. But I didn't even want to know what the air temperature was on that fateful evening, knowing wasn't important. All that mattered was little Ruby's body was found rigid under the snow, the latest winged angel in heaven, her spirit now freed to morph into, how had Franklin put it years ago, a lively butterfly, the Indian symbol for everlasting life.

The End

CPSIA information can be obtained at www.ICGtesting.com
Printed in the USA
LVOW090031100312

272435LV00001B/76/P